Wall Street Main Street
AND THE
Side Street

A MAD ECONOMIST TAKES A STROLL

by

Julianne Malveaux

Pines One
Publications

PINES ONE PUBLICATIONS
Los Angeles

For the young'uns . . .

Anyi Malik Howell
Armand Marcus Howell
Matthew Elijah Brown

Grateful acknowledgments are made to the following for permission to reprint previously published material: —USA Today, King Features Syndicate, The Progressive Media Project, Crisis Magazine, San Francisco Sun Reporter, Black Issues in Higher Education Magazine and National Black MBA Magazine.

Books are available to organizations, corporations and professional associations at quantity discounts. For information, contact the sales department at Pines One Publications (213) 290-1182; Fax (213) 295-3880; or E-mail Pinesone.worldnet.att.net

Library of Congress Cataloging-in-Publication Data

Malveaux, Julianne
Wall Street, main street, and the side street: a mad economist
takes a stroll / columns by Julianne Malveaux, 1994–98
p. cm.
ISBN: 1-890194-22-0

1. United States—Economic conditions. 2. United States—Economic policy—1981–
3. United States—Politics and government—1994– 4. United States—Social conditions.
5. Discrimination in employment—United States. 6. Afro-Americans—Economic conditions.
7. Labor market—United States. I. Title

HC106.82M35 1999 98-50213
330.973—dc21   CIP

Pines One Publications, 3870 Crenshaw Blvd., Suite 931, Los Angeles, CA 90008
http://www.pinesone.com

Cover and text design by Laurie Williams/A Street Called Straight

Printed in the United States of America
10 9 8 7 6 5 4 3 2 1
FIRST EDITION

CONTENTS

CHAPTER THREE: PLATITUDES, POLICY AND PRIORITIES 61

Foreword

That which is in Julianne Malveaux, that which has made her a journalist, should be in each human being and may in fact already be in each human being to some degree. That penetrating insight and daunting courage which she exhibits would make us better friends, better neighbors and better citizens if we had those virtues in good measure.

As I read these articles, I was reminded of Langston Hughes and the character he created, Jess B Simple. Hughes examined the human condition critically, its foibles, failures and triumphs, then allowed Simple to comment upon his findings. Most often, Simple's expressions were humorous, but they were always pointed. He remarked on the loutish ignorance of racism and the folly of believing that power lasts forever in the same hands. Admittedly, Malveaux never, or at least seldom, uses humor. There is about her and her writing the same "getting to the point immediately" that Hughes employed in both prose and poetry.

Malveaux's passion carries her beyond the realm Hughes established, for she sets out to upset the status quo when that status quo bespeaks injustice, mendacity, cruelty and other social abuse. She is acute in probing cause and effect which works in our national and local politics and policies. She targets unchecked greed and runaway nepotism with incisive intelligence and has no hesitation about making suggestions on how to uproot the evil and right the wrong. Whether or not she would agree with the statement, Malveaux has the safety and security of all people in her mind when she spears the brute and lances the bigot.

It is said that Napoleon stated that he would rather confront six cadres of heavily armed enemy soldiers than six angry journalists. He could have reduced the latter number to one if that was Julianne Malveaux.

Maya Angelou, November 1998

Introduction

Why do I call myself a "mad economist"? Because you've got to be either angry or crazy or some combination thereof to interpret economic data and keep a level head. Some days I want to scream at the bifurcation and trifurcation in this country, the double standards and triple meanings, the way that the rich get richer, the poor, poorer and the rest of us more complacent. I want to scream, instead I write. I write two columns a week for King Features Syndicate, once a week for the *San Francisco Sun Reporter*, monthly for *USA Today* and for *Black Issues in Higher Education*. I haven't run out of things to write about. Not yet.

Why not? These are wonderful, wild, wacky, painful, poignant, frustrating, energizing times. Apathy seems to be at an all-time high, with more than half of us choosing to stay away from the polls. On the other hand, there is a new and exciting grassroots activism that might yet transcend the '60s habit of simply taking it to the streets. Many are frustrated that one of the tools for black economic progress, affirmative action, is being dismantled; still others find a real challenge in the new "multiculturalism". There is an excitement that comes with the new millennium, yet the year 2000 will be little different from 1998 (except all the computers might go bonkers) unless someone chooses to take an affirmative action toward the year 2000.

Semantics are both funny and frustrating. We demand performance standards for women on public assistance, but not for manufacturers of B2 bombers. We decry "preferences" for people of color, but in the international arena demand them for some terms of trade. That's not a stretch—some of those who suggest that African Americans, Latinos, Asians, Native Americans and women do not need a level playing field can develop elaborate arguments to justify the breaks they seek when they want to export their goods to other countries.

Then there's economic reality. And the real deal is always economic. For the past four years, the economy had been expanding by at least 3 percent growth per quarter. In the first quarter of 1998, growth was 5.4 percent. In 1995, 1996 and 1997, the Dow Jones Industrial Average grew by 20 percent per year. Half of all Americans are participating in this stock market, either directly or indirectly, and the stock market has created thousands of "401-k millionaires," working people whose pension investments have created large portfolios for them. The real fat cats aren't the workers whose pensions have multiplied thanks to a healthy stock market. The CEOs whose compensation is in the dizzying nine-figure neighborhood are the ones whose pay might be carefully probed. Especially when they earn these dollars for laying people off, exporting jobs and generally undermining the structure of the economy of the United States.

While Wall Street prospers, and the revival of the mega-merger movement suggests the consolidation of power at the top, wage growth has only weakly sputtered past its stagnancy, growing by a mere 2 percent in 1997. Despite record-breaking low unemployment rates, talk of labor shortages, and inflationary fears on the part of the Federal Reserve Board, wages haven't risen enough to either trigger inflation or allow workers to catch up after years of economic stagnation. While consumer confidence gets stronger and stronger, the amount of debt that Americans shoulder is also growing, and our savings rate is declining. Wall Street prospers, Main Street falters.

If it's weak on Main Street, consider the Side Street. Ten million Americans earn the minimum wage, a wage Congress resists raising. We treat the poor as if they are our enemies, not fellow citizens, and too frequently sneer about handouts without offering a hand up. Despite much-touted economic prosperity, there are still at least a million homeless people in our country. At the end of 1997, with the stock market soaring, the National Conference of Mayors reported a 3 percent increase in requests for emergency housing and food assistance. We watch the minutiae of rises and falls in the stock market, but rarely fluctuations in the state of the poor. Out of sight, out of mind. We simply don't see the Side Street often enough, and when we do focus on it, we see it as a minority thing, forgetting that there is more poverty among whites than among people of color, that most Americans know someone (or are related to someone) who lives on the Side Street. We're too busy treating the Dow Jones Industrial Average as if it were a score in a football game, obsessing over whether the indicator has moved up or down a few points, instead of dealing with long-term structural issues. The inner workings of the Federal Reserve Board are so micro-analyzed that Alan Greenspan can cause chaos by simply clearing his throat in a way that implies that short-term interest rates are rising or falling.

When the lens of national attention veers away from our robust economy, it is too often focused on the trivial. I sometimes tell folks that I live with the devil, and that has nothing to do with my personal living arrangements. Living in

Washington, D.C., though, you sometimes feel as if people are collectively possessed by some demonic energy as their focus waxes and wanes, and manages still to remain on the inconsequential. How else do we explain the nation's fascination, at the beginning of 1998, with allegations that President Clinton had sex with intern Monica Lewinsky, allegations that came from surreptitiously taped conversations with a "friend"? How do we explain the document dump of thousands of pages of pornography in the name of justice? How do we explain the Congressional red-faced rush to sputtering righteousness about the President's ill-advised peccadillo, especially when accompanied by steely silence about the growing gap between haves and have-nots in our country? It is much easier, of course, to grasp at the trivial than roll up our sleeves and struggle with the struggle. Better, perhaps, to focus on the details of a tawdry affair than the inevitable outcomes of economic division.

While the press corps seemed caught up with the minute-to-minute unfolding of the Lewinsky case, President Clinton went to Africa, Latin America, China and Russia, and attempted to broker peace in the Middle East and in Ireland. On each of these continents he made significant foreign policy inroads. Still, his historic Africa trip, the first ever of its length undertaken by a United States President, was substantially ignored and overshadowed by allegations, accusations, leaked tapes, broken confidences and a smug self-righteousness on the part of those pundits who would make indiscretions an impeachable offense.

The real deal is economic, yet the economy is being shaped by those who would consolidate power in a few hands, change policy to lock people out, utter pronouncements to reinforce their own sense of false superiority, and hide behind markets and technology to assert that economic bifurcation is the result of some natural order of things. Nothing can be shaped without the acquiescence of "the people," that large and rather silent group of folks with often unexercised economic and political power. If these people ever decide to exercise their collective power, we'd probably see a different set of laws and policies. If those unemployed and disenfranchised, regardless of race and gender, started talking about wages, prices and access, we might have more branch banks, higher minimum wages, better public transportation and a more vibrant civic life. Too many of those on Main Street and the Side Street have yielded their power to others.

Main Street and the Side Street give up their power when they suggest that only markets matter, that the golden rule means that he who has the gold makes the rules. I learned a lot about Main Street, though, when I worked with the AFL-CIO and their "America Needs a Raise" rallies in 1996, and talked to a fiftysomething white man who thought layoffs meant other folks until it happened to him, and a thirtysomething Latino man who struggled to support children on a part-time janitor's paycheck. These men would hardly have described themselves as disadvantaged. But they had no advantage in an economy that prides itself on revering profits and disrespecting people.

Some of my readers assume that this left-of-liberal, African American woman writer has more concern for race matters than for the dozens of other complex issues that confront our society. Not. Race certainly matters to me, but it matters because it often shapes the way we are able to deal with other matters in our society. Biases about race often reverberate into other areas. Assumptions about race, overlaid by assumptions about gender and ethnicity, often yield warped results, "strange fruit." So a man like Timothy McVeigh, who was convicted of killing 168 people in the Murrah Building in Oklahoma City, has jocular conversations with his jailers while Mumia Abu-Jamal, convicted of killing one police officer, lives in isolation. While race matters dictate these comparisons, nothing is simply a matter of race. The real deal is economic, and the economy is a challenge for white folks, black folks, brown folks, older people, the technology-challenged, women and just about everyone else.

These columns touch on a broad range of issues, but their common thread is a challenge to the unspoken assumption that this is as good as it gets. It isn't. Frederick Douglass said it best: "Power concedes nothing without a demand, it never did and it never will. Those who want freedom without agitation are like those who want the ocean without its mighty roar." Each of these columns is not a roar, but in each I sought to provide information, pose a challenge, shed light on that which is fractured and flawed. This is an exciting time to write a column, to observe and analyze economic social, and demographic trends. Our times will be all the more exciting when Main Street and the Side Street take on the Wall Street assumption that power should be concentrated in just a few hands in our society.

Julianne Malveaux, November 1998

CHAPTER
1
AN IMPRESSIVE ECONOMY?

When I hear the word "impressive," I think of something riveting and imposing, grand and majestic. I don't think of an economy that, despite its expansion, still generates a significant amount of misery in our society, and a high level of poverty, especially in the African American and Latino communities. One headline says the economy is impressive; the other trumpets the layoff of ten thousand people. One headline says the unemployment rate is lower than it has been in 28 years; the other says consumer debt is rising. We keep getting mixed messages about the economy because it seems that only Wall Street reactions count in describing the economy as impressive. Still, Wall Street doesn't trickle down, and the economy that is impressive for one person is a situation of agony for another.

Is our economy truly impressive? Can we associate majesty with a bifurcated economy that generates so much inequality and poverty? To be sure, the past six years of economic expansion can be considered unusual, even impressive, in historical terms. However, this is the first economic expansion that has failed to significantly alter the status of people at the bottom of the economic distribution. Further, the focus on balanced budgets has meant a curtailing of government programs at a time when such programs are affordable. Finally, the illusion of prosperity has pushed many women on public assistance into the labor market, but usually in precarious low-paying jobs that provide neither benefits nor stability.

An impressive economy, or a contradictory one? The fact that this economy has generated such different realities for different people in our society suggests that impressive is as impressive does, and this economy has yet to do the right thing!

CAN U.S. EXPANSION SURVIVE WORLD ECONOMIC INSTABILITY?

BY JULIANNE MALVEAUX

When Russia's central bank decided that it could no longer support the ruble, it forced the world to take that nation's economic crisis seriously. Those United States corporations that have investments in Russia can expect their profits to drop as quickly as the ruble does. And the announcement that Russia can't afford to spend more than the $8.8 million it has already spent propping up the ruble had almost immediate consequences on Wall Street.

Russia is a major player in the world economy. The G-7 group of world economic leaders was expanded three years ago to include Russia as part of a new "Group of Eight" in recognition of its impact on world prices, productivity and stability. If world economic leaders had misplaced confidence in Russia, we will all feel it as the Russian economy struggles to re-establish stability. The International Monetary Fund and the World Bank have put billions of dollars into propping up the Russian economy. Several United States corporations, enamored of the notion of a borderless, global economy, have invested funds in Russia that they may now lose through this crisis. Already, the Soros Quantum Fund has lost $2 billion. Many major U.S. banks also stand to lose from the Russian economic crisis, as foreign investors hold about a quarter of Russia's $40 billion debt.

Already, there are reverberations in Latin America, where the devalued ruble had an impact on local currencies. Latin America is also affected by the Asian economic crisis. The result of currency devaluations in both Russia and Japan has been to weaken economic structure in countries like Venezuela, Brazil, and Mexico. Interest rates have risen, and growth projections have been revised, because of world economic turmoil.

Can the United States continue its own economic expansion in the face of world economic instability? In the long run, the answer is clearly negative. We have, after all, developed an economic strategy that depends on trade and the development of international markets. President Clinton's round of international trips this year, to Africa, Latin America, China, and next week to Russia all reinforce the notion of our economic mutuality. We can't have it both ways, though. World economic growth is an engine for U.S. economic growth. World chaos and recession, on the other hand, will slow growth in the United States and affect our ability to grow. The Asian economic crisis is likely to affect the job market in the United States, says the Economic Policy Institute, to the tune of a million or more jobs.

That's not many jobs in a labor market of 110 million people, but when this job loss is combined with job losses attributable to other downturns we may be talking significant employment loss.

Some economists are suggesting that the way out of the stagnancy the United States can expect because of world economic crisis is to cut interest rates. Federal Reserve Board Chairman Alan Greenspan, on the other hand, implicitly makes the case that he'd like to raise the interest rate but for the stable inflation that accompanies low unemployment. Greenspan might well be willing to tolerate more unemployment, as his recent public statements have focused on inflationary pressure on labor markets. If interest rate cuts are needed to insulate the United States from world economic fluctuations, they aren't likely to happen and we are clearly vulnerable to economic oscillation as a result of instability in Russia and Asia.

This seems to be an appropriate time, though, to look at the risk that we are willing to shoulder with investments in Asia and Russia. In Russia, especially, United States investment could only be described as highly speculative investment that offered high risk but also high rates of return. Why don't bankers have the fortitude to tackle similar investments in our nation's inner-cities? Would George Soros be willing to take a $2 billion loss because an inner city investment went awry? Would Credit Suisse First Boston be willing to expose a third of its six months profits to fluctuating circumstances in inner-cities, reducing profits by $254 million to $500 million as it did because of the ruble's devaluation? I think not!

In the name of a global economy, United States companies may well have over-invested in Russia, and their losses may well jeopardize our own economic expansion. If United States corporations have the mettle for losing billions of dollars and double-digit percentage points in profits, though, perhaps they ought to look closer to home. They can make a major difference in our nation's inner cities and are far less likely to fail in Harlem, Anacostia, D.C., or San Francisco's Bayview area than they are in Russia.

King Features Syndicate, August 27, 1998

THE MORAL HAZARD IN PROTECTING RICH GAMBLERS
BY JULIANNE MALVEAUX

A month after Long-Term Capital Management L.P. said it had lost 44 percent of its assets, the House Banking Committee turned its attention to the reason the Federal Reserve Bank of New York scrambled to rescue the fund. New York Federal Reserve Bank President William McDonough and Federal Reserve Board Chairman Alan Greenspan both defended the need to arrange the private bailout, because Long-Term Capital Management's borrowing was so extensive that its collapse would cause reverberations both in domestic and global financial markets. But the fact that Greenspan feels no regulation is needed to curtail this legalized gambling indicates his bias for protecting rich gamblers.

Most of us are so far removed from the world of hedge funds that we can't fathom a banking world where a dollar's worth of equity can garner a thousand dollar bet. But this has been, in fact, the case with hedge funds. These investment funds use computer models to make bets on the relative difference of interest rates among securities, and generally provide spectacular returns. In the case of Long-Term Capital Management, $2.2 billion in investments was leveraged into $90 billion in borrowed money. This $90 billion was collateral on bets representing more than a trillion dollars. With the collapse of the Russian ruble and the increasing severity of the global financial crisis, the bets were proving to be bad ones, but since Long-Term Capital Management had so little real money on the table, it couldn't pay up. This necessitated the involvement of the New York Federal Reserve Bank, which coordinated the group of banks and brokerage houses that put up $3.6 billion to prop up the shaky four-year-old Long-Term Capital Management and take control of its assets. Rescuers include Merrill Lynch and Company, Morgan Stanley Dean Witter, Goldman Sachs, Salomon Smith Barney, Bankers Trust, Chase Manhattan and J.P. Morgan. Some of the banks involved may have used funds that are protected by taxpayer-financed deposit insurance, which partly explains the interest of the House Banking Committee. This rescue should also be of interest to those who use these brokerage houses to manage their funds; investors might well ask if they can count on the same kind of loans (at a 1:1000 leverage ratio) and rescue that Long-Term Capital Management had.

Justifications for the private rescue of Long-Term Capital Management are many. The fund is, we are told, too big to fail. Its assets simply can't be liquidated quickly without impacting an already shaky stock market, and without causing international reverberations. But if Long-Term Capital Management is too big to fail and could cause such chaos in financial markets, why hasn't it, and other hedge funds, been regulated? Indeed, hedge funds were specifically designed to avoid regulation and the justification for failing to regulate them in the past has been that the rich can handle the risk. (Participation in hedge funds is limited to people who have incomes of $300,000 a year, or a net worth of $1 million. This represented less than a half a percent of the entire population.)

It seems that the rich have the money to step up to the gambling table, handling the investment. But the concentration of assets in hedge funds like Long-Term Capital Management has such ramifications for the entire system that the rich can't handle the risk without risking the financial well-being of the rest of us. If they could handle the risk, after all, then why are public officials like Greenspan and McDonough scrambling around to rescue them and providing elaborate justifications for their involvement?

Greenspan says no regulation is needed to insulate the economy from other hedge funds collapsing like Long-Term Capital Management did. In his testimony to the House Banking Committee, he described the Long-Term Capital Management debacle and investment strategy as a "dumb mistake." But regulation is often imposed to protect fools from themselves, or more importantly to protect people from market consequences in certain situations. We have child labor laws because markets might well dictate the labor force involvement of poor children, but their work effort is not in the public interest. If the collapse of a hedge fund will cause massive public consequences, then it is in the national interest to consider regulating these hedge funds.

Regulating the rich, though, is always an uphill battle. Putting limits on market gamblers might protect us all—the bailout simply protected the gamblers from the consequences of their foolish actions. Greenspan's testimony acknowledged the "moral hazard" of the bailout. Still, he justified this welfare for the wealthy.

King Features Syndicate, October 1, 1998

AN IMPRESSIVE ECONOMY?
BY JULIANNE MALVEAUX

I wish I could see the world the same way Federal Reserve Chairman Alan Greenspan does. He says the economy is in great shape, "as impressive as any I have witnessed in my near half-century of daily observation of the American economy." The indicators suggest that Greenspan is right. We have not seen an unemployment rate as low as May's 4.3 percent in more than a generation—28 years to be exact. In his testimony to the Joint Economic Committee, he was optimistic that wage increases (just 4 cents an hour last month) are so well contained that they will not increase inflation. He indicated that there is no need to raise interest rates. Even detailed questioning from Rep. Maurice Hinchey (D-N.Y.) on the Asian financial crisis did not tarnish Greenspan's essential optimism. He did not retreat from his assertion that the economy is in great shape.

Many Americans would agree with Greenspan, but the stock market hardly responded to his optimism. Indeed, in the two days after his testimony, the Dow Jones Industrial Average dropped below 9000, though the year-to-date gains in the Dow were more than 10 percent. Still, Greenspan had lots of evidence to support his optimism. With wages ticking up, nearly half of all Americans enjoying stock market gains, and both consumption and investment on the rise, the Fed chair has ample macroeconomics evidence to support his optimism. What he lacks is the perspective that comes when one gets away from the macroeconomics indicators and closer to the gritty reality of too many American lives.

On the same day, for example, that Greenspan testified before the Joint Economic Committee, the House of Representatives passed legislation that will make it more difficult for people to declare bankruptcy and walk away from their debts. Replete with the language of the Contract on America, the Republicans argued that there is too much personal bankruptcy and not enough "personal responsibility" in consumer finance. Yet the increase in bankruptcies may have as much to do with flat wages as with personal irresponsibility. Yet in his question-and-answer session with the Congress, Greenspan indicated little concern about rising bankruptcies and consumer debt. It is as if his reality does not trickle down from the indicators to the people.

President Clinton says he will veto the bankruptcy bill because it provides a set of arbitrary means tests to determine how much relief from debt people can expect. Some Democrats also oppose the bill, which passed on mostly partisan lines, because it will remove any advantage that alimony and child support payments have over other kinds of debt payments. In other words, child welfare and survival may have to take a back seat to Visa and MasterCard payments, and single parents who depend on alimony and child support will have to fight credit card companies for their right to collect money they are entitled to. It is amazing that this legislation passed with so little concern about the causes of bankruptcy, especially in this "impressive" economy. It is also amazing that when asked about growing consumer debt, Greenspan failed to sound an alarm.

If Alan Greenspan is right, and our economic outlook is optimistic, why has this Congress not begun to repair the social service fabric that has been frayed in our nation's attempt to balance the budget and improve our economic prospects? This may be the first time the economy has expanded and the plight of the poor has been ignored, if not exacerbated, by public policy. Under ordinary circumstances, economic good news allows us the flexibility to do things like raise wages or support social programs. The Greenspan testimony seems to imply that "contained wages" are the price we must pay for this economy that he describes as so impressive.

What is impressive about the large number of Americans who earn the minimum wage? About the projections that low-wage jobs are among the fastest-growing jobs in our society? To be sure, impressive is in the eye of the economic beholder. But Greenspan's comments to the Joint Economic Committee indicated that his definition of impressive contrasts sharply with that of millions of Americans who have yet to experience the positive effects of our nation's so-called impressive economy.

Given the macroeconomics indicators, I do not expect Mr. Greenspan to describe our economy in anything but glowing terms. Indeed, some suggest that his exuberance was equivocated by his concession that interest rates are more likely to rise than fall when the Federal Reserve does adjust them. But while Mr. Greenspan is doing his job by placing positive spin on our impressive economy, the rest of us do not have to believe the hype. As this Congress struggles with budget issues and badgers the poor with new bankruptcy laws, they might also consider the fact that too many people are unmoved by our nation's impressive economy.

King Features Syndicate, June 10, 1998

WHO GAINS FROM THE RISING DOW?

BY JULIANNE MALVEAUX

As the Dow Jones Industrial Average flirts with a historic 9000 level, economic policy makers have become smug with congratulating themselves on the health of the current economy. Like physicians who interpret a normal temperature as the sign of a healthy body, these economists see the steadily rising Dow as an index of a healthy economy. But just as people with normal temperatures may have a host of other ailments, an economy with a rising Dow may have underlying weaknesses which go unexamined because of outward appearances of good health.

The appearance of good health is now complicated by an increased participation in the stock market. The percentage of wealth of U.S. households invested in stocks is at an all-time high, with more than half of all households either directly or indirectly (through mutual fund or other participation) participating in the market. Much of this participation comes from 401-k or pension plans. Millions of people with modest salaries have seen their net worth soar because of their participation in employer-sponsored savings plans.

Employer savings plans have been replacing traditional pension plans for workers, as more and more employers shift the burden of savings and pensions onto the individual. Retirement income, then, depends on what workers save, the extent to which employers match their savings, and the performance of the savings in an investment plan. Unlike pension plans, in which employers take the investment risk, in 401-k plans, workers are the ones who either shoulder the risk or enjoy the benefit of the investment.

Typically, employers match employee savings up to a percentage of salary with a contribution of between 25 and 150 percent of employee contribution. They may allow employees to use as much as 10 percent of their salary for purposes of matching. They may begin to match savings as soon as employees start working, or they may choose to match savings only after people have been on the job for six months, a year, or longer. Clearly, the employees at the lowest salary levels may have the most difficulty saving. Income inequality today may well be translated into greater inequality tomorrow based on worker ability to participate in 401-k plans.

What is the basis of the future inequality? In companies with strong unions, high pay, and a tradition of generous pensions, pension benefits are now combined with optional 401-k plans to help workers create a robust set of retirement income options. In contrast, in industries where pay is low and turnover is high neither pensions nor 401-k plans are offered. Since women are most likely to be found in the retail and service industries, but are also likely to live longer than men, it is likely that women will have lower incomes in retirement.

Because both employers and employees can deduct their contributions into 401-k plans, it is important to ask who benefits from this employee perk, which is the second most popular after health insurance. According to a 1996 study by the Social Security Administration, 57 percent of income from company-sponsored retirement plans goes to the 20 percent of elderly with the highest incomes. While this study was based on 1990 income data, and there is other research that suggests the benefit is not as stratified, it is clear that those who have low incomes during their work life will also have low incomes when they retire.

Though employers are not required to offer 401-k plans, an increasing number do. Thus, a growing number of workers have pension, profit-sharing, or 401-k participation. It is through this participation that a growing number of workers have a vested interest in the booming stock market, causing greater trickle-down than we have seen in the past.

At the same time, as many as half of all workers have absolutely no connection to the stock market. These workers are already impaired by low earnings, high turnover, and scant benefits. The uneven availability of pensions and 401-k plans means that these workers will also face issues of income inequality in the future. And it means that even though the rising Dow benefits an increasing number of workers, it still leaves too many out. Every worker certainly has the option of participating in the stock market, but millions simply do not have the means.

King Features Syndicate, March 27, 1998

IT'S STILL THE ECONOMY, STUPID
BY JULIANNE MALVEAUX

A review of the political discourse of 1995 will reveal that some tried to shift conversation from the economy to values. Pundit Ben Wattenberg wrote a book, *Values Matter Most* (Basic Books, 1995), that won him a telephone call from President Clinton and the speculation that things like family values, teen pregnancy, welfare reform, and affirmative action are more important than the bread-and-butter issues that President Clinton was motivated by when someone posted a sign that said "It's the economy, stupid" in his Little Rock campaign headquarters in

1992. Values matter, but if a recent Associated Press report is correct, the economy matters more to most Americans.

According to the AP poll, when people were asked the open-ended question about what issues were most important to them, more than one in four said the economy or jobs. The next highest answer was education. Nearly half of the people chose the economy, jobs, and education as their key issues. Things like "family values" fell much further down on the list of things people were concerned about.

This doesn't mean that people are unconcerned about values. Indeed, the values debate seems to be driving certain economic outcomes. The hundreds of thousands of federal workers who were furloughed for a second time on December 16 are being held hostage to a values debate between the Congress and the President. These workers will take home less than half of what they took home two weeks ago, since they will get half pay but will pay for full deductions in their next paycheck. It may not hit the highest-paid federal workers, but the clerical workers, maintenance workers, and others who earn less than $25,000 are so hard hit that many will file for unemployment compensation to tide them over until the federal government settles the impasse.

These are the workers who have watched our nation's economic values hit an all-time low. Economic growth was robust in the first half of 1995, slowing in the second half. But wages have been absolutely stagnant. People haven't been taking home more money, but they've been reading about the killer profits earned by Wall Street traders. They want to work, want to get paid, want to support their families. Many are frustrated because the opportunities aren't there. Jobs once considered stable are disappearing, and one of the most secure employers in the country, the federal government, has now become extremely unreliable.

Economic insecurity and waning consumer confidence are manifested in retail sales data for the end of 1995. Sales during the six weeks between Thanksgiving and the end of the year can make or break a retail year. But the Conference Board has reported a worsening in consumer confidence, and notes that people are postponing spending on everything from new cars to Christmas gifts. One of the reasons has to be the high level of consumer debt, up about $100 billion from a year ago. People have no more money to borrow, and they have lost the optimism that makes it easy to borrow for consumer spending.

But there is a great divide between those who make public policy and those who live it. While those on Capitol Hill seem obsessed with slugging out a values war, those who live in the shadow of the Hill simply want to make ends meet. While legislators have jetted home to enjoy their holidays, furloughed federal workers are wondering whether they can make it through the new year without stopping by the unemployment office. If legislators insist on rewriting the agenda so that values matter most, the people who go to the polls may have a surprise for them. To let an AP poll tell it, issues of economic security, employment and survival dominate the concerns of the elected, if not legislators.

King Features Syndicate, December 28, 1995

WALL STREET JOY FROM MAIN STREET BLUES
BY JULIANNE MALVEAUX

When AT&T announced that it would lay off 40,000 workers in 1996 because of its reorganization and streamlining, its stock soared. While many celebrate changes that the new year brings, at least one thing remains the same—when Main Street shudders in fear, Wall Street reacts with glee. The relationship between layoffs and soaring stock prices is both short-sighted and frightening. Doesn't Wall Street understand that when Main Street closes down, so will Wall Street?

Maybe not. Stock prices are up 35 percent in 1995, while there have been at least half a million jobs lost to downsizing during the same period. Corporate mergers are at an all-time record, with more than $346 billion in deals recorded by November 1995. By the time 1995 deals are recorded, they are likely to eclipse the $347 billion recorded in 1994, and more than double the $150 billion in merger activity that took place in 1992.

The brisk rate in mergers in 1995 has increased the pace of downsizing that began in 1990, when "streamlining" and "lean and mean" became corporate buzzwords. The American Management Association reports that 15 percent of layoffs can be attributed to corporate mergers. Almost always these mergers boost stock prices, and push thousands of workers onto the street.

In the past decade, AT&T has laid off more than 125,000 workers. The most recent layoffs are the largest the company has ever announced and among the largest any corporation has announced. AT&T laid off 32,000 people in 1986.

Some say these AT&T layoffs are just the beginning. AT&T is breaking into three separate companies, spinning off its computer businesses and telecommunications units. Next, the company may look at unprofitable business centers and sell them or close them off. Some estimate as many as 10,000 more layoffs before the end of 1996. Look out, stock prices!

The problem is bigger than AT&T. Three million jobs have been lost to downsizing in the last five years. Stock prices have risen with layoffs every year. In some ways this has contributed to the bifurcation of our nation's fortunes, to the fact that there is no one truth about the nation's economy. Economic expansion is a mixed blessing for the minority of Americans, mainly for those at the top end of the wage scale, or those who have invested in the stocks that keep soaring. For most people, incomes have been stagnant, benefits have been dropping, and issues of economic insecurity are paramount.

Wall Street doesn't see the human cost of layoffs. It sees profits. Stock prices soar when people lose their jobs because investors feel that streamlined workplaces are more profitable workplaces. They fail to see that streamlining can, in the long run, affect their bottom line and the economic big picture. Even though about half of the workers who lost their jobs to downsizing will walk away with settlement packages, most will count their pennies for the next several months. Their consumption patterns are likely to change. They might not move their telephone service from AT&T, but they are likely to look askance at the array of frills that the telecommunications company markets. From Main Street to Wall Street, here's a message. Workers are consumers. What part of this message is hard to understand?

While AT&T shareholders got a boost from the layoff, it is safe to say there are at least 40,000 workers who will not, in months ahead, thank you for calling AT&T.

King Features Syndicate, January 4, 1996

AN OPPORTUNITY FOR DIVERSITY ON THE FED
BY JULIANNE MALVEAUX

When Federal Reserve Governor John P. LaWare steps down from the Federal Reserve Board at the end of April, it offers President Clinton an opportunity to make a statement about diversity on the Fed. By diversity, I'm not talking race or gender, although with just two women and no people of color on the seven-member board, those matters should not be ignored. But the Fed is overpopulated by bankers and academic economists, people who study money and banking, but don't necessarily feel money and banking issues. And adding an African-American, Asian, Latina or woman banker won't necessarily add perspective to the body charged with regulating our nation's interest rates and money supply. What about putting a worker, a consumer advocate, or a union member on the Fed?

The law, after all, does not require that a Ph.D. economist or someone with a long history of banking experience be appointed. It has few restrictions, except political and geographic balance. LaWare is a Democrat appointed by President Ronald Reagan to the Federal Reserve Board. His background as a Boston banker perhaps moved him to urge the President to replace him with another banker. He wrote the President that "the quality of board deliberations . . . is enhanced by the direct participation of a member with personal private-sector experience in banking."

There are all kinds of banking experience, though. There is the experience of the person who signs off on loans and the experience of the person who can't get one. There is the experience of a person who makes bank policy, and the experience of someone who is pinched by such policy. There is the experience of the person who worries about whether his $100,000 deposit will be covered by FDIC, and then there is the experience of the person who has to scrape $100 together to open a bank account. Yes, banking has changed since the days when the banks were open from ten in the morning to three at night and children saved their pennies and nickels to learn thrift. These days a child's account is likely to be zeroed out by high monthly service charges, and banks are pushing the regulatory process to become "one-stop shops" that sell everything from insurance to stocks and bonds. Some argue that reform of the Glass-Steagall Act makes sense in terms of changing technology, but those who have had to face off monster banks argue that industrial consolidation during a time of deregulation leaves the consumer without much protection.

So who should President Clinton appoint to the Federal Reserve Board? How about a member of Justice for Janitors, the union affiliate that has struggled to get pay for cleaning-service workers above the minimum wage. In Washington, D.C., Justice for Janitors workers closed down commuter bridges to push their case. Such advocates might also be effective in focusing attention on flaws in the banking system.

President Clinton might look to the Greenlining Coalition or ACORN for a possible appointee to the Federal Reserve Bank. These organizations have also developed activists who are both experienced at institutional analysis and direct action. They might not only liven up Federal Reserve Board Open Market Committee meetings, but might also make issues of rising interest rates clearer to other Federal Reserve Board members.

What about a Teamster? A member of the Service Employees International Union? Someone who types for a living? An organizer? These are the voices we need to hear when the Federal Reserve Board conducts those interest rate experiments that provide security for bondholders but rock so many other worlds. There are plenty of people who study markets and know banking on the Federal Reserve Board. In the name of diversity, President Clinton ought to consider adding a people's perspective.

King Features Syndicate, March 31, 1995

THERE'S PORK IN YOUR MORTGAGE DEDUCTION
BY JULIANNE MALVEAUX

Sometimes I don't know why I bother to "debate" conservatives. Debate, after all, implies an exchange of ideas, but my experience with some on the rabid right is that they recharge their brains in the basement of a conservative think tank and come out with a set of canned one-liners like, "There you go again, tax and spend, tax and spend," or "Cut taxes and you'll expand the economy." More recently, as the crime bill agonized its way through Congress, there were allegations that the bill was packed with the "pork" of about $7 billion in crime-prevention spending.

Any bacon in the crime bill was of the turkey variety, because the bill had been so pared that many crime-prevention programs didn't survive. Still, I fumed at the characterization of "pork," fumed until I read the month's *Common Cause* magazine, and its cover story "Home Inequity: A Revealing Look at America's Biggest Special Interest." Do you want to talk pork? Homeowner deductions cost the U.S. treasury $83.3 billion a year. The very same taxpayers who rail about people on welfare and crime prevention programs are as much on the dole as a food stamps recipient. The difference — they don't stand in line, they don't suffer public embarrassment, or spit out "homeowner deduction" as if it has a slightly sour taste. This deduction, though, is regressive, giving people with higher incomes greater breaks than people with lower incomes. It is also regressive because everyone can't afford to take advantage of that tax break. In 1988, 31 percent of all homeowners could not afford to buy a median-priced home if they were to re-enter the market. An overwhelming 90 percent of renters couldn't afford to buy median-priced homes!

Who benefits from mortgage deduction benefits, then? Ten percent of the benefits went to households with more than $200,000 in earnings, just 0.7 percent of the population. Those who earned between $100,000 and $200,000 got 25 percent of the mortgage deduction. Of those 89 percent of households who earned under $75,000, many did take the deduction even when they owned homes. Renters, 35 million of our nation's households, receive no housing benefit at all. Many of these households write a check for rent as high as any mortgage, but because they don't have a down payment, they can't get any of the home ownership pork that the rich get.

The homeowner deduction, despite its drain on the treasury, is as American as motherhood and apple pie. Its supporters say it promotes ownership and stability. But with the number of people using their homes as a borrowing chit, it also promotes inequality. People can borrow on their homes to pay off car loans, credit cards, and lines of credit, deducting the interest. Those who borrow to buy a car the conventional way end up with mounds of non-deductible debt.

There are other ways to promote home ownership and stability than the homeowner deductions that currently exist. A homeowner tax credit could be structured to reduce the tax bill instead of the current structure of a reduction on total income. It would also even out the benefit of home ownership, bringing some low and moderate income people into the housing market who aren't there now. There are also proposed reforms from deficit hawks like the Concord Coalition who would limit the mortgage deduction to $12,000 for single taxpayers and $20,000 for couples. Ross Perot is among those who has proposed capping a mortgage deduction to $250,000 in mortgage principal. That might hurt buyers in higher-priced California, but make the deduction fairer in other parts of the country. The *Common Cause* article outlined several proposals for change, but notes that there are some powerful real estate, banking, and home-building lobbies protecting the status quo. And there is little impetus to change the current situation.

There's been plenty of sneering about "welfare" and "entitlements" by conservatives who would like to eliminate government assistance to the poor with a simple flick of their pen. Who wants to bet they won't be as eager to streamline the entitlement of mortgage deductions that subsidizes the wealthy and ignores the poor?

King Features Syndicate, September 15, 1994

CREDIT FUELS ECONOMIC EXPANSION
BY JULIANNE MALVEAUX

The economic indicators of the past year or two provide a mixed and inconsistent story about the state of the nation's economy. On one hand, there has been rather steady economic growth, but few seem to feel the effects of this growth since wages have been stagnant and many workers fear layoffs and downswings. Consumer confidence faltered somewhat last month, but new home sales grew by 1.4 percent, a two-year record. With confidence down and incomes stagnant, what fuels economic expansion? A look at credit card debt provides an unfortunate answer to the question.

Revolving consumer debt keeps rising, reaching a record $438.5 billion in April 1996, 20 percent more than credit card debt a year ago. Growth isn't up 20 percent. Incomes aren't up 20 percent. If debt is up 20 percent, it means that people are spending faster than they are earning. And some of this debit spending is driving the economic growth that we are experiencing. It might also be driving the trepidation that so many consumers are feeling about their jobs and their futures. And, increased credit debt might explain why, despite uncertainty, consumers are able to keep spending.

Increased spending in and of itself would not be problematic, except for the fact that many consumers are not repaying their creditors on time. Late payments on credit cards hit a 15-year high on March 31. Nonbusiness bankruptcies were up 17 percent from a year ago, and at the current rate there may be as many as a million personal bankruptcy petitions filed in 1996.

Meanwhile, banks and businesses are competing intensely for the nearly 20 percent interest people pay on credit card debt. Airlines, department stores, and even computer companies have combined with banks to offer specialty credit cards with benefits like frequent flyer miles and free on-line time offered for frequent use of credit cards. But banks walk a tightrope between encouraging credit card spending (they don't make any money on the consumer who charges and then pays the bill within 25 days, avoiding both interest and late charges) and tightening up their credit standards to make it more difficult to qualify for cards.

Once people qualify, though, they may never need to carry cash again. Grocery stores, gas stations, and even fast-food restaurants accept credit cards. The increased ease in using plastic may be great for convenience, but it also makes it easy for those on the financial brink to dig themselves deeper into trouble. When someone is paying for groceries with a credit card because they don't have the cash to buy food, bankruptcy can't be far behind.

Despite increased bankruptcies, the banks keep sending the credit cards out, seeking new markets on college campuses and among others with limited ability to repay. Some students report having received several credit cards with access to thousands of dollars in credit. Many students find themselves in serious financial trouble before they have reached their majority because of the easy access they have to credit.

If economic growth is based on the shaky foundation of credit card debt, we can only expect to see growth slow if more people find themselves in financial trouble because they can't pay their bills. Many expected this slowdown in the face of the employment situation, but the availability of credit may have allowed some people to keep spending and to postpone the inevitable, both for themselves and for the country.

King Features Syndicate, June 26, 1996

LIFE, DEATH AND TOBACCO PROFITS
BY JULIANNE MALVEAUX

The relatively unregulated multi-million dollar tobacco industry has been challenged by medical experts on the relationship between smoking and cancer. After reviewing thirty years' worth of internal documents from Brown and Williamson, a company that produces several brands of cigarettes, the American Medical Association has charged "cover-up" saying that there is "detailed and damning evidence" that the industry covered up the addictive and cancer-causing impact of cigarettes for three decades.

AMA president Lonnie Bristow said that the federal government should eliminate all forms of tobacco advertising, block exports of cigarettes, and more strictly enforce laws that prohibit minors from buying cigarettes, "to prevent the tobacco industry from recruiting replacements for the thousands of people dying each year from smoking-related diseases." The AMA, in a series of articles in the most recent *Journal of the American Medical Association (JAMA)*, provides details, including quotes from tobacco executives, about the link between smoking and cancer. They conclude that the American people have been "duped" by the tobacco industry. "We should all be outraged, and we should force the removal of this scourge from our nation and by so doing set an example for the world," an AMA spokesman said at a press conference reviewing findings from its "first scientific review" of Brown and Williamson documents.

The AMA wouldn't ban smoking, but it might support making cigarettes a prescription drug. They were acutely aware of the implications of their findings and recommendations. Said a spokesman, "We recognize the serious consequences of this ambition, but the health of our nation is more important than the profits of any single industry."

Profit is the magic word. So is the way tobacco advertising has infiltrated itself into so many of society's good causes. There's the Virginia Slims tennis tournament that supposedly advances the status of women in tennis. There's the Kool Achievers Award that highlights community service. There are the dozens of ads in magazines that pitch their editorial content toward minorities or women, and the ads in the commemorative program journals of civil rights and women's organization conventions. One might note that since women and people of color smoke, these ads are nothing more than an appropriate recognition of committed customers. Sometimes, though, the ads may entice new customers. The fastest-growing group of smokers is young women, especially young women of color. Do the magazines and organizations that say they want to uplift these women actually shake the hands of those who kill their constituents?

Few eschew tobacco advertising, but those who do don't seem to manage. San Diego-based African American Women on Tours has grown from an annual three-day extravaganza of African American women's vitality to a five-city, fifteen-day traveling celebration. Founder and Chief Executive Officer Maria Carothers deliberately avoids tobacco sponsorship, preferring the support of companies that support a holistic lifestyle. Her underwriters include Reebok, Honda, JC Penney, Allstate Insurance, *HealthQuest* magazine, and the African American Tobacco Education Network.

Carothers has been firmly committed to a course that many are reluctant to risk. Perhaps the unwillingness to create distance from tobacco has been a function of ignorance about the risks from smoking. After all, that Surgeon General's warning that sits on the side of a cigarette box is about as effective a deterrent as the waggling finger of a moral elder aunt. Now, the American Medical Association findings offer more ammunition.

Smoking causes cancer. Cancer causes death. Smoking generates profit.

Profit supports (some) life. The nation's largest medical association says we need to understand the link between smoking and death. Is there any reason to support the link between smoking and tobacco industry profits?

King Features Syndicate, July 14, 1995

POVERTY AND THE ECONOMY
BY JULIANNE MALVEAUX

Poor people have become the nation's latest scapegoat, and the 104th Congress seems determined to punish the poor for their poverty. Welfare recipients are being told to find jobs in an economy that can't generate enough employment for those who don't need public assistance. Deadbeat dads are threatened with lock-up, even if they are unemployed. Some cities have passed ordinances that criminalize panhandling because citizens and tourists are bothered by the intrusion of coins clanging in a cup. Our attitudes toward the poor might change if we viewed the economic impact of their consumption. Millions are employed because of the ways that we regulate the poor, and because of the ways that the poor spend their money. Instead of scapegoating the poor, we might want to scapegoat those who benefit from their poverty.

For example, Howard University professor Ralph Gomes has estimated that poor people spend about $800 million at fast-food restaurants annually. Imagine the employment implications of withdrawing that much money from the economy! Poor people, because of their location, tend to buy at mom-and-pop neighborhood stores instead of supermarkets. They pay more than they should for staples like milk, juice, and bread, but they keep millions of people employed. Poor people who are lucky enough to get Section 8 vouchers for housing (only one in eight of those eligible for Section 8 gets it) pump dollars into the housing market, often by paying rents in homes that might not be as easily rented. Someone gains because the poor need housing.

We might also look at the social service industry, the people employed in it, and the alternative uses of their time in our society. The social workers whose approval is a hurdle the poor must clear to qualify for public assistance are, quiet as it's kept, public servants. Will eliminating welfare eliminate their jobs? How much of public assistance expenditures keep social workers employed? How would a movement to something like a negative income tax impact social service employment? Is that one of the reasons we haven't moved to the most efficient solution to poverty—providing the poor with money?

To the extent that there is a connection between poverty and crime, it is also useful to consider the prison industrial complex. Prison guards in California are paid an average of $45,000 annually, the highest salary in the nation. Teachers in California don't earn the same average pay! The California Corrections Officers made the largest single contribution to a gubernatorial candidate in 1994, giving Pete Wilson $423,000. It seems to be in the interest of prison guards to elect a governor committed to prison, not rehabilitation. If poverty contributes to the crime level, then, it is in the interest of prison guards to elect a governor committed to maintaining a certain level of poverty in the state.

Too many policy makers justify poverty by pointing out that poor people don't work hard enough, that they in some ways "deserve" their poverty. But the people who hold minimum wage jobs (child care workers, parking lot attendants, food service workers, home health attendants) are among our nation's hardest workers. Most welfare recipients have held jobs like these sometime in the past two years. We could increase the minimum wage and eliminate poverty. We could improve the earned-income tax credit and eliminate poverty. But there may be an economic justification to poverty. Poverty may generate too many benefits to be eliminated.

King Features Syndicate, August 18, 1995

IS FLAT FAIR?
BY JULIANNE MALVEAUX

Former Congressman Jack Kemp headed the National Commission on Economic Growth and Tax Reform and just recommended a total rehaul of the national tax system. He says a flat tax makes sense, and in saying so, he joins the gaggle of flat-tax geese led by candidate Steve Forbes and Congressman Richard Armey. On the surface, the flat-tax argument appeals to people. When you remind people how many hours they spend preparing their taxes, then suggest that a flat tax means they can jot their taxes down on a postcard, the flat tax seems attractive.

Kemp suggests that 19 or 20 percent is the appropriate flat-tax level. He advocates a "generous" deduction for the working poor, noting in an interview on the *Today* show that families of 4 with less than $30,000 in income should pay no federal taxes. But Kemp would also keep the mortgage interest deduction. So that flat tax isn't as flat as it might be, with the tax treatment between owners and renters sharply different.

Not that most low-income earners are homeowners. Indeed, the mortgage interest deduction is seen by many as a "mansion subsidy" that gives middle and upper income people a tax break. To be sure, anyone who pays mortgage interest gets a deduction. But it means more to the higher-earning person than to a more moderate earner. If a flat tax preserves the mortgage interest tax deduction, in many ways it passes along part of the tax burden to those who do not own homes. From that perspective flat isn't fair.

But there are many reasons to criticize the flat tax. Some analysts note that flat taxes with "generous deductions" will lower taxes for the poorest and richest taxpayers, shifting the burden to those at the middle, those who earn between $50,000 and $100,000 per year. When the flat tax is combined with the elimination of an array of deductions that middle income people rely on, they further shoulder the burden of this structural shift. Those who get the best deal from a flat tax are the wealthy, especially wealthy shareholders who won't pay capital gains taxes anymore. Republicans have been pushing for capital gains tax cuts since 1981, when Ronald Reagan became President. The flat tax is the ultimate capital gains tax cut. It is a gift to the wealthy.

Jack Kemp offers less of a gift than Steve Forbes does. Forbes would have a simple flat tax, with few exemptions and few deductions. This kind of operation helps people like Forbes, with multi-million dollar incomes and massive wealth, more than any other group in our society. Despite differences in their flat tax concepts, though, both Kemp and Forbes seem to dismiss the notion of a progressive tax system, which suggests that the wealthiest pay a higher percentage tax on their incomes to reflect the greater responsibility they have for maintaining the government that supports the status quo that guarantees their wealth.

Kemp and Forbes seem to forget that government does not simply dole out money to the poor or create giveaway programs for the middle class. Government regulates the financial institutions that help the wealthy preserve their wealth and, through regulatory groups like the Federal Reserve Board, sets the interest rate to, essentially, maintain profits in the stock and bond market. Government creates economic opportunities for the wealthy, not the poor, when it contracts out, shifts regulations, decides to jettison environmental safety and health legislation.

There are dozens of reasons to continue to support the progressive tax system, including one source that some conservatives savor. There is a Biblical verse that says that "much is expected of those to whom much is given." Kemp and Forbes see wealth as an entitlement, not a gift. They seem to feel that the poor and middle-income should pay their fair share for the institutions that support the wealthy. They have spent time, energy, and effort promoting the notion that a flat tax is easy. But it isn't fair.

King Features Syndicate, January 18, 1996

CUTTING TAXES OR STIMULATING ENROLLMENT?
BY JULIANNE MALVEAUX

Cap in hand and gown aflowing, President William Jefferson Clinton made his bid to be the "education President" when he spoke on June 4 at Princeton University. He offered a $1500 refundable tuition tax credit for students and their parents, and predicted that such a credit would make community college attendance essentially free. What he didn't say was that the tax credit would cost about $25 billion in the next seven years, though the President did say that he could pay for the cost by reinstating a tax on international flights and imposing another set of new taxes.

Because issues of educational access are so important, this proposed tax credit merits attention. To be sure, it will help poor young people who don't have the wherewithal to attend a school like Princeton or Yale. But one has to wonder, as one always does when tax incentives are offered to modify behavior, if the tax will stimulate enrollment or if it will do less than is intended.

Let's talk, first, about the mechanics of a college tuition tax credit. How will students claim it? They'll have to file a form on April 15, and get a credit against the taxes that they owe. If they owe less than $1500, they'll get a refund from the government. Sounds good, right?

It sounds good for the parent who sends her daughter to Princeton, whose $5000 tax obligation is reduced by a tuition credit. But what about the parent who has to scramble to make a tuition payment at a community college, or the adult student who, between making ends meet, cannot find the extra dollars to enroll for classes. Despite President Clinton's good intentions in using a tax credit to provide tuition relief, good intentions may not be good enough for those who struggle with day-to-day survival issues.

If this tax credit is designed to help students on the bottom, then community college tuition should be free. The $25 billion that is spent reimbursing people for tuition might well be used to make sure that community colleges are open to everyone who needs a boost or a hand at college attendance. All it takes is a walk through community college halls to understand what I mean. The last time I visited a community college, I ran into a 50-year-old woman who had just finished her GED and hoped her years at a neighborhood college would prepare her for a BA in English Literature. I talked to a young black man who was undertaking a vocational certificate in printing, and living with relatives until he could find employment. I spent time with a Latina woman whose English as a Second Language courses had lit her learning fire and moved her to pursue political science studies. None of these folks had the disposable income to pay for the classes they wanted to take, and their dreams were held together by a combination of financial aid and community support. Few of these folks would see their plight enhanced by a college tuition tax credit. Good intentions sometimes aren't good enough.

And there are other issues. Some economists note that the money spent on this tax credit will have to come from someplace else in this deficit-conscious economy. Indeed, some Clinton advisors argued against the tuition tax credit, suggesting that this could lead to some kind of bidding war on targeted tax cuts for some populations.

The travel industry, which might shoulder the burden for this cut, has already called it unfair. Is there a connection between international travel (the tax on which would rise from $6 to $16 a ticket) and higher education? What about the sale of radio and television franchises? What do we give to get?

The human capital equation suggests that education is one of the few ways that African Americans can improve on the card we are dealt. Educated black folks simply earn more than uneducated black folks do (though less than educated whites), so that any initiative that stimulates black enrollment and encourages black education bears examination.

But it is not clear that a tax credit is the way to encourage the college enrollment of those whose struggles with disposable income are so significant that they don't have enrollment fees. If, as the President notes, a community college credential today is what high school used to be, then community college tuition ought to be free. Not credited. Not rebated. Not deducted. Just free.

Otherwise this new Clinton initiative might stimulate posturing, but not enrollment. Otherwise, those who ought to benefit will find themselves, again, out in the cold.

Black Issues in Higher Education, June 6, 1996

WHAT PRICE A LIFE?
BY JULIANNE MALVEAUX

What value do we place on a life? A limb? The possibility of poisoning from dirty water, leaded paint, poorly manufactured food? The 104th Congress, with its focus on "risk assessment" as a way to curb a generation's worth of food, drug, and environmental regulations, will give us the opportunity to find out.

Republicans argue that government regulations place excessive burdens on business and competition. They say that cost-benefit analysis must be applied to any regulatory process. On one hand they offer to "streamline" government by eliminating regulation, but on the other hand, the risk assessment process may simply prolong discussions about which regulations should be imposed and which should not. The new process for "risk assessment" includes a cost-benefit analysis, a peer review system by panels that may well include representatives of the industry being regulated. Talk about the fox watching the chicken coop! The Gingrich rationale is that the fox knows the chicken coop much better than the chickens do, and so is a logical choice to watch it.

In addition to additions to the "risk assessment" process, there are proposals to simply cut the appropriations of regulatory agencies such as the Food and Drug Administration, the Occupational Safety and Health Administration, and others, rendering those agencies so ineffective that their elimination would make no difference. The anti-regulatory fervor extends to the Safe Drinking Water Act, the Clean Air Act, the Consumer Product Safety Commission, and other regulatory groups. All of this is being done as part of the "Jobs Creation and Wage Enhancement Act" in the Contract on America, on the simple assertion that less regulation will create employment.

House Speaker Newt Gingrich considers the Food and Drug Administration and the Environmental Protection Act the two largest "job-killers" in America, and the witness lists on regulatory policy reflect this bias. Industrialists have dominated the hearings, with environmentalists, consumer advocates and others sidelined until the very end of the hearings when the press (and some members of Congress) have moved on. In some cases, business owners have been handed seemingly limitless amounts of time to babble about the negative effects of regulation, while environmentalists have been held to strict time limits. In other cases, all of the "opposing views" have been compressed onto a panel, while those who abhor regulation as strongly as Newt does were allowed individual speaking time.

Newt's regulatory fervor ignores the reason the federal government first got involved in the regulatory process. Unfettered profiteering in the early phase of industrialization ignored concerns of environmental or consumer protection. The Food and Drug Act of 1906 was passed in response to unsafe and unsanitary working conditions in meat-packing plants. The Child Labor Act was passed because so many children were employed, and injured, in the mines and on the fields. Without these regulations, most businesses seek to make profit no matter who it hurts or how. While some businesses find regulation onerous, many acknowledge that regulations simply balance the concerns of industrialists with the concerns of the rest of society.

The 104th Congress, in voting this risk assessment policy into law, is suggesting that the rest of society should have no concerns. That's not only troubling, it also begs the question. What price a life? An environment? Safety? The Contract on America is nothing more than a Contract with Big Business at America's expense. This is less about a balanced budget amendment or a rules change than about ways the balance of power shifts away from the people and toward the industrialists who funded so many Congressional victories in 1994.

King Features Syndicate, March 3, 1995

WEEVILS IN THE SMALL BUSINESS ENGINE
BY JULIANNE MALVEAUX

Small Business Week is coming up, and people are celebrating, rallying around the theme, Small Business: Building America's Future. Between April 30 and May 6, the United States Small Business Administration will honor the nation's 21 million small businesses with a series of special events around the country, including recognition of a Small Business Person of the Year, a Women in Business Advocate, a Veterans in Business Advocate, and a Minority Small Business Advocate (if minorities are not outlawed by the Contract on America before April 30).

The people at the Small Business Administration are right to note that the small business presence has increased by 50 percent since 1982, that small firms employ more than half of all workers, and the majority of all receipts. They are also right to celebrate the rise of the small entrepreneur. But there are weevils in small business success, weevils that speak to flaws in the theory that the small business engine is the ticket to ride for those locked out of majority corporations. In too many instances, small businesses replicate the occupational segregation and unequal pay that larger businesses set patterns for. Is small business a ticket to ride, or a ticket to static? It depends on your perspective.

A recent Bureau of Census Statistical Brief described a study of small business that spoke to occupational and industrial segregation and separation. Entitled "Two Different Worlds: Men and Women from 9 to 5," the report noted that most men worked for firms that employed men, while most women worked for firms that employed women, and that firms with a higher percentage of male employees paid higher wages and salaries. The gender and education of firm owners often determined the gender of those hired. In other words — men were more likely to employ men, while women were more likely to employ women.

Most men worked in firms that were more than 90 percent male. More than 20 percent of men who worked for small businesses worked for all-male firms. What chance does a woman have to be hired in a firm where macho culture is the name of the game? How likely is her survival?

The coin certainly tosses the other way on this one. Women are more likely to hire women employees. But firms owned by women have lower pay levels and lower profits than firms owned by men. This has less to do with gender, in my opinion, than with bias. In any case, men don't pay the same penalty for their work at an all-male firm as women pay for their work at an all-female firm.

The stratification of workers within firms suggests there is a limit to public policy about equal pay. The Equal Pay Act of 1963 outlaws differential pay for people who work in the same firm. But if people work in different firms, firms segregated by gender or race, the law does not address their pay differences. Occupational segregation in small firms leads directly to pay differentials.

The federal government can't do much to change individual firm hiring patterns, especially when small businesses are so small (with an average of 6 employees) that it makes no sense to come down hard on one or two firms. But when the government celebrates this Small Business Week, it might nudge firms segregated by gender to consider the implication of their hiring patterns. The small business engine of economic growth is slowed by the weevils of gender segregation in small business employment. Somewhere in the Small Business Week celebration, there should be time for that moment of truth.

King Features Syndicate, April 7, 1995

PUSHCART CAPITALISM AND ITS DETRACTORS
BY JULIANNE MALVEAUX

The other day, in downtown Washington, D.C., a policeman ticketed a street vendor whose goods were spread across the street from a small shop that sold some of the same things. Of course the officer couldn't ticket the vendor for having better prices or for unfair competition. Instead, the ticket was for "obstruction of public space" because some of the vendor's display cases blocked foot traffic.

As the weather gets better, that scene is replayed around the country. Small shop owners, and some large department stores, see street vendors as a threat and want to do something to contain them. In New York, Mayor Rudolph Giuliani declared war on street vendors a year ago, first restricting food carts on 57th Street, then removing vendors from Harlem's 125th Street into a more contained public market on 116th Street. Such drastic measures are rare, but the tensions that simmer between pushcart capitalists and their cooped-up cousins are commonplace.

Store owners have overhead much higher than that of street vendors. They pay rent, utilities, and other fees. In most cities, vendors pay a fee for a vending license that ranges from $200 to $1500. They also pay sales tax to cities. But every vendor isn't licensed and cash transactions sometimes slip between the sales tax cracks. So with lower expenses, street vendors can offer far more attractive prices. Just a few steps from a New York bookstore, I saw a vendor with best-selling novels priced at half of the cover price. Around the corner from one of my favorite flower shops, a street vendor offered a dozen roses for just $10, less than half of what I'd pay inside. The playing field, where overhead is concerned, is hardly level between shop owners and street vendors.

Street vendors are trying to make the same living store owners are. They get hassled by law enforcement officers, stymied by poor weather, challenged by the "free market" pressures of finding, and keeping, the right spot to sell from. Yet they offer much to the urban environment, and also to consumers. When the 57th Street hot dog stands were closed in New York City, thousands asked where else they could find such a quick and inexpensive lunch. When the man who sells roses at half price is missing, many miss the $5 pre-wrapped bouquets he offers, since they are simply unavailable elsewhere.

It is amusing to contemplate the differences between street vendors and the stores and wonder if price and service differences reflect the difference in overhead. Street vendors don't offer bags or receipts, there are no quality guarantees, nor return policies. But some are as permanent (and as dependable) as large department stores. With the quality of customer service declining in stores where job insecurity sometimes turns sales clerks into snarling register guards, the street vending experience is much more pleasant than the department store queue.

Many vendors aspire to become shop owners. Their pushcarts, stands, and vans spilling over with goods are the first step to owning a more permanent structure. Street selling is, for some, the entry-level job to a career in retail sales. It's a point some cities need to keep in mind as they try to regulate the pushcart capitalists out of business.

King Features Syndicate, June 4, 1995

SMALL BUSINESSES GENERATE JOBS, NOT CLOUT
BY JULIANNE MALVEAUX

As our nation's small businesses both grow and diversify, it has become popular to discuss these businesses in terms of their economic influence. The raw data seem convincing — the nation's 22 million small businesses make 52 percent of all sales and employ 54 percent of all labor. Small and medium-sized businesses owned by women employ more people than the 11 million or so employed by the Fortune 500. Small businesses are our nation's "economic engine," the place where the jobs of the future will be. Do these facts mean that the pendulum will shift from Fortune 500 businesses to small businesses?

In the latest edition of *Who Rules America: Power and Politics in the Year 2000* (Mountain View, California: Mayfield Publishing, 1998), University of California at Santa Cruz professor William Domhoff argues that power will not shift. The owners of small businesses, he says, "are too large in number, too diverse in size, and too lacking in financial assets to have any collective power that could challenge the corporate community." Thus, while there are reasons to encourage the growth and development of small businesses, the notion that these businesses have a chance to erode large corporate power is laughable. Why does it matter? Because large corporations, through the contributions they make to politicians, too often set the policy agenda. Because what is good for big business is not always good for small business (and is almost never good for workers or consumers). Because the notion that small business can challenge big business simply because of the jobs it generates makes our policy process seem far more democratic than it is.

According to the latest economic census just 18 percent of the businesses tabulated had employees. As many as a third of the businesses counted are part-time businesses. Many of the businesses described as our nation's "growth engines" are actually self-employment opportunities for individuals who have been laid off or downsized from corporate America. Many are concentrated in the services, and many individuals are replicating work they did "inside" Fortune 500 companies for less pay. Indeed, Domhoff notes that some small businesses are part of economic networks that depend on large corporations. They are subcontractors and suppliers who are often dependent on the large corporations that set the policy agenda. Are they likely to bite the hand that feeds them with criticisms of the corporate role in setting the policy agenda? Hardly.

Small businesses may generate jobs, but larger businesses have the power that comes with ownership of assets. Domhoff asserts that the same concentration of wealth that we see among individuals exists among corporations. Three-tenths of one percent of our nation's business entities have 59 percent of total business assets. They intimidate and set an agenda through their sheer size, through ways they relate to smaller businesses in trade associations, and through the ways they can affect the economic health of smaller businesses. The new merger movement, which is causing increased industrial concentration, leaves small businesses at a greater disadvantage.

This is not being written to disparage small business ownership or to suggest that the jobs generated by small businesses are not important. Indeed, the reason many small business owners do not object to industrial concentration and the disproportionate clout big business has is because they hope, one day, to be big business, too. So they don't speak up, organize, or work to their own advantage, to make sure the market operates fairly and that no one has too much power, either economically or legislatively. Small business silence is one of the reasons why campaign finance reform is so slow in coming. It may be one of the many reasons why the tobacco bill could not be passed.

Small businesses may well be our nation's economic engine. They do generate more jobs than Fortune 500 companies do. But they don't have the clout or access that big businesses do. They can't influence the political agenda the way big businesses do. They ought to be the most vocal advocates for campaign finance reforms and for other ways to dilute the concentration of power in our nation. Instead they are busier running their businesses than influencing policy, which may be good for their bottom line but not for the nation.

King Features Syndicate, June 19, 1998

WHAT'S THE MATTER WITH BANKING?
BY JULIANNE MALVEAUX

A careful look at banking practices makes one wonder if banks need, or even want, customers. On one hand, banks have developed a set of electronic services, such as automatic tellers and 24-hour banking by phone to keep people away from banks. ATM machines turn up every place from the grocery store to the gas station, making it convenient for customers to get at their cash whenever they want to. At the same time, many banks charge a fee for the excess use of these services. One California bank allows only 3 calls a month to the 24-hour banking-by-phone line before tacking on a service charge. Another requires a certain balance before telephone banking is available.

At the same time, many banks have developed a debit card capacity. ATM cards can be used to pay for groceries, department store items, concert tickets and almost anything else in a debit capacity. Again, there may be a fee tacked on, but that's the price of convenience?

The most amazing development has been the banking industry's new push to charge people for walking into a bank and using the services of a teller. If the electronic lure to stay out has not been enough, some banks have decided to penalize customers for wanting their services. Last week, First National Bank of Chicago announced it will begin, in June, charging a $3 fee for transactions that involve a teller. Some banks in California and Seattle already charge fees for certain teller visits.

What's a customer to do? Bank fees are on the rise. More and more banks charge for the smallest courtesies — from unlimited checking to the simple act of returning canceled checks. Now they want to charge for "face time." The message that the customer seems to get is "bring us your money, but then let it sit." If you want to take it out via ATM, check, or teller, it's going to cost you!

The irony here is that while banks can't seem to do what they are supposed to do, simple banking, they have been lobbying to do more than the law allows them to do. Some banks want to sell insurance. Others want to push stocks and bonds. They want to offer "one-stop shopping" for financial services. But the one-stop shopping could turn into a one-stop fee splurge if people were charged $3 every time they looked into a "banking service." The simple act of asking too many questions might cause someone's checking account to go into overdraft.

Perhaps I overstate my case. The point is that bankers earn interest on the money that people deposit in their institutions. All these extra fees and charges seem to sweeten the pot for bankers, but do nothing for their customers. In recent years, much has been written about how much it costs to maintain an "average" account, one with an average daily balance of under $1000 with a dozen or so checks written on it each month. Those kinds of thresholds concern me, when many do not maintain an average balance even half that, when the average income for a family of four is such that those balances are out of the reach of many families.

Banks need to come clean with what they call the "costs" of servicing regular accounts, come clean with a rationale for charging customers for getting customer assistance. Most businesses would pay people $3 to walk into the door, but banks seem to want to have it the other way around. And the pack mentality among banking competitors ensures that if one bank asks $3 for a teller visit, it won't be long before every bank asks the same.

What impact does this kind of structure have on teller employment? Are tellers being turned into independent contractors who have to attract a certain number of customer visits before earning a salary?

What's the matter with banking? It seems that bankers have forgotten that customers are the foundation upon which they offer their services. If bankers keep this fee-for-transaction trend up, they make a strong case for the use of alternatives to commercial banks, such as credit unions.

King Features Syndicate, May 5, 1995

CAUTION ON BANK MERGERS
BY JULIANNE MALVEAUX

If Citicorp and the Travelers Insurance Group are allowed to merge by federal regulators, the newly proposed Citigroup would be the world's largest financial institution, offering one-stop shopping where consumers could have access to everything from life and automobile insurance to checking and savings accounts, to investment services. This mega-merger is the natural outgrowth of several other mergers that have happened in the past year (and forthcoming proposed mergers like that between BankAmerica and NationsBank, Inc.), but most critics note that these mergers are good neither for workers nor for consumers. Bank mergers often mean the consolidation of branches and are accompanied by layoffs. Consumers lose with mergers because their options are diminished, there is less competition and higher prices, and it is too easy for one-stop shopping to turn into a one-stop rip-off.

Many of the concerns about mega-mergers are likely to be voiced on April 29 when the House Banking Committee meets to discuss the regulatory challenges posed by the merger boom. These banking hearings are likely to be complicated by pending legislation. HR 10, the Financial Services Act of 1998, proposes to streamline bank regulation and remove some of the firewalls that exist between certain financial services. While bankers have urged the Congress to get rid of post-Depression-era banking legislation that offered an array of structural safeguards and consumer protections, Congress ought to be mindful of the conditions that made such legislation necessary. In other words, one need not be a pessimist to notice similarities between the soaring stock market and increasing financial consolidation of today, and the conditions that preceded the Depression nearly seventy years ago.

Consumer groups have noted that bank mergers and the new financial legislation combine to provide few consumer protections, higher bank fees, and less community reinvestment. Small business groups note that mega-banks are most likely to "bank by the numbers," and the personal touch that many small businesses need to get started or to have access to capital will be missing. While small banks and credit unions may get a boost from the consolidation of major banks, credit unions still must pass the hurdle of new legislation to reverse the February Supreme Court decision that curtailed their operation.

While the Federal Reserve Board has primary responsibility for banking regulation, and the final say on bank mergers (but not necessarily insurance mergers, since state insurance agencies regulate groups like the Travelers), several other regulators can get involved in the banking regulation process. The Office of Thrift Supervision charters savings and loan companies, the Federal Deposit Insurance Corporation guarantees deposits of member banks, and the Office of the Comptroller examines the books of banks. All may want to have a say at next week's hearings on the mega-merger trend. So will California Congresswoman Maxine Waters.

Waters (D-Calif.) has been a member of the House Banking Committee since her election to Congress in 1990. Her focus has been on the little people, banking consumers as well as those who do not have access to banks. When our nation's taxpayers were asked to finance the results of the savings-and-loan debacle, it was Waters who pushed for banks to take some responsibility for their misdeeds. She also insisted that affirmative action policies be used to choose those who cleaned up the S&L mess. Waters was masterful in pointing out the irony of paying banks and accounting firms to clean up the mess that they had recently made.

Now this advocate for the little people has focused on the Citicorp-Travelers merger and made her opposition clear. Mostly, Waters opposes the merger because she feels it will not enhance the well-being of the nation's consumers. Equally importantly, though, she has asked Congress to investigate "the nefarious use of Citibank's private bank system by the world's most notorious drug lords and money launderers." "If any of these devastating allegations lead to criminal conviction," Waters said, "Citicorp never should be allowed to merge or acquire again."

Waters detailed allegations against Citibank at an early April press conference. She referenced an ongoing investigation by the Department of Justice and the Swiss and Mexican attorneys general into potential Citicorp/Citibank involvement with Raul Salinas de Gotari in laundering drug money. Waters notes that Salinas had access to funds despite the fact that he was never asked about his employment or source of income. Imagine how many dollars the average consumer would have access to without providing this information! Indeed, consider the notion that in some communities people do not even qualify to have a bank account because of their lack of income.

Allegations about drug laundering are but one reason why consumers should look askance at a proposed Citicorp-Travelers merger. If these mergers make it more difficult for consumers to get banking services, they should simply be rejected.

King Features Syndicate, April 4, 1998

MIXED METAPHORS AND MICROSOFT
BY JULIANNE MALVEAUX

The Justice Department and twenty state attorneys general are right to go after Microsoft, the software development company that has, in the words of Netscape officials, "a choke hold" on the computer industry. With 90 percent of the world's personal computers using the Windows operating system, and with Microsoft introducing its own Internet browser (Internet Explorer) on Windows, the company can steer consumers in one direction and crush any competitor. In technical terms, there is no "free entry" into the browser business for Microsoft competitors. The government's antitrust suit has a strong legal basis since it is possible for Microsoft, through Windows, to completely control access to the Internet and the World Wide Web.

In the short run, the Microsoft near-monopoly with Windows 98 may seem convenient to PC users who can be frustrated by the process of moving from one operating system to another. In the longer run, though, the near-monopoly may well mean higher prices for consumers. Government's role in regulating monopolies, as established by the Sherman Anti-Trust Act of 1890, was developed to prevent the predatory pricing that monopolists can impose on computers. Competition, theoretically, keeps innovators sharp and keeps prices down. Absent competition, industries can become stagnant, and prices can soar.

The hyperbole surrounding this case, though, has been an amusing and amazing study in mixed metaphors. Bill Gates says that requiring Microsoft to offer information about a competitor is like requiring purchasers of Coca-Cola to put two cans of Pepsi into a six-pack. Not. The more appropriate analogy might be that Coke purchasers would get to see cans of Pepsi at an adjoining display. Gates is overreaching in his analogy, just as he is overreacting in asserting that a compromise with the government would "put everything we've worked for and built for the past 23 years at risk." That statement suggests that Gates isn't confident that he can stand the competition that companies like Netscape are eager for. If the simple provision of information could topple the Microsoft empire, then it is possible that the empire is built on a foundation of sand.

The President hasn't helped matters here, either, by asserting that delaying the shipping of Windows will have a negative effect on the economy. Puh-lease. The so-called year 2000 computer crisis is likely to have a much larger effect, and after much panic about Y2K, as that problem is being called, some are suggesting its effects will be mild. Gates and Clinton have painted a picture of gloom and doom if we can't get Windows 98 soon after its scheduled June ship date. But the fact is that, for many, Windows 95 is working perfectly well. A few of us still use Macintosh computers. Our multi-trillion dollar economy won't grind to a halt sans Windows, no matter what Gates says.

The thing is that the more Gates talks, the better case he makes for the antitrust lawsuit. He may be a brilliant businessman and a technical genius, but his use of mixed metaphors shows some contempt for the competitive process and for concepts like "free markets." His May 19 full-page ad, taken out in newspapers all over the country, touts the "freedom to innovate, improve, and integrate new features into products." The ad would be persuasive if issues of entry had been addressed. Otherwise, it does not persuade consumers that there is no case against Microsoft. Indeed, the Microsoft ad may well have been ill-timed, and it may backfire.

The strongest factor in Microsoft's favor is time. The Justice Department is notoriously slow in settling antitrust cases — it took 10 years to break up AT&T, and 13 years to blow its case against IBM. It has been monitoring Microsoft since 1990, when it investigated the company for possible collusion with IBM. Gates certainly has the resources to drag this antitrust case out, while the Justice Department's chief antitrust prosecutor, Joel Klein, may have other monopoly issues (like code-sharing and consolidation in the airline industry) to consider. Klein is also constrained by his budget, and is already seeking more money to handle his caseload. Technology moves at lightning speed. If it changes the way computers operate, the case against Windows might be moot.

Time may be on Microsoft's side, and consumers may currently be indifferent to the Windows near-monopoly. But the Justice Department rarely brings antitrust cases that it cannot win. This case is important not only in the computer industry, but also in an economy that has seen increasing industrial concentration in the past few years. The "Baby Bells" are consolidating, as are the airlines, and consumers are likely to pay for this consolidation. In the Microsoft case, the Justice Department's success is likely to increase Internet access options for consumers.

King Features Syndicate, May 25, 1998

CHAPTER 2

POLITICS AND PERSONALITY

How can one call politics a science? There is no science to explain the way good intentions, on-paper agreements, and even budgets get complicated by the personalities we call politicians. Combining public policy with personal agendas has yielded us a mess called the Contract on America, a foreign policy shaped by misanthrope Jesse Helms, and by a Newt who has been in-our-face and out-of-control from the time he became Speaker of the House of Representatives in 1994 until he stepped down in late 1998. Science? Is there any science to the ranting and raving that characterize discourse on the floor of the House of Representatives? Or any science to the peculiar double standards that cause adulterers who live in glass houses to throw stones at a flawed and humbled President? Rev. Jesse Louis Jackson once talked about "personaltics" and politics, noting that when the two collide there is only chaos as an outcome. Well, personaltics and politics have been on a collision course for the past four years, with rancor and hostility often ruling the day. When our members of Congress address each other as "my esteemed colleague," it doesn't take a rocket scientist to figure out that in some minds "esteemed" has become a synonym for "idiotic" or "contemptible." Perhaps our times are uniquely shaped by the politics of personality.

Why don't we just call it that, then, the politics of personality? Then we'd have an easier time explaining, for example, how we can trade with Vietnam but not Cuba (Jesse Helms). Then it would make sense to justify why tax-cutting Republicans went dialing for dollars to provide federal support for a Robert Dole public policy chair at the University of Kansas. If we did the personality thing, not the politics thing, we could explain why the rather undistinguished (but both African American and charismatic) J.C. Watt is a rising star in the Republican Party. And if we talked the politics of personality we could explain some, if not much, of that impeachment thang. Impeachment, after all, is as much a political

process as a legal one, and it is a political process driven by personality. So, as much as we'd like to know what kind of person shakes his Psresidential groove thing with an intern less than half his age, we'd also like to know what kind of person writes it down in excruciating detail. And, we'd like to know what kind of person shapes an interrogatory with questions that begin "admit or deny."

POLITICS AND MORALITY
BY JULIANNE MALVEAUX

I keep hearing words like *morality* batted around in Washington. *Morality, integrity, role model, example.* Those who raise those words do so with all upright spine, and all appropriate virtuosity, with tongue-clucking, exasperation, outrage, and anger. What abomination, this Starr report, and its subject President William Jefferson Clinton! What an abhorrence — consensual, adulterous sex, and then lies about it! How despicable that a married man lied about an illicit affair! Give me a break! The moral arbiters in glass houses trying to throw stones are abominable, abhorrent, and despicable. Those who would constrain morality to personal lives and not public ones are the ones who cause me more pause than Mr. Clinton.

I write, of course, of the Washington imbroglio that has resulted from . . . well, what has it resulted from? Independent Counsel Kenneth Starr was authorized to look into fraud in the Arkansas Whitewater land deal. His authority was later extended to consider the firings in the White House Travel Office, and then the unauthorized acquisition of the FBI files of hundreds of Republicans. On these three matters he found so little that his report to the House Judiciary Committee mentions Whitewater exactly twice, and the Travel Office and FBI files not at all. In contrast, sex was mentioned more than five hundred times, and perjury about half as many times. So the Washington imbroglio has resulted from an overzealous and deceptive prosecutor on a partisan mission who was enabled by a flawed President who gave him fuel for the fire.

Still, if the issue is morality, there are lots of moral questions we might ask about legislative life and culture in Washington, D.C. Is it moral for legislators to refuse to raise the minimum wage while at the same time making it more difficult for the working poor to protect themselves from bankruptcy? Is it ethical for legislators to restrict the public's right to sue unscrupulous health maintenance organizations, while at the same time making it more difficult for individuals to get private health care? Is it scrupulous for Congress to pump up defense spending in a post-cold war era while ignoring President Clinton's concerns about smaller classrooms? And how decent is it to spend more than $40 million on a politically inspired investigation that yielded mere salacious drivel, when such funds could have been feeding the hungry, housing the homeless, educating the illiterate, or revitalizing cities?

Our nation seems stuck on a peculiar form of moral McCarthyism that raises an uncomfortable question — are you now, or have you ever been engaged in an extramarital affair? If you are not, do you know anyone who has participated in illicit sex? From a Starr perspective "illicit" is a permeable word. It means sex outside marriage, sex with an intern, sex with a younger person, sex at the desk, sex by the Paula Jones definition. Even I'm getting a little squirmy now, having used the word "sex" more times per paragraph than Kenneth Starr used "Whitewater" in his report. This is not about sex, not even slightly. It is more about a political witch-hunt, and about a Republican Congressional majority using every means necessary to repeal the election of a popular, moderate President.

And if we want to meander down a lane of historical morality, then we might ask about the morality of snatching land that belonged to Native Americans and Mexican people, selling human beings conveniently known as slaves, and importing Chinese people to build California railroads. To many, these aren't moral outrages, just market matters. For those who can't do such moral parsing, though, it is peculiar to watch Senators and members of Congress who have never been exercised about any issue suddenly jumping up and down about morality in the White House. It is as if these somnolent Congressmen were roused from a Rip Van Winkle sleep with a sudden reverence about justice. Their reverence, though, is more about sexual matters than economic justice that they can rail at Congressional microphones about unfairness without ever referencing our nation's deepest unfairness.

The real "fairness cops" are those members of the Congressional Black Caucus who have transformed the African American experience of selective prosecution into a rousing defense for William Jefferson Clinton. There are 37 members of the House Judiciary Committee; 21 of them are Republicans. In addition to ranking Democrat John Conyers (D-Mich.), the only Democrat to serve on the Judiciary Committee during Watergate, other CBC Democrats include Sheila Jackson Lee (D-Tex.), Bobby Scott (D-Va.), Maxine Waters (D-Calif.), and Melvin Watt (D-S.C.). Waters has, perhaps, spoken for the whole CBC contingent, when she noted that "We face Ken Starrs every day, men who run rampant over our rights. Ken Starr is a poster boy for the reckless abusive prosecutor." Sheila Jackson Lee told CNN that the Judiciary Committee is involved, not in a judicial process, but a "political process." "We have put the cart before the horse," she said. "We have released the evidence before deciding on the rules. We did not go into the grand jury room to see Timothy McVeigh testify, but we have gone into the grand jury room to see President Clinton." If there is a double standard, African American legislators are going to be sensitive to it, and opposed to it. Is this, perhaps, the real moral standard in this imbroglio, a standard that insists that the rules be real, consistent, fair? A standard that rejects a partisan, perhaps even personal, inquisition. A standard that draws a "zone of privacy" around personal and consensual relationships.

African Americans lift up this standard both because of the fairness argument that Maxine Waters advances, and because we have always had to grapple with the Biblical concept that the Lord uses flawed vessels through which to communicate his message. In context, President Clinton has done the right thing by the African American community, doing more than either electoral opponents George Bush or Robert Dole would have on appointments, politics, and policies. Thus, it makes sense that the African American community would support the President. It also makes sense that we, targets of our nation's selective morality, would ask questions about the crooked nature of our nation's righteousness. It makes sense, too, that we should deplore the way this sexual imbroglio has skewed discourse about public policy.

Thus, Republicans have attempted to add money to the defense budget while cutting taxes because they perceive this President as vulnerable. They have rebuffed an attempt to raise the minimum wage. They've attached anti-choice riders to the appropriation that would pay our outstanding UN dues and taken to the op-ed circuit to crow that the President need simply conform to their terms to cover our nation's UN obligation. They have attempted to use this President's Starr-induced weakness to compromise his policy positions.

Meanwhile, left-leaning liberals like me have been surprised at the venom directed at this President. He has, after all, tried to play both sides against the middle for much of his administration. He didn't have to deform the welfare system, but he did because he thought he was effecting a compromise that both sides can live with. Assisted by economic expansion, he has seen welfare rolls fall since public assistance was replaced by the flawed TANF (Temporary Assistance for Needy Families) program. Still, this President has not addressed ways that the poor will deal with welfare reform in recession. Why do conservatives despise a President that has reshaped an important income maintenance program on their terms? Why do they so strongly attack a Democrat who has done his best to effect bipartisan compromise?

The answers to these questions have little to do with morality, but much more to do with politics. No moral imperative dictates an impeachment, but the Republicans have sufficient political muscle to maneuver President Clinton's political denouement.

Crisis Magazine, October 1998

GENDER GAP MAY SAVE THIS PRESIDENT
BY JULIANNE MALVEAUX

Liberal women's groups have been taking partisan tongue-lashings because of their support of President Clinton. On CNN's *Crossfire*, Pat Buchanan asked if women's groups were "hypocrites" because they haven't asked for the President's resignation. Comparing this President to Clarence Thomas, who earned the ire of feminists when University of Oklahoma law professor Anita Hill accused him of workplace sexual harassment, Buchanan asked the same question other conservatives are asking — where are women now?

Of course, Buchanan is canny enough to know the difference between the unwanted advances Anita Hill says she was subjected to and the consensual (though inadvisable) relationship President Clinton had with Monica Lewinsky. And Buchanan is partisan enough to understand that he finally has a concrete reason to excoriate this President, and he isn't about to squander the opportunity even though the President's wrongdoing hardly constitutes an impeachable offense.

But recent polls say that leaders of feminist organizations are reflecting the interests of most women when they support the President and his policies. According to a Pew Research Center poll, women are also less likely than men to support impeachment even if it were proved that the President lied under oath. Do women have a different moral standard than men do? Hardly. Women understand the difference between the President's private life and his public policy. They also understand that this President has been supportive of women's issues and causes, and has been especially sensitive to the challenges facing working women.

That's why, when a group of women leaders held a press conference Thursday, they were passionate in their support of President Clinton. Demanding that the Republican Congress back off impeachment, these women were clear that, from their perspective, this impeachment talk is nothing more than a partisan attempt to halt the progress Clinton has made for women. This is a President, after all, who signed the Family and Medical Leave Act into law within days after taking office. This is a President who has appointed more women in senior cabinet positions than any other. This is a President whose philosophy of limited government intervention is offensive to many free-market Republicans. Most women understand that impeachment would serve more than a Constitutional purpose for Republicans. It would also nullify an election in the name of partisanship.

"Women should write, call, telefax, e-mail, shout and tell Congress, 'Do not impeach this president and don't force him to resign,'" said Yvonne Scruggs-Leftwich, head of the Black Leadership Forum Inc., at Thursday's news conference. Patricia Ireland described the Republicans as "mired in a partisan game of chicken." While no feminist leader is prepared to defend President Clinton's inappropriate relationship with Monica Lewinsky, and many are troubled with some of the details of the relationship, feminists were firm that his actions are not impeachable. Further, Fund for the Feminist Majority's Eleanor Smeal said, "We risk the ushering into power of a puritanical or fundamentalist sex police which speaks of freedom but allows government to destroy the right of privacy."

The real scandal, some women say, is the way women's issues have been overshadowed and ignored by the Starr report. Another issue, from where I sit, is the way some have chosen to define morality. How moral is it for women to work full time, full year and still not earn enough to make ends meet? How moral has been the Clinton-supported welfare reform? If I were to fight with President Clinton, it would be over his policies, not over his personal sexual relations. But the Congress prefers the personal fight, and women are telling them to back off.

If women follow the lead of feminist leaders, and if they stick to the opinions they have expressed in the polls, the gender gap may be the salvation of this President. But this hinges on voter turnout in November, on whether women's support for Clinton is stronger than their doubts about him, and whether women are willing to put their votes where their beliefs are.

King Features Syndicate, September 24, 1998

CLINTON: THE PERSONAL AND THE POLITICAL
BY JULIANNE MALVEAUX

If President William Jefferson Clinton had an affair with then 21-year-old intern Monica Lewinsky, he needs his butt beaten with an ugly stick. No doubt, Kenneth Starr will take care of that for him. At the same time, the press corps feeding frenzy around these allegations needs to be probed dispassionately. As repugnant as the President's private life might be, how does it affect public policy?

I've heard the perjury discussion, and I fully agree that no law enforcement official should suborn perjury or encourage it. At the same time, why is a private, consensual affair anybody's business? To be sure, learning that an allegedly libidinous President doesn't even stop at romancing a 21-year-old might tell us something about his character. Will it tell us something that we never knew? Ever since allegations about Gennifer Flowers surfaced about Clinton, there was an acknowledgment that there is something "not quite right" about this President. If the allegations are true, this President can contain the economy but not his sex drive. Far from being an apologist for this President, I'm a realist about him. There is too much playboy smoke out there for there not to be a little fire. Is this fire against the law? Does it render him incapable to serve as President?

If the perjury question is central, let's address it. Don't we force people into perjury when we dig into the marrow of their lives? Former HUD Secretary Henry Cisneros and the woman he had an affair with now both face jail terms because they hid their relationship. Yet, their relationship was no one's business but theirs. In addition to our resumes, must we also turn in our sexual histories in order to qualify for government employment? Must we also disclose that we drank too much one evening, drove without a license, and cheated on an exam a generation ago? The questions that prosecutors are asking people like Cisneros and Clinton are questions that went unasked in the Eisenhower and Kennedy administrations. There were allegations that were simply whispered a generation before that. We idolize leaders who were callous slaveholders but vilify those who got involved in consensual sexual relationships. Sounds like a double standard to me.

I'm as repulsed as anyone at the possibility that President Clinton was involved with an intern in the White House. Given his place at the center of the Paula Jones sexual harassment scandal, one would think that this President would avoid even the appearance of an untoward involvement. Despite the notion that an affair between President Clinton and Intern Lewinsky may have been consensual, I am also disturbed by the notion of unequal power in this relationship. If this President took advantage of a very young woman, however consensually, he ought to be repudiated. And if this President asked Ms. Lewinsky to lie, he has engaged in criminal acts.

Yet, I still want the press to draw some line between people's political and personal lives. Can a public servant have private flaws? Can a good man have bad affairs? Should a young woman who makes a bad consensual choice have her name and her image churned through the media? Why are we so interested in people's personal lives? And might we not focus our interest elsewhere?

I have always had mixed feelings about President Clinton, mainly because of the ways he attempts to be all things to all people. He is racially conscious with African American audiences, racially myopic with larger groups. He talks the talk with Democrats, and tries to cut the deal with Republicans. I think he knows what our nation needs, but I think he is willing to offer politically expedient half-measures. This sex scandal increases, not resolves, my ambiguity. If President Clinton had an affair with Monica Lewinsky he needs a strong reality check. But there are other villains — including wiretap queen Linda Tripp, who may have taken as much advantage of young Lewinsky as the President allegedly did.

If we had not such prurient interest in people's personal lives then women like Linda Tripp would have no role in political discourse. Isn't this reason enough to step back and take a hard look at this story? What integrity exists in a system that rewards a woman for betraying the confidence of a friend? Even as we wait to learn whether allegations against President Clinton are true, can we begin a conversation about the line that must be drawn between the personal and the political?

King Features Syndicate, January 22, 1998

MONICA LEWINSKY: NEITHER VICTIM NOR VIXEN
BY JULIANNE MALVEAUX

The media madness that surrounds allegations that President Clinton had an affair with a 21-year-old intern and convinced her to lie about it has prompted many to leap to judgment, or at least to conclusions. The public has been treated to a slow drip of minutiae about every aspect of these allegations, and to a growing gaggle of pundits who have reached conclusions about these allegations. Two disturbing aspects of the press coverage have been the examinations of Monica Lewinsky's character and the silence of feminists around the treatment of Lewinsky.

Monica Lewinsky has alternately been described as victim or vixen. Her own lawyer has tended to treat her with chivalry, indicating that his client was "only" 21 when an affair is alleged to have happened. Others have talked about the "moral turpitude" inherent in a 51-year-old man "taking advantage" of a 21-year-old. "Poor Monica," it is alleged, was powerless to resist the advances of an amorous President.

Then the pendulum swung. A high school teacher said he'd had an affair with Ms. Lewinsky. An old boyfriend gave an interview that left Lewinsky sounding like a sophisticated vixen, not a naive victim. Lewinsky was charged with sophistication by association, tarred by a book her mother wrote about the personal lives of three male opera singers.

As the pendulum swings, the silence of feminists is almost deafening. When the silence on the left is accompanied by hypocritical finger-pointing from the "take responsibility crowd" on the right, there is little balance in our portrait of Monica Lewinsky. I am intrigued that the same "take responsibility crowd" that would excoriate a pregnant teenager and label her responsible for her actions is willing to give Monica Lewinsky a pass on hers. What needs to be said, as allegations swirl, is that any alleged relationship between President Clinton and Monica Lewinsky was a consensual one. It also needs to be said that 21-year-old women are just that—women, in control of their sexuality and their choices. And it further needs to be said that salacious investigations of Lewinsky's background are distasteful and need to stop. The same attorneys who have argued that past sexual behavior should not be introduced in a court of law now want to introduce Ms. Lewinsky's sexual past into the court of public opinion.

Clinton-hating conservatives would surprise me if they weren't out pointing fingers and making accusations. They must be aware of their hypocrisy in condemning pregnant and indigent teens who make foolish choices while protecting a slightly older, perhaps wise, college graduate for the same kind of alleged foolishness. But the "take responsibility crowd" has always offered a harsher standard for the poor, the disadvantaged, than for anyone else. Why should they change now?

More disturbing is the silence of feminists, especially young feminists. As distasteful as they may find allegations of adultery, feminists cannot suborn descriptions of Monica Lewinsky that make her victim or vixen. To support her portrayal as a victim is to suggest that 21-year-old women are incapable of making choices and are, even in consensual relationships, being "taken advantage of." We don't consider men "only" 21 when we send them to war. We don't withhold college diplomas because 21-year-olds are too immature to have them, nor do we restrict the right to drink or drive for those ill-fated 21-year-olds who haven't yet learned not to do both together. Twenty-one-year-olds are self-directed adults, and it demeans them to be treated otherwise.

If part of the women's movement was about women taking control of our sexuality, and being treated the same way as men, then feminists need to step up to the plate and correct popular images of Monica Lewinsky. To do any less is to yield to the stereotypes that shackled women a generation ago. Lewinsky is neither a hapless victim who was taken advantage of, nor a wily vixen who set out to seduce a President. She is a complicated woman who deserves the right to make personal choices and mistakes without having them scrutinized by a detail-hungry press corps, many of whom have created a profile based on little more than innuendo.

King Features Syndicate, January 30, 1998

IT TAKES BOB DOLE TO DISTORT A PROVERB
BY JULIANNE MALVEAUX

Thanks to Hillary Rodham Clinton's book, all of America has familiarity with the African proverb "It takes a village to raise a child." It doesn't take a village to raise a child, it takes a family, says Bob Dole. As if the concepts of village and family are completely unconnected. Dole tried to repudiate the African proverb with his tales of "personal responsibility," forgetting, perhaps, one of the world's oldest adages, "No man is an island."

I am not sure why the proverb rankles Republicans so. Perhaps they see the village as big government. But those who understand the proverb see it as a way of asserting our interconnectedness. A child grows up in the context of a village, not inside a singular nuclear family. A child grows up in a community full of institutions — schools, churches, synagogues. All these institutions, the libraries and museums, touch the child in some way. The child doesn't grow up inside four walls, three windows and behind a white picket fence. She grows up in a community.

But people like Bob Dole and Susan Molinari don't see community. They see disconnected individuals. And all of the good and well-being that comes with the proverb is distorted by the mean-spiritedness of those who have pimped their personal biographies to get relevance from their own empty lives. It doesn't take a village, they say smugly. It takes a family. But the family is part of the village.

As I listened to Bob Dole, I wanted to ask him about the village that produced him. He genuflects to that village as often as he can. He is a product of Russell, Kansas, and he won't let you forget it. It took more than the parents and family that Dole mentions to produce him. It took institutions, it took the community, it took the world to shape him into the Dole he is today. He speaks of military service as a personality-defining institution, and yet the military is one kind of village. It is part of a community. And although he is now running from his identity as a 35-year Senator, some see the Senate as some kind of institution, some kind of village, albeit a warped one.

If you take the conversation out of the context of the United States elections, the notion of a family, not a village, runs counter to world trends. Futurists keep talking about our borderless economies, and borderless communities, about the fact that our world is growing smaller and larger at the same time. We watch cities make international partnerships and talk about mutual dependence, and we see the same thing in our world. At the same time, we have people saying that the village metaphor is the wrong one. Instead of moving out, they are turning inward. They say that it doesn't take a village to raise a child, it takes a family. Well, I say it doesn't take a village, it takes a world.

The razzle-dazzle of the Republican convention is over, and now it is the Democrats' turn to toss platitudes. But Dole is on the campaign trail, and the line about families will be oft-repeated, with the same smug glow, the same pause for applause. But Dole and his surrogates have hit no home run, but a ground ball with their weak line. It takes a Dole to distort a proverb. And he didn't do it by himself. He had speechwriters. You see, it really does take a village to raise a child, and community to nurture a politician, even when that politician is horribly misguided. He didn't get that way by himself.

King Features Syndicate, August 22, 1996

DELIBERATE, DISGUSTING, REVOLTING CONDUCT
BY JULIANNE MALVEAUX

Help! A sector of American society has, once again, been "Helmsed." In the tradition of turning a name into a verb that captures a peculiar action, let me claim "Helmsed" as a special kind of conduct: extreme and inaccurate verbal abuse. The latest instance of Helmsing happened when the North Carolina Senator put a hold on the Ryan White CARE Act, indicating his unwillingness to support federal assistance to people living with HIV and AIDS because it is contracted through "deliberate, disgusting and revolting conduct."

Thousands of infants are living with HIV and AIDS. What was their "deliberate, disgusting and revolting conduct"? Birth? Isn't it ironic that one who opposes abortion because of the sanctity of birth describes the birth of some children as "disgusting and revolting"? And what about the people who contracted AIDS through blood transfusions? What was their deliberate and disgusting act? Use of the nation's medical system? To be sure, there are problems and inequities in the way health services are delivered in our country. But the system that uses one-seventh of our nation's resources can hardly be called "disgusting and revolting."

Perhaps Helms had neither infants nor those who got AIDS through transfusions in mind. Perhaps the only people Helmsed were members of the gay and lesbian community. Helms has always had a bone to pick with gay and lesbian people, and this most recent diatribe is consistent with other public statements that he has made. The problem? Gay people aren't the only ones with HIV and AIDS. And the pace at which the HIV virus turns into full-blown AIDS is a function of the quality of health care that is available to people.

Helms' absurd comments do raise one question about health care in this country, and that is the piecemeal way we approach some health issues. It makes no sense to have federal authorizations that go disease by disease, providing money for AIDS or money for breast cancer or money for another illness, instead of providing comprehensive treatment for all illness. Many have raised the question of whether those who live with HIV and AIDS should have more favored treatment than those who live with, say, cancer. In Helmsing those who have AIDS, Senator Jesse Helms has raised questions about the way we deliver health care. This may be the closest he comes to dealing with health care policy.

It occurs to me, though, that the "deliberate, disgusting, and revolting conduct" he describes has less to do with the people living with HIV and AIDS than the people making public policy for our nation. The conduct exhibited by the United States Senate during the vote on whether to vote on Dr. Henry Foster's nomination strikes me as especially "deliberate, disgusting and revolting." The threats by those like Senator Phil Gramm to filibuster Dr. Foster out of a vote are extremely "deliberate, disgusting and revolting." The Senate behavior in slashing social programs while increasing defense spending is particularly "deliberate, disgusting and revolting."

Of course Senator Jesse Helms wouldn't Helms his colleagues. But before he goes around Helmsing sick people, he ought to think about that psychological term, "projection," in which one accuses others of behavior he is guilty of. Deliberate, disgusting, revolting conduct? What about it, Jesse Helms.

King Features Syndicate, July 7, 1995

A WHOLE LOTT OF NONSENSE
BY JULIANNE MALVEAUX

Senate Majority Leader Trent Lott (R-Miss.) is obviously flying high because he was able to persuade his colleagues to reject the tobacco legislation that so many had worked on for so long. Describing the legislation as "too harsh" for tobacco companies, he has offered a weak compromise that is unacceptable both to fellow Republican John McCain and to the White House. But if all Lott did this week was kill the tobacco bill, he would not have surfaced on my radar screen. What else, after all, do I expect someone as beholden to tobacco interests as Lott to do? The fact is that the tobacco companies have so completely purchased the Senate that many of these legislators are prepared to ignore the interests of their constituents in favor of the interests of big business.

But Lott wasn't talking business when he talked to conservative commentator Armstrong Williams on the America's Voice cable network. Instead he was talking ignorance, myopia, and hate. Black people on the Gulf Coast of Mississippi, where Trent Lott is from, were treated the same as white people were. He said he didn't see a lot of racial tension while he was growing up on the "tolerant" Gulf Coast. But Biloxi, Mississippi was so segregated that fences divided the beach. When Hurricane Camille devastated the area in 1969, my mom, a Biloxi native, called it "God's revenge" on white folks.

Lott grew up 25 miles from Biloxi, in Pascagoula, Mississippi, the son of a shipyard worker and a teacher. I guess he didn't notice the segregated schools and the fact that the quality of education was starkly different by race. He didn't notice the fact that black students waited for hand-me-down books from whites and that often the school year was shorter for African Americans to accommodate planting and other needs. I guess he didn't notice that his own alma mater, the University of Mississippi (also known as Ole Miss) didn't admit African Americans until the late 1960s, and only after James Meredith fought for the right to attend that bastion of racism.

Lott told Williams that the 1950s and 1960s were a "good time" for America. Which America? These were the days when white folks sicced dogs on black people to keep us in our place. Did Lott forget that in his own state of Mississippi, Medgar Evers was killed by a vile and twisted white man? Or was that just an insignificant blip on his radar screen. To let Lott tell it, I guess these are good days in Texas, too, good days when the Klan is planning to march in Jasper, Texas, hot on the heels of a vehicular lynching that brutally killed James Byrd, Jr. Instead of sticking his head in the sand and talking about the "good old days," Lott could show moral leadership by decrying incidents like these and talking about reasons the Klan should not rally in Jasper.

Instead of leadership, Lott spewed ignorance when he said he believed that homosexuality is a sin that gay people should be assisted in dealing with "just like alcohol . . . or sex addiction . . . or kleptomaniacs." Stealing is a crime, homosexuality is not! Whatever Lott's religious beliefs about homosexuality, his attempt to liken gay people to addicts and criminals is objectionable. And, when couched in religious terms it ignores the central Biblical tenet, which is to love everyone.

Lott's comments reveal why there are such major problems with social policy legislation and this Congress. A man who thinks that the good old South treated everyone in the same way obviously sees no need for affirmative action programs. A man who thinks that homosexuality should be treated just like alcoholism or criminal activity brings clear biases to issues of hate crime and discrimination against gay people. Additionally, a man with such attitudes obviously does not mind dragging his heels when President Clinton nominates gay and lesbian people for positions that require Senate confirmation.

There's a whole Lott of nonsense coming from the United States Senate these days. The American people are being poorly served by the biases Trent Lott brings to the legislative process.

King Features Syndicate, June 19, 1998

ANOTHER UNSIGNED CONTRACT ON AMERICA
BY JULIANNE MALVEAUX

House Speaker Newt Gingrich's Contract on America was a bid for the wallets and pocketbooks of middle America, and for the coffers of the corporations that will be enriched by moritoria on regulation and capital gains tax cuts. Wednesday, the Christian Coalition offered up a new "Contract with the American Family," a ploy for American souls, for the reform of the social agenda. Or at least that's how they'd like to play it, with their "ten suggestions, not ten commandments." It isn't clear that the word "commandment" even belongs in the sentence, but it adds weight to the new "contract" that summarizes the agenda of the religious right.

The Contract on the American Family is not just about school prayer and abolishing abortion. It is also about school vouchers and the elimination of the

Department of Education, ending federal funding for the National Endowment for the Arts, the National Endowment for the Humanities, and the Corporation for Public Broadcasting, and restricting the distribution of pornography.

When Ralph Reed announced his Contract, he was flanked by Newt Gingrich and Phil Gramm, the Texas Senator who, in his own words, is "too ugly" to be President. While Gramm's looks are hardly the point, his investments might be. Hours after he stood next to Ralph Reed, heartily endorsing a contract that would restrict distribution of pornography, it was revealed that he invested at least $7500 in a pornographic film.

Gramm says he lost money on the investment and that he didn't know he was investing in pornography. I say his hypocrisy is not surprising, since the Contract on the American Family is replete with similar hypocrisy. Claiming to be a social and moral agenda to "save the children," it harms children and society by eliminating the Department of Education and the nation's cultural agencies. Implicitly tied to the budget-balancing "Contract on America," the Contract on the American Family would add to, not detract from, our budget woes with bigger deductions for charity and higher tax credits for children. Before this new contract was formulated it was extensively market tested, suggesting that this contract is less about moral and social reform than about political reform. And its real meaning is revealed when Phil Gramm, pornographic investor and Presidential candidate, is a key supporter.

To be sure, Gramm's political career cannot be reduced to the pornographic investment he made. But Gramm is getting a little bit of his own medicine as the revelations of his past have come forward. This man, who never served in the military (neither did Newt Gingrich), is fond of describing President Clinton as a draft dodger. Gramm's investment indiscretions make it clear that those who live in glass houses can't throw stones, that holier-than-thou moralists too often have all kinds of skeletons in their closet, that the religious right is mostly wrong when it tries to mix religion with politics.

The Christian Coalition is showing its political savvy in linking its Contract to the morally reprehensible but politically successful Republican Contract on America. Their ten-point set of "suggestions, not commandments" is another successful skirmish in a media war that the right wing is winning, hands down. But they can win the battle and lose the war when their moralizing is tied to hypocrisy like Gramm's, who seems to want to take the moral high ground for his politics, but the moral low ground for his investments.

King Features Syndicate, May 19, 1995

NEWT GINGRICH — IN YOUR FACE AND OUT OF CONTROL
BY JULIANNE MALVEAUX

House Speaker Newt Gingrich is apparently gearing up for the next Presidential election. He's taken his act from Capitol Hill to the road, and he's been getting rebuffed along the way. In New Hampshire, Democratic legislators walked out on remarks that were an "overly partisan" attack on President Clinton. In Washington, D.C, his appearance at the Frederick Douglass home caused a melee that resulted in the arrest of one of that city's most prominent African American ministers.

Just a few weeks ago, on his book tour, Gingrich was describing himself as "new and improved." He presented a svelte new image, but apparently not a new attitude, and he promoted his book on lessons learned. One of the lessons he has clearly not learned is to keep his foot out of his mouth. Another lesson that apparently escaped him was the lesson to choose your venue carefully.

Since New Hampshire is the site of the first Presidential primary of the year 2000, Gingrich must have thought that he was doing the right thing by attacking President Clinton in his remarks to that legislature. But in describing the President as "not above the law," and in excoriating Web Hubbell as a criminal, Gingrich apparently deviated from his promised remarks, which were billed as a briefing of federal legislative issues. Though the dozen or so Democrats who walked out on his remarks represented a minority of New Hampshire's legislators, the exceptional gesture of discontent was a slap at the House Speaker. Since he wasn't in charge, he couldn't accuse the New Hampshire lawmakers of incivility, as he has accused his House colleagues when they have become disgusted with his bombast. If this is the Presidential act he is taking on the road, he needs to fine-tune it a bit.

Back in Washington, Newt Gingrich made it clear that he has just a limited understanding of our nation's history. He joined Congressmen Richard Armey (R-Tex.) and J.C. Watt (R-Okla.) at a press conference held on the steps of the home of Frederick Douglass. The occasion of the press conference was an announcement that two thousand federally funded school vouchers will be made available to the students of the District of Columbia. Gingrich has been trying to use Washington, D.C. as a laboratory for Republican-supported programs ever since he became House Speaker.

There was an in-your-face symbolism in using the Douglass home as the site of the voucher announcement. Frederick Douglass, after all, was a champion of liberty, but the House of Representatives has trampled on the liberty of the District of Columbia with its high-handed, dictatorial moves. These moves include stripping Mayor Marion Barry of much of his power, and appointing a "control" board to oversee the operations of the city. Ironically the "Out of Control" board has not improved the operation of D.C.'s schools. Indeed, the school deficit is larger than when that board's appointed monitor, General Julius Becton, took over. Instead of allowing the elected representatives of the Board of Education to take care of business, Congress has been busy developing experimental educational programs for two thousand of the District's seventy thousand students.

The racial politics of this matter cannot be ignored. The District of Columbia's population is more than 60 percent African American. For two white Southern Congressmen, joined by their African American colleague, to stand on the steps of the Douglass home is to invoke the plantation symbolism of a "master" doling out goodies to eager slaves. But Reverend Willie Wilson, pastor of Union Temple Baptist Church, was unwilling to let the symbolism go unchallenged. His disruption of the press conference caused his arrest, but it also made it clear that House Speaker Gingrich's judgment in staging the press conference was questionable, at best.

A year ago, as his party groused about his ill-advised slips of lip, Newt Gingrich took a low profile, wrote a book, and tried to reinvent himself. It hasn't taken much for him to revert to the lip-flapping, in-your-face, and out-of-control Newt of 1995. As protesters in New Hampshire and in Anacostia, D.C. exhibited, it's not likely to go unchallenged this time around.

King Features Syndicate, May 7, 1998

JANET RENO HAS GOT TO GO
BY JULIANNE MALVEAUX

The Justice Department's most recent decision to request a special prosecutor for allegations about Labor Secretary Alexis Herman is laughable. Justice says it cannot show that Herman is culpable in any wrongdoing, and indeed asserts that there is "no evidence clearly demonstrating" Ms. Herman's involvement in Laurent Yene's allegations against her; a special prosecutor has nonetheless been requested. There have been lots of times when Janet Reno might have requested special prosecutors. It takes a special kind of racism to only utilize her power when people make allegations against President Clinton's African American appointees.

The power of allegation and accusation is never stronger than when an African American is on the hot seat. When the President is accused, hordes of journalists transmogrify into vultures, picking apart the life stories of any and every accuser. Kathleen Willey was flirtatious and eager, Monica Lewinsky a little more than that. But Laurent Yene, a man, is simply credible. From what I understand, he is a Cameroonian ne'er-do-well, a man who masqueraded as more than he was. He insinuated himself into the life of one of Alexis Herman's close associates, and when spurned he exploited his inner knowledge to exact revenge. Our nation's pundits seem all too eager to cluck about a woman scorned, but far too obdurate to consider the notion that men are scorned, too. If Attorney General Reno takes Laurent Yene at face value, she ought also star in the Washington production of the cow jumping over the moon.

Or, perhaps, she has got to go. President Clinton ought to be impatient enough, now, to get rid of her. The fact that four of the seven special prosecutors she has sought are for allegations against African Americans speaks poignantly to her myopia and lack of sensitivity about the politics of accusation. The fact that Alexis Herman, who has already withstood extreme scrutiny in the confirmation process, is the subject of her most recent inquiry, suggests that Reno doesn't mind wasting taxpayer dollars to reach a foregone conclusion. As both the President and Ms. Herman said, there has been no wrongdoing. As investigations a year ago confirmed, Alexis Herman did nothing wrong. Why the investigation? Perhaps because the Attorney General is incapable of making reasoned and measured decisions.

Consider some of the other investigations. Reno appointed a special prosecutor to go after Commerce Secretary Ron Brown because of "improper financial dealings." The investigation was closed after his death. Incidentally, allegations about improprieties around Brown's death have yet to be investigated. Former HUD Secretary Henry Cisneros was investigated because of an affair he had. Why are his private affairs the subject of public scrutiny? And why is anybody surprised that someone equivocates or prevaricates about private sexual matters? Thanks to Reno's special prosecutors, Cisneros' once promising career has turned to ashes. Former Agriculture Secretary Mike Espy was accused of accepting improper gifts. They amount to pennies here and nickels there, and they were gifts that were proper for him to take as a Congressional representative. The investigation on Espy continues, but again a promising public servant has been taken out. Finally, there is the case against Herman, a case Reno herself says is weak. Weak as it is, she does not know how to back down and say "enough." She has focused her investigative powers on people of color. The Attorney General has become race specific in her inquiries.

If Clinton were to dismiss Janet Reno, he'd be the lightning rod for criticism, but not for derision. Too many Americans are wondering why we are spending millions of dollars on a 24-7 witch-hunt of dedicated public servants. For every detractor the President garnered with a dismissal of Reno, he'd gain two or three supporters who would applaud him for finding long-lost backbone. In the pattern of her independent counsel requests, after all, Janet Reno has indicated that "justice" means "just us white folks." And in her request for independent counsel for Alexis Herman she has indicated that even when there is no evidence, the simple existence of black folks in high places is subject to investigation.

If President Clinton wants a Cabinet that "looks like America," he needs to get rid of a woman who has misused her power to attack those whose diversity makes them vulnerable mostly because of their visibility. After seven requests for independent counsel, I say it is time for Janet Reno to go! Where? Back to Florida to wrestle with alligators for all I care. But I am tired of her using her power to wrestle black and brown people back to the periphery of our nation's public sphere.

San Francisco Sun Reporter, May 1, 1998

FROM NEW DEAL TO NO DEAL
BY JULIANNE MALVEAUX

The Franklin Delano Roosevelt memorial has been dedicated in Washington, D.C., and the President who is ranked among the nation's three greatest now takes his place in marble and stone along with George Washington and Abraham Lincoln. Even as the massive, seven-and-a-half-acre memorial is dedicated, the legislators who embrace FDR's memory are scrambling to reverse his legacy. If today's politicians have their way, the legacy of FDR's New Deal will be no deal for those at the bottom of our nation's economy. Welfare deform, for example, is a direct reversal of the Roosevelt legacy. The raising of the Social Security retirement age, the fraying of the safety net, the reversal of protections for workers all reverse the Roosevelt legacy.

"I see a third of a nation ill housed, ill clad and ill nourished," Roosevelt said during his second inaugural. Now those words are illustrated with a marble tableau of five men in a bread line, their hunched shoulders a poignant reminder of the burdens the poor carried then. The poor still carry those burdens, but now they are our nation's demons, and their poverty is their own fault, according to Washington. Instead of working to eradicate poverty, we are working to increase it with legislation that will force welfare recipients into competition with low-wage workers who have only recently left welfare themselves. A third of the nation is no longer poor — now it is more like an eighth. Nearly a third, though, of all African Americans live in poverty, as do a like number of Latinos. Where Roosevelt saw such large proportions of poverty as a problem, some politicians can ignore this problem because the poor can be easily scapegoated, easily demonized.

Many historians credit Roosevelt with moving the American people away from a customary isolationism as we moved into our status as a world power. Once, addressing a group at the Daughters of the American Revolution, he humorously addressed the crowd, "Fellow Immigrants." Now, too many politicians have made it their business to bash immigrants as a way of garnering votes. Roosevelt would, no doubt, have looked askance at California's Proposition 187, but Congress passed legislation penalizing legal immigrants because of their status. Part of Roosevelt's global legacy is the United Nations, yet the United States still owes UN dues. Even as our nation celebrates Roosevelt, we repudiate him with our contemporary actions.

Franklin Delano Roosevelt was, in many ways, larger than life. In life, though, he was not a large man and his physical stature may have been diminished by the wheelchair that transported him from place to place. The fact that he used a wheelchair did not diminish his legacy; it adds to it. Yet the mammoth monument does not include a likeness of Roosevelt in his wheelchair. Excluding this image repudiates the legacy Roosevelt leaves as the first elected world leader with a physical disability. This exclusion robs disabled people of a source of inspiration, of the notion that despite physical handicap, one can execute massive dreams.

The fact that Roosevelt was elected President for four terms, that he led us through the world's largest war, that he led our transformation to world leader, and that he altered domestic policy to develop the philosophy of an activist government is a mighty legacy worthy of the memorial that was dedicated this week. It is ironic, though, that even as Roosevelt's legacy is memorialized, it is also being repudiated by many of those who were on hand to participate in the celebrations.

The cruelest repudiation is the move from New Deal to no deal for the nation's poor. Instead of dedicating a memorial at West Potomac Park, President Clinton might dedicate memorial legislation at 1600 Pennsylvania Avenue to eliminate poverty. It will take more, though, than a volunteer summit to reduce the level of poverty in our country. Roosevelt understood this; Clinton doesn't.

King Features Syndicate, May 2, 1997

TACKLING THE REAGAN LEGACY
BY JULIANNE MALVEAUX

The Republicans who put a Contract on America now want to put a contract on American history. They are attempting to rewrite history by naming an increasing number of public monuments after the 40th President of the United States, Ronald Reagan. To be sure, Reagan was a standard-bearer for his party, the man whose philosophy is almost single-handedly responsible for the current Republican Congressional dominance. The Contract on America is, after all, little more than a descendant of Reagan's fiscally conservative and deregulatory zeal.

Still, there is a Reagan Library, as well as a white elephant of a Washington, D.C. government building that has a massive cost overrun as a tribute to the fiscally conservative Reagan. Before that term "fiscally conservative" is overused, one might also note that it was under Reagan's watch that the budget deficit nearly tripled. Reagan's brand of fiscal conservatism was restricted to domestic public finance. Some of our nation's more extravagant Department of Defense boondoggles were Ronald Reagan originals.

Given everything else that has been named after Ronald Reagan, why do Republicans insist on attempting to name Washington, D.C.'s National Airport after him? To attempt to rename the airport that serves the predominately Democratic District of Columbia is an astonishing display of Republican arrogance. To attempt to rename the airport without consultation of the people of D.C. (even though the airport, technically, is in the state of Virginia) smacks of colonialism. To rename the airport without dispassionately considering the Reagan legacy and the harm it has done to the nation's safety net is to further scorn the poor that Reagan had little or no use for. There is special irony in naming an airport after the President whose actions single-handedly decimated the air traffic controllers' union and precipitated a downward wage spiral through his further attacks on organized labor.

Not many are willing to tackle the Reagan legacy. Because the former President is now suffering from Alzheimer's disease, many are inclined to view his eight-year attack on the American people through a sympathetic lens. He had already been described as the "Teflon President" when none of the scandals of his administration (especially the Iran-contra debacle and Oliver North's self-righteous attempt to justify his illegal behavior) stuck to him. When Teflon is combined with sympathy, Republicans are left with an untarnished icon to lift up and promote.

The Reagan image only shines if one looks at it through evolutionary, fiscally conservative eyes. If one thinks back to 1981, our double-digit unemployment rates, and President Reagan's insistence that we redefine unemployment to lower the rate, one has a less glowing portrait of President Reagan. If one recalls redefinitions in long-term disability, and remembers that of the thousands cut off, a dozen or so took their lives in actions we then termed "Reagan-related suicides," then this President seems a less benign model of social transformation. If one recollects the mean-spirited comments that Mr. Reagan made about welfare recipients, and the way food stamp guidelines were changed, one must conclude this was a President who deliberately placed himself at odds with the poor. Indeed, thanks to Reagan's deregulation, the number of uninspected workplaces increased during his administration. The Occupational Safety and Health Administration (OSHA) saw its staff of inspectors more than halved — as a result, inspections were mostly conducted "by appointment." The chicken processing plant at Imperial Foods in North Carolina had been uninspected for more than five years when a plant fire (and a locked fire door) killed 24 people in 1991.

Through whatever lens one chooses to view Ronald Reagan, one must acknowledge that he was President of the United States for eight years. For that feat alone, the law allows for the development of a Reagan library and for the preservation of his legacy. It is not inappropriate that a building or two also be named after him. But for the Republicans to use their political clout to rename the Washington, D.C. National Airport is an in-your-face offensive attempt to make the Reagan legacy something more than it is.

King Features Syndicate, November 25, 1997

FROM THE PERIPHERY TO PODIUM STATUS: BLACK DELEGATES IN 1984 AND 1996
BY JULIANNE MALVEAUX

What a difference a decade makes! When Rev. Jesse Jackson spoke to the 1984 Democratic National Convention in San Francisco, some white delegates were determined to sit on their hands and applauded only with Jackson's redemptive line "God isn't finished with me yet." In 1996, there was hardly a seated delegate when Jackson finished his poignant 22-minute message. Jackson had moved from the periphery to the podium, in more ways than one.

In 1984, I joined two other commentators in doing a "morning after" the convention day. I represented the Jackson position, and the other two represented the views of Gary Hart and Walter Mondale. The tension was so palpable between the Mondale representative and me that he once shouted that the Jackson delegates needed to "sit down and shut up" because we "didn't have the numbers" and had already "lost a shot at the nomination." I recall snarling back, "We may have lost the nomination, but you will lose the election if you don't wake up and smell the coffee." In 1996, black delegates were the ones who took a strong whiff. Jesse Jackson's fiery rhetoric was muted by his support for Bill Clinton. Congresswoman Maxine Waters gave a spirited critique of welfare reform as we now know it, then pledged her support to the President. For many, the sentiment is that Clinton, for all his flaws, is the "last line of defense" for working people, poor people, people of color.

It isn't all about Jackson. Not anymore. Jackson may have been the bridge that some African American politicians used to cross into office, but Jackson was but one of the African American stars at this convention. Indeed, some would suggest that his star is falling, while others are rising, that Jesse Jackson is a symbol of what might have been, not what will happen. African Americans were about 16 percent of the convention delegates, and played prominent roles in every aspect of the convention. This is part, in some ways, of the Jackson legacy. People who were volunteers in 1984 are now department heads in 1996. Thanks to Rev. Jesse Jackson, some of these new department heads are black, brown, and female.

In 1984, African American women were so incensed by the way they were treated by white women colleagues that the National Political Congress of Black Women was founded by former Congresswoman Shirley Chisholm and C. Delores Tucker. In 1996, African American women play a key role in political strategy.

President Clinton's Director of Public Liaison, Alexis Herman, was on the scene in 1984, but she ran the show at the 1992 convention, and played a key role in 1996. And the podium lineup reflected the black woman's presence in 1996, much enhanced from a decade ago. We heard from Senator Carol Moseley Braun, Alma Arrington Brown, San Francisco's Doris Ward, Congresswomen Maxine Waters and Eleanor Holmes Norton and several others.

While we have come a long way since 1984, I found myself as piqued in 1996 by the role race played in this convention. Several gospel choirs performed, making me wonder if the President and Democrats know many white entertainers, or whether the Democratic "illusion of inclusion" includes the Amos and Andy stereotype of black folks buck dancing and otherwise performing for acceptance. The very moving tribute to late Commerce Secretary Ronald H. Brown made me wonder if an African American can only get recognition after he dies. And when the assembled delegates heard no reference to affirmative action in the President's acceptance speech, I wondered if some Democrat thought that African Americans could be pushed back to the periphery, at least for the evening, in the name of prime-time television.

Race resonates in 1996, but in different ways than it did in 1984. African Americans may have learned political pragmatism in the twelve years that separated the two conventions. In gaining pragmatism and podium status, have we lost the ability to push the party toward embracing our issues?

King Features Syndicate, August 30, 1996

CHAPTER 3

PLATITUDES, POLICY AND PRIORITIES

When rhetoric and reality collide, we end up with armed youngsters in the name of the Second Amendment, incarcerated addicts (who ought to be in hospitals) in the name of the war on drugs, welfare "deform" in the name of ending handouts, and platitudes in the name of public policy. It is as if our Congress has substituted rhetorical facility for substantive policy. Legislation titled "civil rights" would actually slam doors in the faces of those who should be helped by civil rights. "Family flexibility" legislation would deprive workers of overtime pay. In the Congress of rhetorical excess, poverty has become a near-crime, with poor people excoriated as willful indigents, not victims of a flawed economy. In the name of balancing the federal budget, billions are cut from programs that help the poor. At the same time, the military gets more money than it requests, all in the name of national security.

The clichés would be amusing were it not for the fact that our futures depend on setting national priorities. Thus, it is amazing to watch substantive policy conversation degenerate into discussions of motherhood and apple pie, family values and law and order. Those on opposing sides of the political fence attempt to mollify each other and weaken arguments by asserting that "reasonable people" all agree on a common set of values. What values? Can one honestly cling to family values while devaluing the families of the poor? Can one really talk about law and order while wading, thigh deep, through seas of private money "contributed" to influence legislation? What would our national policy conversation be like if platitudes and clichés were simply eliminated from our vocabularies, and if politicians had to say what they mean?

PLATITUDES, NOT POLICY
BY JULIANNE MALVEAUX

In the aftermath of both political conventions, I remain amazed at the platitudes that were offered by speakers at both conventions. Make sure your kids do their homework. Turn off the television. Wear school uniforms. Support adoption. Family values. Family values. Family values. Instead of public policy, we've been offered a steady stream of platitudes and common sense, platitudes that differ little by political party.

But, who can quarrel with the exhortation to turn the television off? With the average American watching some 40 hours of television a week, the directive to reduce our television consumption makes good sense. Who can quarrel with the directive to make sure that children do their homework? Even if, according to Hillary Rodham Clinton, you may not have much time because you are too busy taking the dog to the vet. None of the platitudes are wrong, they are just trivial examples of the way that minutiae have taken over much of our nation's political thinking. Instead of rhetorical highs that inspire a nation, we've got Presidential candidates as parents trying to tell us how to live our lives.

Presidential candidates aren't the only ones who seem mired in the minutiae. The rise in the number of self-help books suggests that our nation has been collectively lobotomized, anytime you need someone to tell you to "love each other" and "be kind." Some of these basic truths can be found in tomes as old as the Bible and the Koran, but since those authors are unavailable for the talk-show circuit, we prefer repackaged pabulum and recycled basic truth.

The alternative to platitudes, apparently, is name-calling, as a few hours of CSPAN viewing of Congressional deliberations will illustrate. Instead of navigating our nation through the troubled waters of an industrial transformation, we have our elected leaders describing their constituents as "alligators" and "wolves," and describing each other as "draft dodgers" and "Communists" to name just a few.

It is as if our elected leaders had a strong dose of George Bush-itis and are all avoiding "that vision thing." Where is the vision that talks about the way our nation will look in a decade? Who is grappling with the aging of the baby boomers and what that will mean to our society? Who is looking at the increasing diversity of our nation and talking about race relations in challenging ways? Whoever those people are, they were hard to find during the political conventions (with the notable exception of Rev. Jesse Jackson at the Democratic National Convention).

The other trend seemed to be policy by autobiography. While many people treated us to moving personal stories, it takes more than an up-from-poverty bootstraps story to make policy toward the poor. And it is more than a little smug to offer oneself up as a symbol of a system that works. Democrats and Republicans alike buried us in platitudes and autobiography because neither party was prepared to talk about public policy.

Once upon a time, we heard rhetoric about "a chicken in every pot and a car in every garage." This was a vision of prosperity that many Americans could relate to. Contrast that with the chiding exhortation to "make sure your kids do their homework." Good advice, but poor public policy, and completely devoid of vision.

King Features Syndicate, September 6, 1996

MENTAL DISORDER IS NOT A CRIME
BY JULIANNE MALVEAUX

NBC sportscaster Marv Albert has brought the sordid case of his sexual assault to a close with a plea-bargained admission of guilt to misdemeanor assault, but some of the questions raised by the case remain unanswered. Is it always necessary to character-assassinate a woman bringing charges of sexual assault in order to defend an accused man? Been there, done that with William Kennedy Smith and Patricia Bowman, Mike Tyson and Desireé Washington. Despite the fact that these cases were resolved differently, they have something in common. Both the accuser and the accused are tarnished by the legal process.

The same Roy Black who defended William Kennedy Smith is now defending Marv Albert. This time his character assassination includes use of the alleged victim's mental health history. "When did you stop taking Prozac?" he sneered, as if the taking of an anti-depressant drug is a crime. From Black's cross-examination, we also learned that the alleged victim had also taken Paxil, an anti-anxiety medication.

I wonder if Black, with the same vigor, would have asked if the alleged victim took insulin, high blood pressure medication, or penicillin. Probably not; there is no stigma attached to physical illness. Despite the fact that 22 percent of all adults are affected by a range of mental disorders, though, such disorders have a negative connotation in our society. In contrast, the 20 percent of adults who have cardiovascular diseases, or the 50 percent who have respiratory disorders experience no such stigma. They are simply sick, while those with mental disorders, are, by Black's implication, so impaired that they perhaps can't distinguish between consensual sex and forced sex.

Such attitudes make it difficult for those who experience mental disorders to seek help. Though depression is successfully treated by medication in 65 percent of cases, too many people think depression is a character flaw, something they can "snap out of" if they put their mind to it. Yet depression often has physiological roots, and needs to be treated by medication. Still, the nation is just learning how important our unbiased consideration of mental disorders is. Some health plans allow nearly unlimited assistance for physical illness, but limit the number of mental health related visits to 10 or 12, and limit payment to mental health professionals in a way that payment to other physicians is not limited.

African American women are among those who suffer in silence when we experience mental disorders. Our image as strong, broad-shouldered women who can "make a way out of no way" often limits our ability to set our burden down and seek help. Motivational writers like Iyanla Vanzant, Julia Boyd, and Susan Taylor have spent the last decade reminding African American women that we can't be effective in the struggle for racial economic justice unless we are kind to ourselves and willing to seek help when we need it.

Our society needs to reconsider attitudes toward mental disorders. They are as much a sign of character flaw as a physical diagnosis of arthritis or hypertension, and the consequences of ignoring mental disorders is often as severe as the consequences of ignoring physical disorders. Taking anti-depressants or anti-anxiety drugs is often the solution, not the problem, for people with mental disorders.

USA Today, September 25, 1997

THE HEALTH DEDUCTION HOAX
BY JULIANNE MALVEAUX

The 104th Congress recently voted to give self-employed people a 25 percent deduction on the cost of health insurance premiums. Their action would cost the treasury millions of dollars, but the Congress says they have a way to pay for it. They'll simply rescind the tax benefits offered to those media outlets as an incentive to do business with minority-owned firms. Describing the tax breaks as a bonus to millionaires who know how to play the game, the 104th Congress rallied to slam the door that was only recently cracked open to allow minorities access to airwaves previously dominated by just a few.

To be sure, when diversity replaces white millionaires with millionaires of color, there are class issues that need to be considered. But the fact that the federal government, through the Federal Communications Commission, distributed licenses based on race and class in the past makes an argument for their involvement in deciding who should now control the airwaves. They can't take back the licenses they gave in the past without prompting howls of unfairness, so the route of offering tax carrots seems a reasonable way to redistribute media influence.

Except this is the 104th Congress, the Congress that took out a "contract" on America. Affirmative action isn't mentioned in the contract, but somewhere on the path between "personal responsibility," "job creation," and "common sense legal reform," the Congress took a detour down the affirmative action path, perhaps because they'll find more consensus on further scapegoating the African American population than they will on keeping their promises on issues like term limits. The recent vote to take away a tax break from those who share the wealth with minorities is a perfect example of such scapegoating. The implicit message in the vote is that we could afford more social policy if we didn't have to make all these special concessions to African Americans. The problem is that the social policy that the Congress wants to offer, a partial deduction on health care premiums, is a paltry, class-biased premium that benefits only a few.

Why offer a deduction to self-employed people, but not to people who work for companies that fail to offer them health insurance? In offering a 25 percent uncapped deduction, the Congress panders to the high-rolling self-employed who can afford "sky's the limit" packages. Why not cap the deduction at $1000 or so, allowing those who want to pick top-of-the-line health plans to pay for them themselves, instead of having the taxpayer pay? It seems like another rich person's giveaway to me, but it passed on the hoax that people were gaining at the expense of another minority set-aside.

Newt Gingrich and Bob Dole have been whipping up a frenzy against affirmative action and the need to balance the playing field for black employees and entrepreneurs. Thus, the notion of helping the self-employed while putting minorities in check must have been appealing to that majority of Congressional representatives who bought the health deduction hoax. The vote to offer a deduction for a portion of health care premiums for a portion of the population warrants careful examination, though. It helps fewer people than it appears to, provides no access for the people who currently have no insurance, and slams the door on minority participation in telecommunications. There are other ways that this Congress could help the uninsured pay for health insurance. They'd have to spend more money than the millions they snatched away from the tax deduction to companies who sell media outlets to minority entrepreneurs. The purpose of the health deduction hoax was not to provide health access, but to make a point about minority set-asides. And so the debate on affirmative action begins, with a vote that compares the cost of health insurance premiums with the cost of minority business participation. The future debate promises to be even more confusing, as the 104th Congress continues its contract to obfuscate.

King Features Syndicate, February 23, 1995

HEALTH CARE AND THE GULF WAR SYNDROME
BY JULIANNE MALVEAUX

Ever since our troops returned from the Persian Gulf War in 1991 and 1992, we've been hearing about a "Gulf War syndrome" that has affected thousands of people. Possibly a result of the chemical warfare some say was waged in the Persian Gulf, the syndrome has symptoms like fatigue, skin rashes, memory loss, headaches, and nausea. Some say the symptoms also have emotional side-effects, others suggest the system may cause a partial breakdown in immune systems and nerve damage. But while hundreds have trekked to Washington to testify about Gulf War syndrome, the Defense Department has been busy denying its existence, and denying veterans the disability payments they deserve if they fell victim to GWS.

Now, research shows that there may be some medical basis to GWS. Medical researchers at Duke University and at the University of Texas can simulate GWS by exposing animals to a set of chemical combinations. And now, thanks to the private donors who financed this research, the Defense Department is ready to sit down and talk about whether GWS exists.

Why has the Defense Department resisted the notion of GWS? Perhaps they do not want to take financial responsibility for those veterans who, completely disabled, are now entitled to full health care and disability payments. Would Defense resist GWS so firmly if cost were not a consideration? If they knew that disabled veterans would have access to health care whether or not they could classify their disease, might people be more open to the concept of GWS? Perhaps.

It seems to me when 30,000 people report a set of common symptoms, the Defense Department's goal ought to be to serve them, not try to make them think they are crazy by denying that the symptoms exist. It seems to me that when people who were willing to fight in a conflict many considered dubious come back unable to function at their former level, they deserve something other than skepticism. And it seems to me that if we had universal health coverage, the focus might be more on curing people than shifting blame for the source of their symptoms.

It helps, though, to remember who these Gulf War veterans are. A disproportionate number of them are black and brown subjects of the economic draft that makes the military an opportunity of last resort. Many in the reserves were workers who needed the extra couple of hundred dollars a month of reserve pay to make ends meet. Those who fought in the Gulf War are hardly the most powerful members of our society. Because their war was unpopular, their post-war concerns are at the periphery of our consciousness.

Health care and health reform have been pushed to the periphery, too, at least until the introduction of new legislation this month. Of course, the failure to make progress on national health care reform is a singular shortcoming of the Clinton administration. To be sure, Bill and Hillary Clinton were hindered by everything from their own inexperience to the catchy commercials sponsored by those vested in the status quo. The fact that our health care system limps along piecemeal distorts all kinds of behavior, from the "job lock" that is addressed by the tepid Kassebaum-Kennedy bill to the distorted Defense Department response to those affected by Gulf War syndrome.

When people don't have insurance coverage, minor illnesses become the catastrophic urgencies that are often treated in hospital emergency rooms where it costs more to deliver health care than it does in a doctor's office, clinic or hospital. It frightens me to think of someone suffering from Gulf War syndrome seeking health care in a hospital emergency room both because the Department of Defense doubts their symptoms and because our heath care system has no room for them. But the possibility is clearly there, and while the Kassebaum-Kennedy health insurance reform bill is a step in the right direction, it is simply not enough.

The research that suggests that Gulf War syndrome is real raises questions both about our treatment of veterans and about our medical research and health care system. What has happened to those who have not been able to receive treatment for a syndrome some thought did not exist? What about those whose claims for disability have been ignored? If they are sitting in hospital emergency rooms, we ought to be ashamed.

King Features Syndicate, April 18, 1996

DON'T ISOLATE MEDICAL SERVICES
BY JULIANNE MALVEAUX

I want to get my teeth cleaned, but hesitate at the thought of parking at the dentist. The plaque protection forces are on the alert again, randomly shooting people who dare endanger plaque outside dental clinics that are located between Brookline, Massachusetts and Parkersburg, West Virginia. My physician assures me that if the plaque isn't scraped from my mouth, my teeth will be endangered and eventually pulled, but because of the violence surrounding dental clinics, I'm being asked to choose between my mouth and my life. Of course, if my dental services were available at the same facility where I get all my other medical services, I wouldn't stand out like a sore thumb when I go to get my teeth cleaned. If my dental services were seen as part of a comprehensive set of medical services, then this particular procedure might not be singled out as a lightning rod for misguided protests. But medical practitioners have insisted on segregating, not integrating, medical care. And the result is that I shudder every time I go to get my teeth cleaned.

Granted, abortion is a far more serious procedure than tooth cleaning. Otherwise, though, I think the analogy holds. Between the onset of menstruation and menopause, women spend some 40 years managing their reproductive systems. Unintended pregnancy isn't the only reason a woman may need a surgical procedure to ensure proper functioning of that system. Women who suffer from endometriosis or fibroids may need a dilation and curettage, also known as a D&C. Women who desperately want to conceive may find their uterus being poked, pushed and scraped in the analysis process. Obstetricians and gynecologists offer women a range of services, most often in their offices or clinics. It is only the women who don't have access to regular medical services or a sympathetic doctor who end up with their reproductive health isolated from other health procedures, stuck at clinics. Their isolation is compounded by the zealots who have decided to make medical centers a killing ground in the name of saving the lives of the unborn.

Smug Paul Hill smirked through his sentencing after he was convicted of killing a physician and his escort in Florida. Perhaps his supporters and his elevation to martyrdom inspired John Salvi III to shoot into an abortion clinic in Norfolk, Virginia and allegedly kill two women at a Brookline, Massachusetts clinic. People who call themselves "pro-lifers" refuse to denounce the massacre of people who are simply seeking medical services. Their inflammatory rhetoric may, in fact, be partly responsible for the madness of extremists like Hill and Salvi III.

Paul Hill and John Salvi III are "angry white men," as angry as those who went to the polls to elect Newt Gingrich and his colleagues to rule the House of Representatives. Many of these angry white men want to click their heels three times and return to a simpler past, a past where people — women, minorities, the poor — stayed in their place and did the predictable thing. They want to return to a past where biology is destiny, where ability and technology are dwarfed by some Byzantine "natural order" of things. Words like civil rights and planned parenthood are an anathema to them, because they threaten the 1950s' sense of order — women barefoot and pregnant, black folks silent and easily controlled.

Women's ability to control their reproductive systems ought to have the same priority as our ability to take flu shots, schedule tooth cleanings, or arrange inoculations. One set of services ought not be isolated from the other. When planned parenthood or abortion clinics stand apart from the rest of medical services, we who care about reproductive freedom send the signal that these services are separate and distinct from other health services. We send the signal that these services can be attacked because they are different, and more vulnerable, than other services.

John Salvi III sent women who care about their health a wake-up call about how some services are delivered. He reminds us that it is critical to demand comprehensive health services, not a clinic here, a clinic there, to be picked off at the whim of any madman determined to claim an old world order.

King Features Syndicate, January 5, 1996

WELFARE REFORM RHETORIC MISSES THE POINT
BY JULIANNE MALVEAUX

Republican rhetoric about public assistance exploits the myth that all of those who receive welfare are lazy ne'er-do-wells living on the public dole. They've exploited racial fears by painting welfare as a "black" program, though there are as many whites who receive public assistance as African Americans. Like President

Clinton, they've failed to connect the size and composition of the welfare rolls with the job market. If 9 million Americans who seek work can't find it, what makes anyone think welfare recipients have some superior knowledge of the labor market?

The women who receive public assistance fall into three distinct categories. Discussions about how to fix welfare must acknowledge the differences in solutions for the three groups. The easiest group to deal with is the best prepared group. These women are forced onto welfare because of death or divorce, stay on welfare for a few months, then leave, usually never to return. They may be well educated but lack marketable job skills, or they may have several children and no child care plan. A few months of aid gives them time to develop a game plan for a life that has been drastically altered. At any time these women represent about one in six of all welfare recipients.

At the very bottom there are women who are the lazy ne'er-do-wells so often depicted as the typical welfare recipient. They've dropped out of school, and also out of life, and haphazardly care for their children, perhaps abuse drugs and alcohol, and never met a job application that didn't repel them. Like the group at the top, they are in the minority, representing about one in six of all recipients. A two-year up-or-out system might make them homeless, or might motivate them to find new attitudes. But what about their children?

But the typical welfare recipient is someone who has experience in the labor market. She rides a merry-go-round between welfare and work, holding low-wage jobs or juggling part-time jobs until her patchwork existence is threatened by something she has no control over. Her car dies and she can't get to her cashier's job in the suburbs. Her child falls off a swing and she has no health care. She is sick for a week and is fired as a result. A child care arrangement unravels and she has to take time away from work to make another arrangement. Women with more resources than she are rattled by such problems, but they have a safety net and employment benefits to cushion life's blows. Most low-wage jobs do not provide health care or child care, and so the low-wage woman on the welfare merry-go-round has public assistance to fall back on. Draconian measures remove her safety net, but don't get to the root of the problem. Health care, child care, and a higher minimum wage improve her material circumstances.

Two-year up-or-out policies ignore the realities of a woman on the welfare merry-go-round, ignore the fact that this woman desperately wants to work and does so, no matter how low the pay. Instead of treating women on welfare as deviant, we ought to look at the deviance of an economic system that pays workers so little, and provides so few benefits, that they cannot survive. We can't really talk about welfare without talking about downsizing, layoffs, and the erosion of the wage base. Rhetoric that treats low-wage workers as the enemy ignores the fact that there's an employer somewhere paying low wages.

Nobody likes "welfare as we know it." But from where I sit, reform can't proceed unless we recognize the different realities of welfare recipients, and understand the fact that a better labor market could reduce the number of people who receive aid. Rhetoric that focuses on punishment misses the point that most welfare recipients really want to work.

King Features Syndicate, November 17, 1994

CLINTON CAN VETO WELFARE DEFORM
BY JULIANNE MALVEAUX

By a vote of 74-24, the Senate passed "welfare reform" legislation. Calling for the greatest changes in welfare since its inception during the New Deal, the Senate version of the legislation would give states new power to run their own welfare and work programs with federal funds. The most important change in welfare policy is that the federal guarantee of cash assistance for poor children has ended. It will be up to the states to decide whether or not poor families receive cash or any other benefits. Also, heads of families on public assistance would be required to find work in two years or lose benefits. Lifetime welfare benefits would be limited to five years, and states could set even shorter lifetime limits. States are also no longer obliged to make payments to unmarried teens.

Senator Carol Moseley Braun was eloquent in her attack on this legislation. She reminded her colleagues that "67 percent of the people receiving welfare are children, and 60 percent of those children are under six years old. This bill makes a policy assault on nonworking parents but it uses the children as the missiles and as the weapons of that assault." Braun noted that real welfare reform would have a commitment to job creation, adequate child care, job training, and job placement. Instead, the Senate has allowed myths to shape their policy of punishing those who cannot find work.

The Senate has also bought into a disturbing xenophobia by denying legal immigrants a range of public assistance benefits. Their rhetoric has been that people who come here need to be able to support themselves, but what happens when self-supporting people collide with economic hard times? Are they then expected to return to their country of origin? The Congressional Budget Office says that $60 billion would be saved by cutting food stamps and benefits to legal immigrants, but few have calculated the tax payments that legal immigrants make into the system. The tone of this "reform" is punitive, exclusionary, and indifferent to children.

Since last Tuesday's vote, the D.C.-based Urban Institute has released its analysis of the legislation, estimating that at least a million more children will enter poverty because of the punitive provisions of this welfare reform, even if their mothers find work. "States have flexibility but far fewer federal dollars," noted senior fellow Isabel Sawhill and her associate, Sheila Zedlewski.

President Clinton spoke, in 1992, about "ending welfare as we know it." In 1993, he proposed welfare reform that included limits for recipiency, but also provided the resources needed to move welfare recipients into jobs at fair wages, including child care and job training. The President's initial plan cost more than the current welfare system, and so it failed to get broad support. Instead, this poorly conceived legislation saves money and places lives in jeopardy. The Senate is willing to substitute "welfare as we know it" for welfare as we don't, just to say they are doing something.

The Senate and House versions of welfare reform go to a conference committee next week, and the compromise legislation is likely to land on the President's desk by the end of next week. He can allow politics to place him in the uncomfortable position of signing this legislation because he said he would, or he can do the right thing and exercise his veto power. "You can put wings on a pig, but that doesn't make it an eagle," President Clinton said this week in describing the legislation he will have to consider. And you can call it reform but that doesn't make it right. If the President stops playing politics and acts in the national interest, he will veto this flawed legislation.

King Features Syndicate, July 26, 1996

WHO CARES FOR THE POOR?
BY JULIANNE MALVEAUX

When President Clinton said he would sign a welfare reform bill that has, in his own words, "serious problems," he put politics above principle and turned his back on the poor. To be sure, he couched his comments in the lofty rhetoric of changing welfare as we know it, and even indicated that "this bill is a real step forward for our country, our values, and for people who are on welfare." What a pity that this step forward must take place on the backs of more than a million poor children!

Clinton isn't the only culprit in this welfare reform debacle. Fully half of Congressional Democrats supported legislation that discriminates against legal immigrants and cuts food stamp spending by $4 million a year. Some of those who supported welfare reform with their votes have been skeptical of it with their rhetoric, suggesting that when poor people are concerned, you can talk the talk without walking the walk.

New York Democrat Charles Rangel had it right when he said that the only losers in this legislation are children, and that's because they do not vote. Despite the thousands that thronged with Marian Wright Edelman and the Children's Defense Fund in the June Stand for Children, too many Democrats understood that our national antipathy for poor people is far greater than any compassion we have for poor children.

What happened to the Democratic Party that was once the party of "the people"? Does the President so little value the votes of people from the civil rights, women's rights, and labor communities that he would thumb his nose at them and sign a punitive bill? In an election year, he is secure that his supporters in those communities have no alternative to his flawed leadership. Indeed, some have placed so much focus on Congressional races that those who abhor Clinton's action can't risk staying home if they want Democrats to have a chance to take the Congress.

But this legislation makes it clear that Democrats aren't often very different from Republicans and raises real questions about what Democrats stand for. People who are going door-to-door trying to persuade people to vote now have a much harder time making the case for the Democratic Party with Clinton's support of this welfare reform legislation.

Of course, some Democrats will say they voted for the welfare reform legislation (which might more accurately be described as "welfare repeal" in the words of New York Senator Daniel Patrick Moynihan) because of their concern that handouts are debilitating to the morale of poor people. Those members of the Congressional Black Caucus who supported welfare reform may not be guilty of the same indifference as some of their colleagues, but they are certainly guilty of myopia. Nobody likes the notion of people getting handouts, but unless welfare repeal is coupled with job training, child care, and other provisions, it simply won't work.

We won't know how flawed this bill is until two years from now. By then, Clinton, a lame-duck President, can wax eloquent about his caring for the poor, powerless to do anything about his caring because the states will then control public assistance. At the current pace of legislative change, it would take a full three years from the time we feel the effects of welfare reform to remedy its flaws. President Clinton will be on center stage with the rhetoric, but off the hook in terms of his ability to show legislative compassion for the poor.

So who cares for the poor? Who cares for poor children? Neither Democrats nor Republicans, it appears. The dime's worth of difference between the two seems to be that Republicans don't bother to conceal their indifference, while Democrats bury theirs in quasi-compassionate rhetoric. And the bottom line is that one million more children will experience poverty next year in the name of welfare reform.

King Features Syndicate, August 1, 1996

SCAPEGOATING THE POOR
BY JULIANNE MALVEAUX

President Clinton's promise to end "welfare as we know it" was easy to offer, but difficult to realize. With citizen Dole on the hustings attacking Clinton for broken promises, welfare is being treated as a wedge issue of the 1996 campaign. Both Clinton and Dole have heaped rhetoric and scorn on the poor, tinkering with the welfare system to make people "less dependent" and "more responsible." It makes little sense to scapegoat the poor, though, without exploring alternatives to public assistance that include work at living wages, affordable health care, and affordable child care.

Instead, former Senator Dole proposes drug-testing welfare recipients. Imagine how he'd howl if someone proposed drug and alcohol testing for members of the United States Senate! We've heard President Clinton propose that teen mothers be forced to live with an adult instead of establishing separate households, a proposal that, perhaps, ignores the home conditions that contributed to a teen pregnancy in the first place. There have been other proposals, including efforts to penalize welfare recipients who don't finish school, or whose children don't attend classes. It has also been proposed that immigrant workers who have economic hardship be excluded from all federal programs, including public assistance, subsidized education, and community health care.

There seems to be a contest between some Democrats and Republicans over who can offer the most draconian measure to reform welfare. The notion that the poor need to be penalized, though, does not deal with the reality that most welfare recipients experience. Most have worked sometime in the last two years and are receiving public assistance because the low-wage jobs they held simply could not sustain their families. Penalizing them by cutting the levels of public assistance and forcing work at sub-minimum wages does not improve their abilities to support their families in the long run. All it does is make life harder for them in the short run.

Instead of looking at penalties and forced work (and where will the jobs come from?), those who would reform welfare should look at the reasons people seek public assistance. Many need further education and training to find better work. Others find that work is simply unavailable. Health care and child care enable single mothers to find and keep even low-wage employment, but President Clinton's health care proposal had little success, and the child care provisions have been so faulty in the welfare reform bills that have reached the President's desk that he has vetoed that legislation.

The image of women working very hard at low-wage jobs differs sharply from the image that former Senator Dole has advanced in his statements on welfare reform. Dole has focused on drug use, illegitimacy, and other deviant behavior as if it is the rule rather than the exception. But penalizing hardworking women struggling to keep families together doesn't earn the same political mileage as getting tough with drug-using laggards who are dependent on the tax dollars of the overburdened American. Dole is exploiting the very economic malaise he helped create as a Senator by suggesting that people whose greatest crime is poverty need to be punished to preserve American "values."

To be sure, the welfare system "as we know it" is far from perfect. Recipients, their social workers, and the public are dissatisfied with the very flawed system that makes the transition from welfare to work very difficult. But those who would end "welfare as we know it" haven't tried to fix the flaws that penalize school attendance, and discourage work and savings. In talking time limits for welfare recipients, they have often ignored economic reality, and embraced the tiresome double standards that turn assistance into the pejorative "dependency" only when people (instead of corporations) are involved.

In an election year, we can forget the idea of real welfare reform. President Clinton will continue to accept waivers from states that would alter their welfare system, just as he has already accepted 60 waivers from 38 states. The

President will also continue to talk about requiring recipients to work, and rhetorically embracing aspects of the Wisconsin system when it serves him to do so. Former Senator Dole will continue to castigate welfare recipients as examples of failures in values and come up with schemes like drug testing to communicate his derision for those who are guilty of economic crimes. Reacting from economic insecurity, many Americans will support this scapegoating of the poor, mostly because of our own fear of poverty. But the fact is that if public assistance were eliminated tomorrow, the budget wouldn't balance, the deficit wouldn't disappear, and the values Bob Dole speaks of so frequently wouldn't be automatically restored. This contest over who can get tougher on the poor diverts attention from longer-term and more important economic issues. But it makes good rhetoric.

The Progressive Media Project, May 28, 1996

POSTSECONDARY EDUCATION IS WELFARE REFORM KEY
BY JULIANNE MALVEAUX

In early December, my travels took me to Gateway Technical Community College in New Haven, Connecticut. I'd expected it to be a campus trip like any other campus trip where a speaker comes in, hangs out a bit, gives a talk, entertains questions, packs up her glad rags and goes home. This doesn't mean that the lecture circuit is rote. Every location brings interesting people with memorable personalities. Some trips bring reunions with old friends, and others bring contacts that sometimes develop into rich friendships. There was much of that in my Gateway trip, but there was something more, as well. One of the deans at Gateway Technical Community College shared her powerful personal story with me and reminded me that, in these days of "welfare deform," postsecondary education ought to play a much greater role than it currently does.

Dr. Susan Lincoln married early, and had four small children and a broken marriage by the time she was twenty years old. The child of Maryland migrant farmers, she also had tenacity and a determination not to be defined by her circumstances. So she collected public assistance from a system she found "harsh and humiliating." But she also finished high school, then college, and earned a Ph.D. Now she is Dean of Student Services at Gateway Technical Community College, an institution she has served for more than 25 years. In her late fifties, Dr. Lincoln has the energy and attitude of someone a decade younger. But she has the warmth and compassion of a woman who has raised children, who enjoys two grandchildren, and who has seen quite a bit in her time. To talk with Dr. Lincoln is to envy the nurturing wisdom that she so clearly shares with her students, a group of folks she speaks of both fondly and sternly. She is dismayed that more African American and women students aren't immersing themselves in technology, disturbed that more women on public assistance don't investigate the community college option as a ladder out of poverty. "Believe me," she told me in a crisp voice reminiscent of Eartha Kitt's storytelling voice, "if I could make it so can they. They just need to understand that education is an option."

Women on public assistance aren't the only ones who need to understand. Policymakers bent on punitive versions of welfare reform need to be clear that low-wage jobs are a revolving door for poor women and no way to encourage self-sufficiency. Pathways to education and decent-paying jobs are permanent pathways out of poverty. Researchers at the Washington, D.C.-based Center for Women Policy Studies have been making this point for years. But the point is made more clearly, more compellingly, when someone like Dr. Susan Lincoln tells her story. The problem is that there are lots of Dr. Susan Lincolns out there, women who saw the welfare system as a means to an end, not an end. But many of these women are ashamed to tell their stories because there is a stigma attached to having received public assistance.

It is a false stigma. If there is any shame in public assistance it is the shame that our country does so poorly by those who are at the bottom. There ought to be shame in the way people are treated when they go to get aid, as if they are contemptible human beings, not people in need. There ought to be shame in the media portrayal of people on welfare. And there ought to be shame in the people who have become rich from their exploitation of the poor. But a woman who receives public assistance, who raises children with few resources, ought feel no shame but a motivation to improve her circumstances. And the motivation must now be compounded by the mean-spiritedness with which some states approach "welfare reform."

In California, for example, welfare checks will be cut by a flat 10 percent on January 1, except for people who live in large cities, who will see cuts of 4.6 percent. The cost of living will rise, but people on public assistance will be cut and they have no choice but to "live with it." Eloise Anderson, the head of the California Department of Social Services, says that poor people need to "learn how to be poor" and cites her own case of rising early to bake bread and make cupcakes to save money when she had to stretch a check after her divorce.

California Governor Pete Wilson seems to have a talent for finding African Americans with iconoclastic views like Anderson and UC Berkeley regent Ward Connerly. I'd love to sit Anderson and Dr. Susan Lincoln in a room and watch the fur fly or, at least, find out whether Eloise Anderson has considered the redemptive power of postsecondary education in the welfare reform discussion.

And I'd like to put women like Dr. Susan Lincoln on a poster, to tout her achievements and accomplishments and to remind people that public assistance, for many, has been a means to an end, not an end. Sisters like Susan Lincoln ought to be the ones leading the welfare reform debate. Sisters like her ought to be the ones shaping the reforms. After all, Susan Lincoln survived public assistance, and triumphed over it, with the help of postsecondary education.

Black Issues in Higher Education, December 11, 1996

WHO WILL COLLECT SOCIAL SECURITY?
BY JULIANNE MALVEAUX

Former Colorado governor Dick Lamm wants to carry the banner of Ross Perot's reform party in the 1996 presidential election. Echoing Perot's rhetoric of four years ago, Lamm has been talking about the fiscal austerity needed to eliminate the federal budget deficit and get our nation's finances in order. Like Perot, Lamm uses homespun homilies and "common sense" to make his points about government spending on things that range from public assistance to Social Security. Some of Lamm's logic on cutting spending is flawed, though, and imposes heavy burdens on some sectors of society at the expense of others.

Take, for example, the Lamm assertion that the Social Security retirement age ought to be raised to 70. People are living longer, says Lamm, and so they ought to work longer. We can't afford, he says, to have people retiring at 65 or even 68. We can't afford the pay- as-you-go system, either. If Social Security is collected at 70, not 68, we can save billions of dollars.

It is easy for a politician, someone who talks for a living, to talk about working until age 70. Indeed, if some politicians (Senators Strom Thurmond and Jesse Helms come to mind) could be persuaded to retire at 70, the policy process might be much improved. But what about those people who still do hard, physical work in our society? There are men who, at 63, look forward to coming off the assembly line, or women who, at 64, are waiting tables at diners or typing for a living. College professors, politicians, writers, or business executives shudder to think of being "put out to pasture" at 70, but many other workers are unequal to the physical challenges of their work after age 65.

Lamm isn't the only politician to argue that the Social Security retirement age ought to be raised. Several federal commissions that have investigated the structure of Social Security have called for the same thing, and the retirement age is scheduled to rise, first to 68, then to 70, within the next ten years. But Lamm says it needs to happen sooner, and many agree. These comments largely go unchallenged because so many fear that the Social Security system will be in real financial trouble as the baby boom ages and the dependency ratio falls. Once, six people supported an individual on social security. By the year 2010, two workers will shoulder the burdens of one retiree.

Still, demographic differences in life expectancy suggest that raising the Social Security retirement age will reduce the chances some workers have of ever collecting Social Security. Life expectancy for African American men, for example, is 66, which means that most African American male workers will pay into a system they will not collect from. Native Americans have an even lower life expectancy. They, too, can expect to contribute to a system they will not live long enough to collect from. Proposals like Lamm's suggest an income transfer from those with shorter life expectancies to those who will have longer lives. Such proposals may save the system, but only by imposing a burden on some groups of people.

There are alternatives to the proposals that the Social Security retirement age increase. The system would be more fiscally sound if more workers contributed to it. Federal policy to encourage the development of more full-time jobs would place more workers in the system. Job training initiatives that provide work options to people who have dropped out of the labor force would also increase the number of workers who pay into the Social Security system. These options require a federal investment in our nation's human resources, not the punitive approach that people like Lamm are taking to find a more fiscally solid footing.

Lamm's approach to fiscal stability may well increase the number of elderly poor. It raises questions about the kind of reform we can expect from Perot's Reform Party, and makes me wonder if this reform is nothing more than politics as usual.

King Features Syndicate, July 12, 1996

MORE FOR THE MILITARY?
BY JULIANNE MALVEAUX

While Republican budget-balancers seem all too eager to cut funds for the arts, public assistance, public broadcasting, foreign aid, and any other program they can wield their axes on, they aren't as eager to accept President Clinton's budget when it comes to the military. Despite the fact that the President has asked for about $40 billion more in military spending (for military pay, and "readiness"), Republican members of the House Committee on National Security (which was formerly known as the House Armed Services Committee) wanted to know why the President didn't want more.

Ohio Republican John Kasich grilled Joint Chiefs of Staff Chairman General John Shalikashvili and Defense Secretary William Perry, asking whether or not the United States is prepared to fight in two wars in two different regions of the world, if we didn't need more money and weapons for "military readiness," and whether our country would be more "secure" if the defense budget were larger. We have the largest military in the world, and the largest weapons arsenal. If we're in an arms race, we're racing with ourselves. Russia is more involved with economic development and democracy issues, we are technologically superior to the rest of the world, and so the notion that we need to spend more on our military makes no sense.

As with domestic public policy, though, the Republicans have been shrewd in seizing rhetorical control of the discussion. By changing the name of the Congressional committee that has military oversight from the House Armed Services Committee to the House Committee on National Security, Republicans have made the military-industrial complex seem a benign set of institutions designed to guarantee our security. Thus, security spending takes priority over any other kind of spending, and even balanced budget concerns take a back seat to the mission of protecting people. But we're overprotected, at least with weaponry. The Pentagon neither needs nor wants Seawolf submarines, but there is $1.6 billion in the military budget earmarked for them. The Center for Defense Information has described a new attack submarine that is budgeted for as a "cold war relic" and suggests scrapping that $704 million program. They say proposed increased military spending should be offset by savings in the military budget, and suggest that the $257.8 billion requested for national defense (which is about $5 billion a week in spending) is excessive.

To be sure, many see military spending as a public works program. Communities with military bases, while pushing for balanced budgets, push to keep bases open because of the deleterious effect base closings have on the economic environment of communities. Military spending is the most ineffective form of public works spending, though. Far more jobs-effective is spending on infrastructure repair, social services, or other public works programs.

The Contract on America has a provision, the National Security Restoration Act, that would prevent U.S. troops from serving under UN command and "strengthen our national defense and maintain our credibility around the world." With the biggest military operation in the world, and the most sophisticated technology, there is absolutely no evidence that our $5 billion per week expenditure needs to be maintained. The House Committee on National Security nearly begged Defense Secretary William Perry to ask for more money for military (or "security") spending. They don't seem to understand that a strong military isn't the only way to ensure national security. A healthy, educated population also goes a long way toward ensuring security. But that costs money we can't spend because we're balancing the budget and trying to win an arms race with ourselves.

King Features Syndicate, February 10, 1995

BOMBS BEFORE BOOKS — B2 PRIORITIES
BY JULIANNE MALVEAUX

Why is the United States committed to spending billions of dollars on the flawed B2 bomber? This is not a rhetorical question. The so-called "stealth" bombers that cost $2 billion each two years ago suffer from a radar system so warped it could not distinguish between a cloud and a mountain. Now, the radar problem has been fixed, but the B2 bomber apparently has a weather problem. It can't go out in the rain without being at least subjectively damaged. Given all its flaws, the fealty that some members of Congress have to further subsidies of B2 weaponry speaks more to their relationship with the B2 manufacturer, Northrop Grumman Corporation, than to any concern they might have for our country's "national defense."

Our country started building B2 bombers back in 1981, when 132 of them were supposed to cost $22 billion, or about $1.67 million apiece. But eight years after the initial contract, the Air Force had spent $22 billion and had just one plane to show for it, and the plane they had didn't really work. According to some, the plane cost three times its weight in gold. And the tragedy is that this plane is one that is not needed in terms of our nation's military strategy.

Those members of Congress who rely on contributions from defense contractors need B2 bombers, though. So do those districts that house manufacturing plants. Isn't the argument, then, that we keep funding the bomber because it creates jobs? Not really. Weapons like the B2 bomber are capital intensive, not labor intensive. We could get a much bigger bang for our buck by spending on services. A bomber costs about $2 billion. So does 100,000 entry-level social workers at $20,000 each. So does 72,000 teachers at $28,000. So does 16,000 HMO doctors earning $125,000 each. So does 66,600 librarians earning $30,000 each. And so on, and so on, and so on. One doesn't need a brilliant imagination to divide $2 billion by the prevailing salary for a range of people — teachers, nurses, social workers, doctors, construction workers, university professors. Or we could talk about what we could buy, like groceries for 400,000 families for a year, or summer jobs for 420,000 kids. We could send 65,000 students to college for four years, or build 13,000 average-priced homes. It doesn't take a rocket scientist to know that $2 billion goes a long way. But it boggles the brain to think of the material difference $2 billion, the cost of one bomber, could make. If we lose one B2 bomber, imagine what an impact that might have on our society! If we lost all 22 of them, imagine how enriched our lives would be!

Some are concerned that losing bombers would mean losing jobs and opportunities. But anyone who can build a bomb can also build an X-ray machine, a school, or a library. Anyone whose science can figure out how to tell the difference between mountains and clouds ought also be able to figure out how to distinguish between benign and malignant cells in a flawed body. If we can waste money developing a bungling bomber, shouldn't we invest money in finding a cure for AIDS, cancer, or something else? Why have our imaginations been so limited? Partly, it seems, because we have left our brains at the starting line of the status quo and tried to move ahead from there.

We are limited in our thinking when we repeat the fractured clichés of a ruptured ruling class. We need weapons to fight the cold war? Last time I looked, Russia was a welfare recipient, hand out, mouth open, waiting for international aid. If we need to defend ourselves against the Russians, or the other former Soviet countries, we certainly don't need to do it with a further military buildup. Indeed, one might argue that our pace of armament is what broke the former Soviet Union. Now that we "won" why don't we declare victory and put our money back into our pockets and back into our society?

The truth is that neither the Pentagon nor the President wants to spend more money on the B2 bomber. Still, the Pentagon, maintaining an infrastructure, will not protest so much about the extra money it gets if the B2 is approved. And the President, ducking military antipathy about his own commitment, will not cut the military budget unless he absolutely has to. We are left buying a weapon that doesn't work, spending $45 billion for a lot of folks to save face.

Think of $45 billion wasted when you think of why we must cut social spending; think of $45 billion wasted when asked whether there are funds available for school construction. A B2 bomber is not only a symbol of a military anachronism. It is also a symbol of our nation's misplaced priorities—bombs before books, before nutrition, before housing. Bombs because profit-seeking defense contractors too often direct our economy.

King Features Syndicate, September 19, 1997

LOCK UP THE GUNS, NOT THE KIDS
BY JULIANNE MALVEAUX

Fifteen-year-old Kip Kinkel, the alleged shooter in the Thurston High School massacre in Springfield, Oregon, was by all accounts a troubled youth. His crimes have made headlines and sparked commentary about the string of school yard shootings we have seen this academic year. Even President Clinton has gotten into the fray, noting that "school shootings are more than isolated incidents" and partly blaming "changing culture" on these shootings.

School yard shootings in small-town America are garnering the kind of headlines that inner-city school violence never garners. In the inner city there have been drive-by shootings, missing children, and murdered children, but most of this violence is treated as business as usual. If we were truly alarmed at adolescent violence, then the violence that plagues inner-city communities, and especially young black men, might have caused more alarm earlier on. Had we looked more carefully at this violence, we might have looked more carefully at the effect that ever-available handguns have on the violence in our country. There are 222 million handguns available for some 250 million Americans. That's almost a gun apiece, with too many in adolescent hands.

I know that guns don't kill, people do. I also know that not every adolescent who handles a gun does use it to create mayhem or murder. But there is a fatal combination between adolescence, pathology, and handgun availability. In adolescence, young people are already volatile, often irrational, and extremely demonstrative. Acting-out behavior often takes the form of minor criminal activity and clashes with parents and teachers. Adding a gun to this mix is as explosive as placing a lighted match on gasoline-soaked kindling. It is, if nothing else, an argument for keeping guns out of the hands of adolescents.

Based on what I've read about Kip Kinkel, though, taking the guns out of his hands might not have prevented him from doing any damage. He is, by all accounts, an extremely troubled youth who enjoyed torturing animals and building bombs. His parents, teachers by training, couldn't control him and had about given up on him. His peers voted him "Most Likely to Start World War III." Even without guns, Kip Kinkel was danger walking.

But I am intrigued by the news coverage of Kinkel and his family, the efforts made to "humanize" this young assassin. We have seen his family pictures, read about his outstanding parents and his caring sisters. For all the information about his pathologies, we have also seen his human side, something we rarely see when the violence conforms to America's stereotypes and the alleged villain is African American or Latino. Then, there are no families, no humanizing factors. Then, it is as if the villain has either dropped from the sky or emerged from a faceless, nameless community of indistinguishable criminals. There is this rush to "understand" Kip Kinkel, a rush that is rarely there to understand inner-city violence and its perpetrators.

Instead, for inner-city violence, the Senate has proposed the Violent and Repeat Juvenile Offender Act. Some are using the Kinkel incident to spur the passage of legislation that would allow 14-year-olds to be tried as adults, would house children in adult jails (where they are more likely to be sexually assaulted and to commit suicide), and scapegoats African American children, who are most likely to be turned over to the adult criminal justice system. The legislation requires schools to expel students if caught with cigarettes, alcohol, or drugs and makes no provision for alternative education. And the legislation would "scar" alleged offenders for life, even if their arrests don't result in convictions, by requiring that records be shared with schools, colleges, and employers. The Violent and Repeat Juvenile Offender Act doesn't invest in after-school and summer opportunities, nor does it have strong provisions to protect children from guns. Yet, momentum is building for this legislation.

There is a profound irony in using Kip Kinkel's alleged crimes to punish millions of other students, many of whom had neither his advantages nor his opportunities. Had Kinkel managed to graduate from high school, his parents would have been able to pull strings to get his record expunged, and to get him admitted to college. Although he was arrested at school, his father's call to the Oregon National Guard about a boot camp program suggests the groundwork was being laid to avoid a sentence for gun possession with some form of alternative or community "service." Inner-city youth don't often have that option. They are more likely to be arrested, to serve time in public facilities, to be transferred to adult court. While minority children are just a third of the youth population, they are two-thirds of those in long-term custody.

We should lock up our guns, not our kids. And we should find compassion for those youngsters who have come to see violence as a way of life, not as an earth-shattering isolated incident. The Violent and Repeat Juvenile Offender Act would not have stopped Kip Kinkel's rampage, but better gun control laws might have.

King Features Syndicate, May 28, 1998

LIFE IS NOT A BASEBALL GAME
BY JULIANNE MALVEAUX

I thought "three strikes you're out" was a baseball rallying cry, but in a country that ranks crime as its number one problem "three strikes you're out" is a sentencing credo instead of a rule at a ball game. The credo has been adopted by Washington state, discussed by the United States Senate, and now embraced by President Clinton in his State of the Union Address. If one commits three "dangerous felonies," then do not pass go, do not collect $200, take yourself directly to jail and stay there for life.

For those who have been victims of dangerous crimes, and for those whose relatives have been killed by dangerous felons, the rallying cry of "three strikes you're out" makes sense. And if this sentencing credo were limited to the most heinous crime— murder—I'd be a proponent, too. The problem is that the definition of "dangerous" crimes gets broader and broader. Pretty soon someone caught possessing drugs three times will be branded a dangerous criminal and incarcerated for life. While that may satisfy the societal cry of an eye for an eye, it makes no policy sense.

The trend toward mandatory sentencing ignores the flaws in our so-called criminal justice system, in the random way that many are pressured into plea bargains even on dangerous felonies. Those who can't afford legal representation are often pushed to plead guilty to a lesser crime instead of clogging up the court system. Too often, they agree to the plea bargain because they know that criminal justice means "just us" for many prosecutors. What's two years in exchange for a life, they ask themselves. Unfortunately, many find out the hard way that the stigma of two years of time served puts the rest of life in peril.

The point came home to me a month or so ago, when on a long ride in a taxi, the driver began to talk about his life. I don't know how we got on the subject, but once I mentioned my alma mater, I had to fasten my seat belt and listen to a 30-minute monologue.

The cab driver went to college a stone's throw from me, and graduated the same year I did. He worked as a social worker, but after a divorce "fell in with a bad set." He drank too much, used drugs, and tuned off life. When he was arrested for drug distribution, he said he "copped a plea." But he wasn't distributing, he was carrying drugs for his personal use. He says the big fish swam past law enforcement, while the lemmings paid. More importantly, he said he has a felony on his record, a felony that prevents some employment and some educational opportunities. He spends his days alternating between bitterness and optimism, and grunted at the mention of "three times you're out."

"Life is not a baseball game," he told me. "The police play a game with misdemeanors and felonies, with what is dangerous and what is not. If I had been standing in the wrong place, I could have been charged as an accessory to a robbery. Dangerous felony. Maybe two felonies. Then I'm walking the rest of my life on a tightrope because three strikes puts me out.

"You forget that the police believe that if you committed one felony, you can commit two. My name is on a list, just like the names of young gang members. If something goes down in my neighborhood, someone will be looking for me, just for questioning. If they can't find another suspect, and the perpetrator was black and burly, I might spend some time at a police station. It isn't three strikes you're out, it's just one strike you're out. From now on I'm guilty until proven innocent."

Our nation's fear of crime has been manipulated into a frenzy so visceral that we all ignore the fact that crime rates have been falling. President Clinton has found his "Willie Horton" issues in welfare reform and crime reduction, but his Willie Horton blinders screen out the reality. Life is not a baseball game. Justice must be tempered with compassion. And unless we're talking murder, we can't afford, fiscally or morally, to lock up all those we call "criminals," unless we are willing to reform our criminal justice system.

King Features Syndicate, December 7, 1994

TREAT DRUGS AS DISEASE, NOT CRIME
BY JULIANNE MALVEAUX

Mandatory sentencing for nonviolent drug charges has been the impetus behind the current prison construction boom in the United States. But we can't build prisons fast enough to incarcerate those whose illness exposes them to the scourge of mandatory sentencing. The data are astounding and disturbing—385 percent more African American women were incarcerated in 1995 than in 1985. Seventy percent of those women were incarcerated for nonviolent drug offenses. They didn't rob anyone, they didn't kill anyone, they did damage mostly to themselves. During their incarceration, little is done to rehabilitate them or offer them treatment. Indeed, anecdotal evidence suggests that drugs are as available in prison as they are on the streets. Why incarcerate these women, then? Apparently, simply to keep the prison-industrial engine churning, to provide construction jobs for those who build prisons, as well as employment for those who guard prisoners.

My views on the "drug war" are only confirmed by a recent, powerful ethnographic study of a year on a Baltimore corner that has been ravaged by drug availability. David Simon and Edward Burns' *The Corner* (New York: Broadway Books, $27.50) chronicles how quickly hope is extinguished in a place where drug use has become part of the way of life. Children are exposed to their parents' drug use, while pillars of the community cannot spare their own children from the ill effects of drugs. Those rare spaces that are oases against drugs are not sacred ground, either. A community center, with one dedicated staffer, has its meager resources stolen by drug "fiends."

Yet when some of those on the corner search for help, it is nowhere to be found. The waiting list for drug treatment is months, not days or weeks. The same government that will pay $50,000 a year to incarcerate a drug fiend will not pay a fraction of that to help that same fiend get clean. Cleaning up the corner, though, is low on anyone's list of priorities. Law enforcement, educational, civic, and other institutions accept the proliferation of drugs as a reality, the consequences of drugs as inevitable, and the "drug war" as a way of keeping themselves employed. Should the paradigm shift just a bit, so that there were rewards for weaning people off drugs instead of for arresting them, places like the corner might have hope.

Addiction is a medical problem. Corporate America has had to grapple with that, often offering "employee assistance programs" to those who drink or drug too much. Professional sports provides counseling and treatment for its players who have trouble with drugs and alcohol. Repeat offenders, certainly, get less help and may lose their contracts. But initial addiction is treated as a medical problem, not a crime.

The same should be true in the streets. Instead of building jails that offer little rehabilitation or drug treatment, it makes more sense to build drug treatment centers. Instead of employing prison guards, it makes sense to employ medical professionals and counselors to help people make the transition away from drug use. Instead of increasing the number of police officers who patrol places like "the corner," repeatedly making the same kinds of arrests, why not employ architects and urban planners to bring the corner back to life?

Policy makers have quickly and easily demonized inner-city drug users like those on "the corner," using rhetoric to make them subhuman and unworthy of our assistance or concern. Mandatory sentencing denies judges the ability to distinguish between those who truly want rehabilitation and those who have surrendered themselves to a drug culture. Few speak, anymore, of prison reform, abandoning millions of Americans to an increasingly harsh system, often for nonviolent crimes. Much of this would change if we treated drug addiction as a medical problem, not a crime, if we treated the people on "the corner" in the same way we treat addicted corporate executives or basketball players.

King Features Syndicate, December 19, 1997

THE REAL DRUG WAR
BY JULIANNE MALVEAUX

I keep hearing the term "drug war" used to describe a national effort to rid the streets of drugs. But there are just some drugs and some streets that have attracted ire. The drug war is a war on the African American community, and the casualties of this war are listed in a recent report released by the Sentencing Project, a Washington, D.C.-based public policy organization that conducts research on criminal justice issues.

Five years ago, the Sentencing Project reported that almost one in four young (20-29) black men were under some form of criminal justice supervision — in prison, in jail, on probation or parole. Their most recent report, "Young Black Americans and the Criminal Justice System: Five Years Later," says that despite lots of intervention activity, the number has increased. Now, nearly one in three (32.2 percent) of all young black men in their twenties are under criminal justice supervision. This incarceration and supervision costs $6 billion a year. Drug policies are the single most important factor contributing to the rise in criminal justice populations in recent years.

In many ways, it is a "race" thing. There are 4 million crack users in this country, more than 2.2 million of whom are white. But in Los Angeles County, not a single white person has been arrested for crack possession since 1986. L.A. is not the only county to take a pass on white drug use. Nationally, the African American proportion of arrests rose from 24 percent in 1980 to 39 percent in 1993, much higher than the percentage of African American drug users. Black drug possessors and users are simply easier to catch than white ones. They are more visible, more likely to ply their trade on the streets, and subject to the random racial police harassment that makes every African American suspect.

If the police were as diligent in cruising the malls as the hood, the profile of those incarcerated in the name of a drug war would look extremely different. But cruising the malls means rattling cages, suggesting that drug problems transcend the black community. There is a set of decisions that range from where arrests are made, to the types of prosecution and sentencing policies that are employed, that lead to the increase in the number of African Americans who are incarcerated. It is also official U.S. public policy to disproportionately punish African Americans for drug possession.

Many have characterized the drug war as a war against crack cocaine and powdered cocaine. The only difference between the two is that crack is powdered cocaine plus baking soda. The possession of five grams of crack cocaine will get you five years in jail. It takes 500 grams of powdered cocaine to get you the same five years in jail that five grams of crack cocaine will get you. If the difference is simply baking soda, then those convicted for having crack are being sentenced extra time for the crime of cooking baking soda! This is not to diminish the devastation of crack cocaine, but simply to wonder about the sentencing disparity and President Clinton's failure to consider the recommendations of the U.S. Sentencing

Commission. They asked that the disparity between crack and cocaine possession be narrowed. The President responded by making a passionate speech about the effects of drugs on our society. Wrong answer.

The right answer requires a look at the uneven effects of this drug war. African American people shoulder the greatest burden because the police lens is focused on young black men (and women, whose incarceration rates have almost doubled), and because the cheaper drug gets a greater penalty according to sentencing guidelines that the President agrees with. If we don't like drug use, we ought to stiffly punish those who distribute and sell cocaine. We ought not decide that those who possess forms of the same drug get a different sentence.

Is this a drug war or a war on inner-city men of color? The Sentencing Project report suggests the latter and challenges us to examine "drug policy." Even as he fights a set of budget battles, President Clinton is a misguided general if he doesn't deal with the contradictions of drug war.

King Features Syndicate, December 7, 1995

CHAPTER 4

BLACK BUSINESS, BLACK BOYCOTTS

The economic status of African Americans is something like the classic economic production-possibility curve. Racism and discrimination have limited the shape and space of the curve, but African Americans still live inside the curve, in an inefficient space, because we don't make the most of what we have.

Public policy often constrains African American businesses, especially by limiting the few minority business set-asides that were designed to level the business playing field. But African American people could use the roughly $400 billion we earned in 1997 far more efficiently. For example, we spent 10 percent of our income on black-owned businesses. Do we think the white man's ice is colder, are we seduced by the Afro-packaging of majority firms, or do we simply not care about our own economic development? We reward firms that punish us, patronize firms that discriminate against us. What kind of sense does that make?

African Americans can both make a point and flex our economic muscle by buying black and boycotting those who discriminate. When we harness our economic power, we can demand dignity and respect in economic markets. That's the bottom line.

SYMBOLS WITHOUT SUBSTANCE: AFRO-PACKAGING
BY JULIANNE MALVEAUX

African American people had, in 1996, income of over $373 billion. That's a hefty sum — so much that it would rank us in the top 20 nations of the world. We talk about our dollar power, but do more talking than strategizing. Indeed, we behave as if we are powerless to change our reality, as if the dollars we spend can do little to improve the economic status of African Americans.

While we behave as if we are powerless, others are more than aware of our spending power and the impact it has on their bottom line. Thus, targeted marketing, marketing specifically "spun" to African American consumers, with the hope that these consumers will reward racial symbols with product loyalty. Thus, the Kentucky fried kente, an experiment at some KFC branches where commercial soul food was paired with touches of kente in an attempt to get black folks to buy more of their chicken done "right." I don't know how many conversations I had with friends who told me how thrilled they were that KFC had "recognized" our community, and how many countervailing conversations I had with people who felt that KFC had ripped us off.

Things are even more blatant in the beauty aid market. Not too long ago, Revlon threatened to drive black hair care manufacturers out of business. They failed, of course, but it wasn't for lack of trying. A group of courageous black publishers went after Revlon and called their bluff on the woof. But Revlon still appeals to many of us by using black models in its packaging, some say to create the deliberate impression that they have some African American ownership.

Charles Johnson, a Dallas-based brother who produces the "non-greasy skin care lotion" Ashaway, says he is frustrated by his attempt to get his products into African American hands. At a recent conference, he was handing out not only samples of his product, but also sheets detailing the health and beauty aid products produced by white manufacturers. Nothing against white manufacturers, but Johnson was objecting to the fact that many of these companies are thought to be black-owned. As Revlon does, TCB, Bump Fighter, Shades of You, Murray's Hair Pomade, Ambi Skin Creams, Stay-Soft-Fro, Black Opal, and TC Natural combine the use of black models with Afro-packaging to create the deliberate impression that companies that manufacture products targeted to the black market are black-owned.

Johnson isn't just operating from the sour grapes tip of a small manufacturer who can't get his foot in the door. He charges that the playing field is hardly level, since drugstores like Wal-mart, Kmart, Walgreen's and Eckerts court black customers but ignore black manufacturers. Even though African Americans buy some 40 percent of lotion and other products, Johnson said buyers want to restrict his "Ashaway" product to the limited, ethnic shelves because white people don't understand what ash is. Buyers want to force Ashaway through ethnic distributors, limiting its market, and often suggest that another lotion product is not needed because there are so many products out there already.

Still, African Americans are the top users of lotion and other skin softeners. And mainstream companies are beginning to adopt "our" language, referring to skin as both dry and "ashy." At the bottom line, Ashaway can't compete with Lubriderm, but it can't even get into the game without access to shelf space. Why shouldn't African American manufacturers have a shot at the lucrative lotion market? We spend more than $1 billion a year on hair care, and another $5 billion on personal care, but black manufacturers are able to cash in on only 4 percent of this market. Why? Partly because they are small, but partly, too, because they don't have elbows sharp enough to muscle into the distribution game.

It takes Charles Johnson, a 10-year veteran of the shelf game, to talk about the hurdles African American manufacturers must clear. He has been manufacturing Ashaway since 1987, and trying, all that time, to get drugstores to produce his project. Although he has mostly been striking out, there have been regional successes. Ashaway can be found on the shelves in Dallas, Johnson's home base. And it could be found in more places if some of us would write the big drugstores and ask that they carry it, or if we stopped to ask managers in stores where the Ashaway is.

It ought to take more than Kentucky fried chicken or Afro-packaging to earn black consumer loyalty. We ought also be prepared to support black-owned manufacturers. Charles Johnson is one of those who is fighting the uphill battle to get us seen as both consumers and producers. In supporting his product, we also support ourselves.

For more information about Johnson Enterprises and Ashaway, write to: P.O. Box 5339, Dallas, Texas 75222, or call 214-855-0083.

San Francisco Sun Reporter, September 24, 1997

WHEN THE "N" WORD IS RELEVANT
BY JULIANNE MALVEAUX

Sixty-two years ago, a group of visionary African American women formed the National Association of Negro Business and Professional Women's Clubs, Incorporated. In 1935, when this organization was founded, the Census identified a scant 2,000 African American women who owned businesses or worked in the professions. Now, with the business and professional ranks of African American women far surpassing the million-woman mark, and with the organization meeting at the New York Hilton Hotel, where the law might have prevented our gathering 40 years ago, some ask whether organizations with the "N" word in their name are still relevant.

I'm president of the National Association of Negro Business and Professional Women's Clubs. I'd rather be called African American than Negro, but I embrace the word "Negro" to describe my organization, because Negro is part of our history, and because some of the conditions that motivated women to form a Negro organization in 1935 still exist in 1997. While things have changed, African American women are still underrepresented in business and the professions. Some still must hurdle the barriers of discrimination in lending to get the money sufficient to open businesses. Some still face a pay gap—African American women who work full-time have median weekly earnings of $362 per week, compared to $428 per week for full-time white women and $580 per week for full-time white men. As long as disparities like this exist, the goals of my organization's founders, to achieve equity through advocacy, remain unmet. The word "Negro" remains a reminder of how much more work we have to do.

Our goals may be the same, but our tactics must shift as we move toward the 21st century. There is as much exclusion by economics and technology as there once was by race and gender. Shifting labor market conditions also challenge the notion of job security; now, civil rights organizations must look at business development as closely as we once looked at the employment arena.

Our search for economic opportunity must also have global dimensions. Legislation is pending that will treat the African continent as a trading partner, not just an aid recipient, in the global marketplace. With the 5 percent growth rates in southern Africa exceeding those in the United States, there are clear opportunities for African Americans in international business development. The door of affirmative action may be closing, but the window of international opportunity is being pushed open. Women of color around the globe see similarities in our situation, and these similarities provide the basis for both organizing and entrepreneurial opportunities.

Because economic justice is a more complex concept than it once was, the role of black women's organizations is different, but still relevant. Even as we challenge disparity, we must also have an eye on emerging opportunities, just as our founders did 62 years ago.

USA Today, August 7, 1997

DO BLACK ISSUES GET SWALLOWED IN DIVERSITY MOVEMENT?

BY JULIANNE MALVEAUX

The February issues of a small business magazine commemorated Black History Month by including articles on diversity, discrimination, and multiculturalism. One article exhorted small companies to implement costly human resource procedures to ensure that a disgruntled minority employee could not sue for discrimination. Another article pandered surface clichés about the behavior of people of color, advising strategies to counter the fact that Asian Americans are supposedly silent, African American women belligerent, and so on. The most amusing of the trio of articles is one that talked about diversity in the broadest of terms — diversity, the writer said, could help white women from different regions of the country understand each other. It could help blondes understand brunettes. It could help younger bosses understand the older employees who resisted them. Race was not mentioned a single time in the entire 2,500-word piece.

Race has everything to do with diversity, but too many people are primed to forget it. The diversity movement is a direct outgrowth of the civil rights movement, and though diversity encompasses more than the simple issues of black-white racial differentials, from where I sit these differences are at the core in the development of understanding about diversity. But at some corporations, diversity means getting white women into the mix. In other settings, much of the diversity effort focuses on gays and lesbians. Depending on who is running a human resource office, diversity can focus on Asian American concerns, Latino concerns, or maybe even African American concerns. All too often, though, African Americans are treated as just one of a group of demanding minorities who want "in."

The public seems wearied of African American concerns, and the media makes the weariness even worse. If there is a pathology, it must be an African American pathology, be it welfare, crime, or the urban condition. The media coverage of the O.J. Simpson case illustrates, if nothing else, the racial bias in the media. One pundit mused that she thought O.J. was immune to the rage that consumed "people of his background," and then regretted aloud that she was mistaken. She didn't go so low as to call him just another n———r, but that was clearly the implication, another black man with misplaced rage. Some African American writers have written much the same thing. He had it all, some say, but black rage got him into this predicament. Everybody has the man convicted on circumstantial evidence, even before he has a trial. And while that ferocious image of black rage is discussed, the real deal is economic. The O.J. publicity may cut some black men out of consideration for employment and opportunity. The diversity movement marches forward, benefiting almost everyone but African Americans.

Data about the new tolerance suggest that the multicultural umbrella doesn't often cover the African American presence. When the *Wall Street Journal* did a study on job losses as a result of the 1990-91 recession, it found that every group except African Americans gained jobs. To be sure, there were reasons for black jobs losses. Plants in the inner city closed. People used family contacts to find new jobs. It wasn't racial, they noted, it was economic. But the economics had an ugly racial undertone.

The companies that laid African Americans off were the same ones who advertised "We are an equal opportunity employer," the same ones who sponsored diversity workshops and forums. On the surface, everything is diverse. Beneath the surface, African Americans are losing jobs, but it isn't racism, some posit. If it were racism, after all, why would the companies initiating the layoffs still be doing diversity work?

Some do it because they have to. Flagstar, the parent company of Denny's, seems to be involved in diversity work because they've been caught with their racism out, although they deny it. After they failed to serve African American customers on several occasions, and got caught at it, I was amazed and amused to learn that they begin diversity training with a sappy crooner singing "We Are One" (I sat on a panel with a Flagstar representative who actually played the saccharin music, then read from a sheet of paper about nondiscrimination) instead of inculcating folk in the hard realities of equal opportunity law. No matter what they do, someone, somewhere, will dismiss discrimination as benign or an honest mistake.

The result of this discrimination, though, is racial economic differentials, the kind that public policy ignores and the diversity movement is too mild to tackle. Many of those who benefit from the diversity movement benefit from the inequality that African Americans experience without doing anything to reverse the inequality. Too many people have used the African American inequality that justified passage of civil rights laws to benefit themselves and bypass the African American population.

I am all too aware of the story folks tell about the white dog who threw a slice of bread at the black, brown, yellow, and red dogs and then sat back to enjoy the rest of the loaf while he watched them scrambling over the crumbs. In the nineties, with the persistence of high African American unemployment rates, one might spin a companion tale of a black dog who snatched a slice of bread from the white dog, brought it back into the courtyard for the other dogs to share and ended up with less than a bite. The diversity movement will ignore black concerns unless African Americans push our own interests with the same passion that we push coalition interests, and until we demand reciprocity from our allies.

I'm not a curmudgeon or a nay-sayer when I note that a diversity movement that excludes African Americans, or pushes our concerns to the periphery, is no diversity movement at all. In many ways, diversity addresses issues of white male hegemony in America's most important institutions. Where is the movement, though, that addresses the racism that is as American as the Fourth of July? Where is the awareness that this racism affects African Americans in a way it affects no other minority?

Black Issues in Higher Education, July 11, 1994

BIG CHILL IN MINORITY BROADCASTING OWNERSHIP?
BY JULIANNE MALVEAUX

The National Association of Black Owned Broadcasters (NABOB) has smaller groups from which to draw its membership than it did just a year ago. In 1995, 109 AM and 86 FM stations were owned by African Americans; a total of 185 AM and 129 FM stations were owned by minorities. Just a year later, 101 AM and 64 FM stations were owned by African Americans. Meanwhile, while the number of minority-held AM stations was constant at 185, the number of FM stations had dropped to 86. Most of the drop in the number of FM stations owned by minorities came from a drop in the number of stations owned by African Americans.

Why, in just one year, has African American ownership of AM stations dropped by 8 percent, while the number of FM stations dropped by a staggering 25 percent? In a presentation to NABOB, Kofi Asiedu Ofori of the Civil Rights Telecommunications Forum suggested that the 1996 Telecommunications Act may have something to do with the drop in ownership. That legislation, for all its hype about increasing access, removed national ownership caps which made it possible for single owners to buy up dozens, if not hundreds, of stations. The legislation also allowed the development of "super duopolies," allowing individual owners to have as many as 8 stations in any single market. Before this year is out, it is likely that the Federal Communications Commission will also approve joint ownership of television and radio stations, newspaper and radio stations, and other combinations that reduce the diversity of ownership in media markets.

The Telecommunications Act of 1996, for all its bipartisan support, was the work of the 104th Congress and its Contract on America. The basis of the legislation is the erroneous assumption that the most efficient markets are unregulated markets. The legislation ignored the fact that the reason media markets have been regulated is because everyone does not have access to radio and television ownership, because monopoly or duopoly ownership in markets may not be in the public interest. African American and other minority broadcasters have been media's "new kids on the block," so new that when Inner City Broadcasting's Percy Sutton bought a station in New York City two decades ago, he acquired only the 13th station owned by an African American. Minority broadcasters have had special concerns about maintaining diversity in ownership. Many of them are too small to compete with the media moguls who, after passage of the 1996 Telecommunications Act, are buying up everything they can get their hands on.

Media observers say that there has been an "aggressive concentration" that started a year ago. Thomas O. Hicks, for example, controls 413 stations through CapStar Broadcasting, Chancellor Media, and SFX broadcasting. The top five radio station owners control 898 stations, and a year from now, their monopoly control of the industry is likely to grow. Where does that leave minority-owned stations? NABOB says the consolidation tendency has caused a "big chill" in the ability of minorities to improve the tiny toehold they now have in broadcast ownership.

It doesn't help that the Congress changed rules that once provided incentives for owners to sell to minorities. Partly because of hostility to affirmative action, partly because some had played fast and loose with the rules — the tax breaks that once made sales to minorities profitable. The rules shift won't eliminate minority ownership, but the status of minorities in broadcasting suggests that a review of the rules is in order. According to *Electronic Media Magazine*, there are 11,000 television and radio stations, only 330 of which are owned by African Americans, Native Americans, Asian Americans or Hispanics. "Aggressive consolidation" is likely to make that number smaller in the next five years.

Who benefits from this consolidation? According to Tom Castro, President and CEO of Los Angeles-based El Dorado Communications and a participant in a recent NABOB conference, "There are no benefits for the consumer or for the community. The only beneficiaries are people who own publicly traded stock."

A decline in minority broadcasting ownership may well be "market driven" given the new deregulation, but we are all poorer when consolidation narrows the voices that have access to airwaves. The provisions of the Telecommunications Act of 1996 that have chilled minority participation need to be reversed.

King Features Syndicate, September 10, 1997

WHEN WILL WE STOP CONFERENCING?
BY JULIANNE MALVEAUX

I just came from the NAACP convention. Glad to be there, too. Glad to be with friends and comrades who are partners in the struggle. Glad to see folks who came sick the year before last (I missed last year) and are looking well now. Glad to see throngs of black folks active, engaged, focused.

And yet, as glad as I be (ebonically speaking), I hear the tinkle of silver as African American people ride buses to this Pittsburgh Convention Center, the shuffling of dollars as we pay for hotel rooms, the sound of credit card imprints being pushed against the imprinter as we buy meals. NAACP President and CEO Kweisi Mfume has made the point more clearly than anyone when he noted that black folks spend $4.3 billion on travel, tourism and hospitality. Conservatively speaking, that means that when black folk come to conventions like the NAACP, we are supporting some 172,000 people in their employment situation. How many of those people are African American? How many of them are running things? How clear is it that our dollars don't get the leverage we deserve?

I'm not picking on the NAACP. I'm president of an African American women's association that will pull hundreds of folks to New York for our conference. We'll drop our tens (no, hundreds) of thousands of dollars, and we will enrich the Hilton Hotel, lots of local restaurants, taxi drivers and others. Will we make a point about black women's economic leverage? I hope so, but to be honest, I wonder. As long as people feel the need to converge, to conference, to convene, hotels are sitting in the catbird's seat. We're not going to meet in the booth in the back in the dark on the fly. We are going to do it big-time, visible, loud. Should we? Must we? What would happen if we didn't? And what would we learn about our own economic leverage?

If half of the money that we spend on travel and tourism is spent on conferencing, then we're doing $2 billion of conference activity a year. If we held our dollars back, negotiating better deals with hotels, airlines, and others, what would that mean? If we simply insisted that those who sling plates at us at official closing dinners look more like us, how many jobs would it generate? Do we think we have the power?

I'm convinced the bottom-line question has to do with what we think we have. Do we, frankly, have the power? Can we, seriously, make a difference? Do we dare conceive it, believe it, achieve it? Sounds like a cliché or a bad Jesse Jackson speech, but that is not the intent. The intent is to wonder whether we realize that we have a tiger by the tail, an economy that we can influence by showing our preference for black economic development. What if we spent our money on us? Where would we be?

I speak with 40 or 50 folks each Tuesday on Net Noir (if you don't know about Net Noir, check it out, via America Online; use keyword NetNoir to learn about a black-run online service). We talked this week about the fact that internationally noted Sylvia's restaurant is taking a product line national, as well as opening restaurants around the country. Though our conversation was mostly positive, parts of it were downright annoying. Some people tried to trivialize the conversation by saying that we were simply talking about food. Yeah, we were talking about food at some level, but we were also talking about the ways people make money. But some folks didn't really want to hear that, not at all. Because food isn't glamorous.

Well, isn't it about time black folks got past some of the glamour? Food isn't glamorous, but it makes money. We spend some $40 billion on foodstuffs a year, about $14 billion on eating out. We will walk into a Kentucky Fried Chicken looking for soul food, or into something catchily named hoping to find ourselves. But when we sit down at one of our own restaurants, we have problems with service, problems with prices, problems really with ourselves. We are so convinced that the white man's ice is colder that we will slurp up warm water and call it cold before we buy cold water from the brother on the corner.

Glamour and a quarter will get you a paper in only some of our nation's top ten cities. In New York the paper costs a quarter, and enterpreneurial development costs hard work. That's it, hard work, elbows to the grindstone. Not meeting and greeting, not schmoozing and cooling. Hard work. So those of us who are not interested in the marketing of food are not interested in $40 billion sitting on the table. Who can afford that level of disinterest?

Let's take it just a step further. What would happen if we stopped having conventions? Not forever, you understand. Some of us couldn't do without our dose of networking melanin. But for a year, for a month, maybe even for a week. For long enough for someone to holler ouch when black folks hurt them by not spending money. We need to flex our economic muscles. Part of that flexing may be about staying home.

When will we stop conferencing? When we find a more powerful way of making our presence known. Let's see . . . how do you spell boycott?

San Francisco Sun Reporter, July 16, 1997

ECONOMIC DISRUPTION IS THE POINT
BY JULIANNE MALVEAUX

After meeting with Texaco's chairman, Peter Bijur, last Tuesday, the Rev. Jesse Jackson urged consumers to boycott Texaco. Jackson feels that Bijur is not doing enough to settle the discrimination lawsuit brought by some 1,200 Texaco employees, and feels that Bijur's condemnation of the tone and tenor of a taped meeting where racist and anti-Semitic comments were bandied about is too small a step toward economic justice. In commenting on Jackson's call for a boycott, the Texaco CEO noted that "Boycotts are divisive. Boycotts, in my view, cause economic disruption." Clearly, Peter Bijur is clueless. Doesn't he understand that the point is to cause economic disruption, to hit a company where it hurts?

When negotiation fails, when lawsuits fail, when conscience fails and when good sense fails, economic boycotts are a way to send companies a signal that they can't ignore. Faltering stock prices, divested stock, and lower sales send a much stronger signal than lunch meetings. They are also an effective way to mobilize people around a common goal. And the best thing about a boycott of Texaco is that it can be more than a black thing. People of conscience all ought to be appalled by the tone and tenor of the Texaco tapes, and a boycott is a straightforward way to make this point.

Are there innocent victims in economic boycotts? When anti-apartheid activists urged divestment of stock in companies doing business with South Africa in the early 1980s, some argued that companies that did good work in other areas would be hurt. Those of us who urged divestment, though, were acting at the direction of the African National Congress, whose goal was to make the apartheid system "nongovernable." Companies who did good work in other areas had to understand that the price of doing business with South Africa was pickets and stock disruption.

Now, with Texaco, we have learned that many independent station owners who merely purchase gas from Texaco might be hurt by a boycott. Again, that's the price of corporate identification. If the boycott works the way it should, some of those who purchase gas from Texaco will now buy it elsewhere. Others will pressure Texaco to take care of business regarding the black employees' lawsuit and their employment policies. Still others will stand with Texaco, rationalizing that you can't punish a whole company for the actions of a few people. If the boycott is effective, those who continue an association with Texaco while the company shilly-shallies around its employment policies will pay a price.

To be sure, boycotts have mixed results, and companies like Texaco are often reluctant to acknowledge that consumer protests affect them. Mr. Bijur is advised, though, to review the history of the Montgomery bus boycott which took place more than 30 years ago. When Rosa Parks refused to go to the back of the bus, she sparked an economic action that lasted a full year, and caused "economic disruption" for the bus company that relied on black riders for revenue even as it implemented discriminatory policy. The boycott was inconvenient, at best, for those who had to walk or find other ways of transportation to get to and from work, but it sent a signal that discrimination in public transportation was unacceptable. When black people started riding the bus again, the "back of the bus" policy had been eliminated as unacceptable. Thirty years after the Montgomery bus boycott, consumers have the opportunity to make a point about discrimination in employment. If it takes "economic disruption" to make the point, so be it.

King Features Syndicate, November 18, 1996

WHAT PRICE DIGNITY?
BY JULIANNE MALVEAUX

When Alonzo Jackson went to an Eddie Bauer store two years ago, he wasn't thinking about shoplifting or "consumer racism." Instead, he and his friends were thinking of doing a little shopping. He'd found some good buys the day before at the Eddie Bauer warehouse store, and he'd brought friends back to check out the merchandise and the prices. But he collided with a Prince George's County police officer who was moonlighting as a security guard for Eddie Bauer. The collision between young Alonzo Jackson and the police officer who accused him of shoplifting left Jackson stripped of both his shirt and his dignity, and Eddie Bauer with a deservedly tarnished image.

Security guard Robert Sheehan confronted Alonzo Jackson in October 1995, and accused the young man of stealing the new-looking shirt that he sported. Despite the fact that a cashier remembered Jackson buying items the previous day, Sheehan forced Jackson to remove his shirt, go home for the receipt, and return with it before he could claim the merchandise he paid for. It took weeks, and a pointed column by *Washington Post* writer Cortland Milloy, to produce a reaction from Eddie Bauer, which is part of Spiegel, Inc. The reaction was a tepid public apology and a donation of Eddie Bauer merchandise to a D.C. homeless shelter. At no time did Alonzo Jackson get a private apology. That's why Eddie Bauer had to go to court.

A jury ruled that Eddie Bauer did not violate the civil rights of Alonzo Jackson and his friends. They also ruled that Jackson is entitled to damages for the treatment he received. The combination of compensatory and punitive damages leaves Jackson with an $850,000 award. The friends who witnessed his mistreatment won $75,000 each. It has taken two years and the faith of lawyers who worked without many resources, but Jackson and his buddies, Rasheed Plummer and Marco Cunningham, prevailed.

What lessons can we take from their case as we look at the consumer racism that poisons our society?

Some say there is little to learn. The civil rights claim was not upheld by the jury. But Jackson attorney Donald Temple says he may appeal the jury's finding that race was not a factor in the treatment his client got from Eddie Bauer. In any case, it is rather obvious that the jury didn't find against Bauer simply because they were rude. Whether race was implicit or explicit, it played a role in this case.

More importantly, I think that youngsters like Alonzo Jackson need to be applauded for keeping an eye on the prize. How many would have blinked or shrugged and decided that a lawsuit was not worth it, not likely to yield any gains. The process of finding a lawyer, convincing him of a case, and sticking with the process for two long years has not been an easy one. Too many people twice or three times Jackson's age would swallow the racism rather than prosecute it. My hat is off to Jackson and his attorneys. He reminded us that "power concedes nothing without a demand." His demand to be treated with dignity won him some cash but also the attention of a callous corporation whose flagrant disregard of its customers is deplorable.

"I'm happy we won but it doesn't give you your dignity back," Jackson said outside the courthouse after the verdict. The young man cried when his attorney asked him to re-enact the experience of removing his shirt because of the misplaced suspicions of the police. How much should dignity cost, and what should be done when our dignity is violated? Think Texaco, Avis, Motel 6, UPS, and the cash register racism that confronts black people wherever we spend our money. I say we need to stop spending with the fools who don't think our money is worth much, who feel that they have to insult us in the process of accepting our cash. Unfortunately, though, too many black people think we have to spend our money to wear the labels of companies like Eddie Bauer who make a habit of insulting us.

The news reports of the Eddie Bauer case seem to only scratch the surface of ways this company and its parent, Spiegel, colluded to violate the rights of three young black men. The man who managed the Eddie Bauer store in Maryland apparently lied under oath when he said he had no knowledge of the collision between the rent-a-cop and the three black youngsters. The company's president and attorneys seem also to have engaged in unethical behavior in their attempt to clean up the very tarnished act of some Eddie Bauer employees.

The bottom line? When I see people wearing the media-described "woodsy" Eddie Bauer plaid shirts, I'll see people who are subsidizing consumer racism, paying for the disparate treatment young Alonzo Jackson experienced. Surely there are people of conscience who value dignity above those tired plaid shirts and even tireder corporate policies. Through boycotts and shunning, Eddie Bauer and Spiegel need to be reminded that they can't mistreat those consumers whose purchases add to their bottom line.

Although Alonzo Jackson and his friends won their lawsuit, the $1 million they were awarded is just a fraction of the profits Eddie Bauer collected in 1996.

Those who buy Eddie Bauer clothes need to think about that, and perhaps strike a blow for dignity by switching brands.

San Francisco Sun Reporter, October 15, 1997

COMMERCIALIZING KWANZAA
BY JULIANNE MALVEAUX

I did not have second thoughts when I plunked the money down for a couple hundred Kwanzaa cards. Indeed, I was exhilarated that the United States Postal Service commissioned artist Synthia St. James to design a Kwanzaa stamp and put on the full court press to let everyone know that the stamp is out there. To be sure, there were a couple of wrinkles, like a group of folks who didn't like the stamp because the colors of the nationalist flag, red, black and green, were not in order. But I still thought the stamp was a wonderful idea and couldn't wait to address my holiday cards and affix the stamp to them.

Then I attended a marketplace designed to encourage Kwanzaa spending. The hall brimmed over with wonderful goods by African American and African vendors. It also bubbled through with people eager to spend dollars on Afrocentric goods. Part of me applauds at our willingness, sometimes newfound, to support our own. Part of me bristles, though, at the consumer underpinnings of our nationalism and at what it means in the long run for black economic development.

African American people are, if nothing else, spenders. Thus, Kwanzaa cards (many marketed by Hallmark, thank you), Kwanzaa gifts, and even Kwanzaa stamps well address our consumerism. And yet one of the Kwanzaa principles, Ujamaa, or cooperative economics, speaks to our need for economic development. Another principle, Kujichagulia, speaks to self-determination. What does our spending determine, in the short run and in the long run? Generally it determines the way that others will profit and develop their economies.

I'm not saying that we shouldn't celebrate Kwanzaa with our greetings to family, friends and colleagues. And since I love gifts so much, I'm certainly not nixing them. I am just concerned that a celebration that was designed to commemorate the gathering of first fruit has become as commercial as the day that commemorates Christ's birth.

Of course, this is American, and the greatest tribute to American assimilation that can possibly exist is commercialization. Witness Disney attempting a slavery theme park in Virginia, or the Martin Luther King Day sales that mar celebrations of the civil rights leader's birth. Witness the commercialization of Kwanzaa.

Having said all that, I still think the Kwanzaa stamp is a good thing. I still think that Kwanzaa is an important celebration and find criticisms of the holiday churlish and self-centered. There are some folks who pass themselves off as African American intellectuals whose claim to fame is throwing stones at glass houses, then wrapping themselves in the title of cultural critic when others differ with their views. Some of the conversations about Kwanzaa clearly have this flava'.

Still, I caution African American people about consumerism and commercialism. I caution us to understand that we are part of the engine that drives the American economy, part of the engine that isn't being especially recognized, nor sharing in the benefits of the macroeconomic expansion everyone is celebrating. The November unemployment rate was 4.6 percent, but the black unemployment rate was 9.6 percent. The black youth unemployment rate is more than 30 percent. The National Council of Mayors has reported that the number of requests for emergency shelter and food has risen for the thirteenth year in a row, and that requests for food are up by 16 percent. In celebrating Kwanzaa, the first fruits of the harvest, we might well think about providing some of those fruits to those who don't have them, helping those African American people locked out of our nation's economic progress. That would be one way to ensure that Kwanzaa is more than a commercial celebration, it is really an embracing of our values and those qualities about African people that we are willing to celebrate.

San Francisco Sun Reporter, December 20, 1997

MARKET GIANTS OR MARKET MIDGETS: DO BLACK DOLLARS MAKE A DIFFERENCE?
BY JULIANNE MALVEAUX

Whenever a group of African American people get together to talk about economic empowerment, we bandy about an income statistic that seems awesome. African Americans, we tell ourselves, have an annual income of between $350 billion and $400 billion per year, depending on how you count it. Counting conservatively, the $373 billion U.S. government sources said we had would have placed us at the table of the Summit of 8 (formerly G-7) meetings, right along with the

Russian Federation, which had an income of $331 billion, more than 10 percent less than black folks in the United States.

While African Americans are about 13 percent of the United States population, we earn only about 5 percent of our nation's income, and hold only 3 percent of our nation's wealth. We don't have our fair share, but I am as concerned with the way we leverage the dollars we have as I am with whether we have our "fair share" of dollars. In other words, African American people have economic muscles that can be flexed, making the difference between profit and poverty for a range of companies. Whether we choose to flex those muscles or not determines whether we can be described as market giants or market midgets.

Consider travel and tourism. According to Ken Smikle's *Target Market News*, African Americans spend $1.05 billion each year on air travel, $746 million on out-of-town lodging, and $182 million on out-of-town car rental. Other travel expenses include meals, admission fees to tourist attractions, local transportation and other fees. All told, African Americans spend about $4.3 billion on travel, tourism and hospitality.

A case can be made that there is representative employment for African Americans in the travel, tourism, and hospitality industry. African Americans represented 15.9 percent of the transportation industry in 1995, though we were more likely to drive buses (African Americans were 25.9 percent of all workers in bus service and urban transit) than work on airplanes (12.7 percent of all workers). We were one in six of those employed as service workers in hotels and motels, and about 10 percent of those employed in food services industries. But as NAACP CEO Kweisi Mfume said when he unveiled that organization's "economic reciprocity" initiative with our nation's major hotel chains, "jobs are not enough." For all the representation African Americans have as hotel workers, we are absent at the top—on boards of directors, as senior managers, as site managers in hotel, food, and transportation services. Are we market giants or market midgets? It depends on whether $4.3 billion worth of muscle in hospitality, travel and tourism is allowed to get flabby or if it is flexed.

Flabby African American consumers accept whatever condition the market generates, including underemployment, insufficient partnerships, and scant leverage. We contract with hotels and restaurants because we need space for our functions, not because we are making strategically wise decisions. After an event is over we grouse that the service was poor and bemoan the paucity of black service personnel. That's the market midget position, one that is passive, not aggressive in targeting our dollars.

Market giants are a different breed of spenders. When our muscles are flexed we take a proactive point of view. When soliciting bids for a function, we are as concerned about relationships with the African American community as we are about menu and parking. We insist, as a condition of contracting, that certain partnerships are developed. These may include internships, scholarships, and other bridges to African American participation in the travel, tourism, and hospitality industry. Our position is that our dollars are commodities that are sought after, and that we must use those dollars to leverage opportunities for African American people.

The NAACP's recent economic reciprocity initiative is the position of market giants, because it is a position of power. It suggests that we bring something to the table that others must compete for and respond to. Market midgets, instead, take the positions of asking corporations to "give" (not invest). The difference between market giants and market midgets is as simple as the difference between quid pro quo and status quo.

African Americans have disproportionately heavy spending on a range of goods and services where use of our economic leverage might make a significant difference. We are twice as likely, for example, to spend money on auto rental. Did the company that tries harder know how much we spend when some of its franchisees discriminated against African American renters? We are 26 percent more likely than whites to have bought new color television sets in 1995. You wouldn't know that we buy these big-ticket items if you walked into the stores where we can't get a salesperson's attention (although the shoplifting patrol is always on the alert). There is also no apparent correlation between the profits our money brings to some establishments and their ability to employ African Americans. (The line that "we can't find any" doesn't quite wash when retailers know how to find black customers.) We spend three times as much as whites on public transportation, yet urban transportation schedules are less convenient in inner cities.

What's a consumer to do? One suggestion might be to curtail consumption to the extent possible. One way of flexing economic muscles is to simply stop spending. According to my rather parsimonious estimates, only $138.9 billion of our current spending is necessity spending. Based on Smikle's *Target Market News,* I feel that only housing, heath care, and education spending should remain at current levels. We spend more than $40 billion on food, $28.7 billion on food consumed at home. Though gourmands might take issue, I have included only food consumed at home as necessity spending. We spend nearly $20 billion a year on clothing, but an austerity budget for black Americans might slash clothing spending by 80 percent, leaving only $4 billion as necessary spending.

I can already hear the moans and groans of those brothers and sisters who believe that shopping is a contact sport. Indeed, the 1997 Gallup poll on race relations suggested that shopping is one of the more common activities where African Americans experience discrimination; 30 percent of those surveyed experienced racist behavior in the shopping process. But we keep shopping, and shopping, and shopping. We spend $380 million a year on men's suits, $377 million a year on stockings and pantyhose, $282 million on CDs, records, and audiotapes, $328 million on film rentals. Black folks are known to shop until we drop, but that's the behavior of market midgets, not market giants. We allow advertising along with our own self-esteem and role definition issues, to determine what we want, as opposed to what we need. And in the process of shopping, we are often supporting some of the very corporations that wouldn't invest in our communities unless it were made perfectly clear that their profits depended on it.

What if we stopped shopping? The $234 billion of discretionary income that African American people have conservatively represents employment for 10 million people, a full 10 percent of the current labor market. That $234 billion represents daily spending of $641 million a day. The withdrawal of such an amount from the American economy could have tremendous implications in terms of profit and employment. It could also have tremendous implications in terms of the dollars that could be diverted to African American economic development.

This is why the corporations become nervous at talk about economic boycotts. Texaco stock faltered and lost a few points after Rev. Jesse Jackson made boycott noises because of racist sentiments expressed in a corporate boardroom. Kmart cut Fuzzy Zoeller loose after he got into the chicken business, some argue, because of the disproportionate amount of African American spending that takes place at Kmart. If African American people randomly picked a product or corporation to boycott because of its record of economic reciprocity with the African American community, we'd be flexing economic muscle and putting retailers on notice that we want our fair share of economic opportunity. A "boycott of the month club," targeted at those who are the most offensive might restore the balance between African Americans and the economic mainstream.

Perhaps a quarter of African American hotel, tourism, and hospitality spending comes from spending at annual conventions of groups like the NAACP, the Urban League, the National Black MBA Association, and others. What would happen if we stayed home one year, preferring to put our dollars into developing a black-owned and operated hotel chain. What if we stayed home and put the billion dollars we spend on conventions in an interest-producing money-market fund or a venture capital fund? What if the money were used to fund black-owned businesses? While most of us chafe at the notion that our networking opportunities might be eroded by the cancellation of conferences and conventions, a look at the big picture might persuade some of us to at least put the issue on the table. Creatures of habit are likely to grouse that "we have always met each year." Pragmatists might note that if black people did what we have done every year since 1850, some of us would still be picking cotton!

Are we market giants or market midgets? Do black dollars make a difference? African American consumers have enough money to make a difference in the profit margin of virtually every good or service that is currently offered on the market. But our economic strength is a function of our collective will. Are we prepared to deal with the inconvenience of a boycott, to maintain enough righteous rage to find a leisure activity instead of shopping, to make demands instead of requests? If we keep on doing what we have been doing, we are market midgets, as our current economic situation suggests. When we flex our economic muscle, we are mighty market giants.

National Black MBA Magazine, September 1997

CHAPTER 5

THROUGH A GLASS DARKLY: RACE, RAGE AND AFFIRMATIVE INACTION

"What happened to a dream deferred?" wrote Langston Hughes. This view of contemporary race matters suggests that too many dreams are still deferred when the treatment is unequal, the comments are unwarranted, the remedies attacked. From the trivia of television to the pressing problems of prison life, race is a factor in our society. Moreover, conversations about race often simply further defer the dream because they so painfully illustrate how intertwined, yet how distinct, our realities are.

Consider the affirmative action conversation. Many whites see affirmative action as reverse discrimination. African Americans see it simply as an opportunity to get a foot in the door. Whites use the word "qualified" to diminish African American achievement. It is a word rarely used to describe whites. Some white people behave as if affirmative action means giving a street person a scalpel and propelling him into the surgical unit at the nearest hospital. They are so vested in white privilege that they can't see it, much less let it go. In addition, the conversation is no longer a conversation in black and white, since the Latino minority will be larger than the African American minority in the near future.

It is amazing, though, that even as some assert the so-called "color-blind" society, evidence of society being not so blind is as blatant as ever. Recent studies of homeownership suggest that African Americans are two or three times as likely as whites to be rejected for home mortgages, all else being equal. The black unemployment rate is twice the white rate. African Americans are three times more likely to receive public assistance (though the majority receiving public assistance are white), and more than twice as likely to be unemployed. Who says race doesn't matter? Exactly what do they mean?

Race is at the roots of our nation's organization and flows from the pores of our nation's Constitution, blighting laudable sentiments like "all men are created equal" with the acne of describing some people as fractions. Like Frederick Douglass, I wonder about the meaning of the Fourth of July for the Negro, and can only episodically muster up enough patriotism to appreciatively pledge allegiance to our nation's faulty flag. Patriotism comes to me in a late-night plane circling Washington, D.C. before landing, when our gleaming monuments are stark contrast to a starry sky. At moments like that, I am capable of thinking kindly of our slaveholding and flawed founding fathers, consoling myself with the thought that perhaps they didn't know better than to live with racist contradictions.

Their descendants, though, have no excuse. The attacks on affirmative action are as vicious and mean as the new American racism—the racism of the *Seinfeld*-like invisibility of African American people. W.E.B. DuBois said the problem of the 20th century is the problem of the color line. Here we sit, at the cusp of the 21st century, still grappling with 20th-century problems.

DR. MARTIN LUTHER KING'S ECONOMIC LEGACY

BY JULIANNE MALVEAUX

Dr. Martin Luther King. Jr. will perhaps best be remembered for his "I Have a Dream" speech, in which he said that he dreamed of the day when people would be judged by the content of their character and not the color of their skin. Few would argue with King's sentiment, but many of those that have trumpeted it have taken Dr. King's remarks out of context. After all, while Dr. King spoke of his dream of a color-blind society, he also reflected that the path to a color-blind society might mean taking color into consideration.

Further, Dr. King never viewed race in a vacuum. He viewed race in a context of work and the labor movement, of poverty and policy, of imperialism and international relations. Those who are eager to speak of Dr. King's dream about color blindness are reluctant to note that he was killed after his participation in an action designed to raise the wages of garbage workers in Memphis, Tennessee.

In contemporary discourse, though, Dr. King's words are often used as an excuse to dismantle some of the very programs that Dr. King was supportive of. Opponents of affirmative action, for example, have used Dr. King's words to suggest that "in a color-blind society" there is no need for a focus on the status of minorities in college admissions, government contracts, or employment. They have also often used King to support free-market policies, especially in international markets, while Dr. King clearly saw the connection between low wages domestically and low wages internationally.

The movement to strip Dr. King's message of its content has especially ugly roots in California where proponents of the California Civil Wrongs Initiative attempted to take one line out of Dr. King's voluminous work to justify their perfidy. Their obsession about King's concept of a color-blind society ignores Dr. King's own scathing analysis of the myth of "bootstraps." In December of 1967, at a mass community meeting, he asserted that white immigrants had a helping hand:

"Remember that nobody in this nation has done that. While they refused to give the black man any land, don't forget this: America at that same moment, through an act of Congress, was giving away millions of acres in the West and Midwest to white peasants from Europe. Never forget it. What else did they do? They built land grant colleges for them long before they built them for us, in order to teach them how to farm. They provided country agents long

before they provided them for us, in order to give them greater expertise in farming. And then they provided low interest rates for them so that they could mechanize their farms. And now, through federal subsidies, they are paying many of these people millions of dollars not to farm. And these are the very same folk telling Negroes that they ought to lift themselves by their own boot-straps, but it is a cruel jest to say to a bootless man that he ought to lift himself up by his own bootstraps . . . Emancipation for the black man was freedom to hunger."

One of Dr. King's biographers, Richard Lischer, notes that Dr. King's rhetoric evolved from moral suasion and identification to unfettered rage. Writes Lischer, "In earlier sermons he might have condemned the individual behavior of those who engaged in rioting or looting, but his later sermons condemn the system that makes riots inevitable. Like the Hebrew prophets who assailed the structures of enslavement in Israel, King shows how the woes of the fathers are visited upon their children in urban America; the disturbances in Watts are voices of anger from children who have grown up in fatherless homes, because the fathers were unable to find work and often had to leave home so that their families could qualify for Aid to Dependent Children." The "take responsibility" crowd that loves King's "content of our character" message may have differences with Dr. King's refusal to blame those whose riotous behavior is a function of social, not simply individual, mal-functions.

It is ironic that the very President who has prided himself on welfare deform will have his inaugural celebration on Dr. King's birthday. When Mr. Clinton, a man fond of quoting Dr. King and tearing up at the very mention of his name, takes his second oath of office, will he remember Dr. King's angry attack on poverty? King reminded us that:

"The curse of poverty has no justification in our age. It is socially as cruel and blind as the practice of cannibalism at the dawn of civilization, when men ate each other because they had not yet learned to take food from the soil or to consume the abundant animal life around them. The time has come for us to civilize ourselves by the total, direct and immediate abolition of poverty."

People are quick to quote Dr. King but not so quick to remember that in 1996, one in four American children lived in poverty. Though black poverty rates fell in 1995, 29.5 percent of the African American community is poor. The poverty rate has oscillated since King made his comment, but it is higher in 1996 than it was in 1974. I have often claimed Dr. King as an economist, because his Nobel Peace Prize acceptance speech lays out an economic program:

"I have the audacity to believe that peoples everywhere can have three meals a day for their bodies, education and culture for their minds, and dignity, equality and freedom for their spirits."

Once upon a time, we had audacity. We marched and we fought and we protested and picketed, we drew lines in the sand and made it clear that there were some transgressions we would not accept, not under any circumstances. Dr. King's Poor People's Movement attempted to unite poor people, but now the contemporary thrust is to look down on poor folks and attempt to ignore them. Thus, Dr. King's audacity has been eroded by the demonization of poverty in our society. In California, for example, those on public assistance will experience a 10 percent cut in their benefit levels on January 1, 1996. Meanwhile, education is increasingly inaccessible as tuition rates rise.

It isn't popular to think of Dr. King as a fire-breathing populist economic critic, but you've got to take King's cajoling along with his excoriating. Those who quote Dr. King ought to be clear that even as he spoke passionately about content and character, he spoke all the more eloquently about economic injustice. This is Dr. King's true legacy, his criticism of capitalism, of inequity, of unfairness. It is a legacy that we must embrace as firmly as we embrace his social message.

San Francisco Sun Reporter, January 14, 1997

CAMILLE COSBY'S PAINFUL TRUTH
BY JULIANNE MALVEAUX

I am one of those African Americans who can find racism anywhere. In the air, on the ground, in the speed of sound. Don't ask me why, it is either my altitude or my attitude, but more often than I'd like to admit, I am persuaded that race matters too much in the way our country is constituted. I rail and rage at the lynching in Jasper, Texas, look askance at the deliberations of the President's race commission. Race matters and there aren't enough people saying or doing anything about it. I've become so comfortable with the fact that the world disagrees with me that I don't raise the matter very often.

I could. I could talk about the racist minutiae that is a simple fact of life in America. I could talk about men I know who are stopped because they are DWB—that's driving while black, on the wrong highway. If their license and registration is in order, they are allowed to move on, but often they are held up for five, ten, fifteen minutes in a hassle that could have been avoided if a racist cop had decided to check his biases off the job. I could mention the fact that if I walk up to a sales counter a few seconds before a white woman, that white woman is likely to be served first. I mention the number of times flight attendants have asked to see my first-class ticket before I've settled in a seat, while ignoring the throngs around me who are also sitting down. But conversation about these things has become churlish in a post-affirmative action era, with a President who feels our pain and a Congress that would exacerbate it. If you're feeling racism, the general mood seems to be, suck it up and get over it. White folks are bored by race conversations and assimilated black folks are embarrassed by them.

Thus, I was encouraged and astounded to see Camille Cosby's column in *USA Today* on Wednesday. Cosby's column, titled "Prejudice Permeates American Culture," was a scathing indictment of the many subtle ways that white superiority is both taught and accepted in the everyday rituals of American life. The fact, for example, that Christianity is popularly portrayed as a "white" thing, with a blond or stringy brown-haired white Jesus, is a way of making the connection between "right" and "white." The fact that slaveholders are the featured photos on our nation's money is a subtle way of asserting the legitimacy of these slaveholder positions.

Camille Cosby isn't saying anything that hundreds of black activists haven't said over the years. Her comments are outstanding because they come from the pain she feels from her son Ennis' death. Her comments are riveting because it seems as if her pain has forced her out of the comfort zone that her money, access, and reputation often leverage for her. White America needs to sit up and take notice. When renegade black folks like me "cry racism" our comments are dismissed as sour grapes, bean counting, and whining. What can they say when people like Mrs. Cosby, people they have heretofore considered "good" black folks, peep their game and call them on it.

Mrs. Cosby asserts that racism may have killed her son, Ennis William Cosby. The man who was convicted of killing Ennis Cosby bragged about it to his friends, saying, "I shot a n——r. It's all over the news." Markhasev had attacked a black man before, serving juvenile time in 1995 for stabbing a black man who was standing at a gas station. But Markhasev wasn't convicted of racism toward Ennis Cosby, but of murder and robbery. What does race have to do with this? For Camille Cosby, everything. Her son's murder reminds her that African Americans, regardless of status or income, live in this country at tremendous risk.

I don't think Camille Cosby has overstated her case. Instead, I think she has demanded honesty in these conversations on race that our President seems to be having. Look at our institutions, she pleads. Look at our churches, our money, our institutions, our issues. Mrs. Cosby has been more honest than any advisory council, any study group. She has adhered to the writer's tenet to "cut a vein." I'd offer her applause, but I'm sure she is indifferent to the accolades that will come from her searing column. She seems to be asking, simply, for the racism to stop. Too many fail to acknowledge that she is raising a set of legitimate issues.

King Features Syndicate, July 10, 1998

SNATCHING BACK THE WELCOME MAT
BY JULIANNE MALVEAUX

When my mentor, Dr. Phyllis Ann Wallace, decided to major in economics, the state of Maryland offered her four full years of tuition, room and board at New York University rather than have her enroll in her state school, the University of Maryland. The reason—rigid segregation. Wallace wasn't the only black Marylander denied the opportunity to attend the state's best school Thurgood Marshall couldn't go there, nor could former Congressman Parren Mitchell. Thousands attended historically black colleges, while hundreds more received state subsidies to leave.

It more than states the obvious to note that the University of Maryland has been hostile to African Americans. It is hostile still, but some signals have been sent that black enrollment is not as unwelcome as it was in the days when the state would pay to keep blacks away. For awhile, through its Benjamin Banneker scholarships, it seemed to reverse the trend by paying outstanding African Americans to come to the University of Maryland. The Banneker program offered tuition, room, board, book money and mentorship to students with a "B" average, at least 900 on their SAT tests, and recommendations stating outstanding promise.

The Banneker scholars are the intellectual descendants of folk like Phyllis Wallace and Thurgood Marshall. Their foremothers and fathers were paid to leave the state, but Banneker scholars were being paid to stay. The past tense is being used because the Fourth Circuit United States Court of Appeals says the scholarships are unconstitutional, and now the University of Maryland will have to cut and paste another program together if they want to reach out to the black students they once repelled. The court says there is no clear connection between past discrimination and the scholarships. The court, clearly, has decided to ignore the experiences of folks like Phyllis Wallace who could not, in 1940, enroll in the University of Maryland. Thurgood Marshall's legal work desegregated the University of Maryland's law school in 1935, but the rest of the campus was closed to black students until the early 1950s.

The university's ugly legacy is reflected in its enrollments. While the population of Maryland is more than 20 percent black, the enrollment at the university is just 12 percent. Racial incidents on campus are not uncommon. The student newspaper has been at the center of controversy because of its uneven coverage of campus events, especially campus unrest and crime. A year ago, black students burned copies of the paper to protest unfair coverage.

The challenge to Banneker scholarships came from a "Hispanic" student, Daniel J. Podberesky, who brought suit against the university with the help of the conservative Washington Legal Foundation. It is dubious that Podberesky qualified for a Banneker scholarship on the basis of his academic record, since most of those students who have challenged academic affirmative action were marginal admits in the first place. His challenge is couched in "fairness" terms, but it actually comes from the economics of resentment and the politics of denial. Should black students get special treatment? the Podberesky lawsuit seemed to ask. The answer is that black folks got especially unfair treatment from the University of Maryland since its establishment. Thirty paltry Banneker scholarships don't begin to reverse the trend or compensate for that unfairness.

If the court would outlaw Banneker scholarships, would it outlaw other discretionary scholarships that make monies available to veterans, women, or other groups? Or is this just a deterrent on African American participation in higher education? Double standards are alive and well at the Fourth Circuit Court of Appeals. Is it any wonder that so many African Americans distrust the "just us" system? This time "just us" is being used to tell black students that the welcome mat that was just put out has been snatched back. People like Phyllis Wallace and Thurgood Marshall, who never stepped across the welcome mat, would not be surprised.

Black Issues in Higher Education, November 7, 1994

DO WE STILL NEED AFFIRMATIVE ACTION?

BY JULIANNE MALVEAUX

In Washington, William Pendley argued before the Supreme Court that minority business set-asides ought to be eliminated, saying that they are based on an "impermissible racial stereotype" and that minority firms can't compete without help. The attorney for the plaintiff, a Colorado highway construction firm, in the *Adarand v. Pena* case, says his client cannot compete on equal footing if firms that subcontract to disadvantaged and minority firms get a bonus that others do not get.

In California two white male professors are circulating a state ballot initiative to eliminate racial preferences in aspects of state business, including hiring, admission to universities, and business set-asides. There is regular railing in the *Wall Street Journal* and other conservative publications about the horrors and evils of affirmative action and diversity, all designed to raise the question—has affirmative action outlived its usefulness? My answer—I think not.

Let's start by looking at the myths about affirmative action. Many say it brings "unqualified minorities" into the workplace, and deprives others of opportunities. But affirmative action merely asks employers to look at the applicant pool for workers, to diversify as if by casting a net broader and wider, and to hire equally qualified people from underrepresented groups where possible.

In contracting the issues differ slightly. "Old boy networks" have excluded minority contractors from many of the federal and state contracts available. Set-aside programs attempt to open doors, offering a small slice of the total pool of funds available for businesses owned by minorities or women who have been excluded from competition by bonding requirements, "prior work" requirements, and other ways of maintaining status quo. At the federal level, minority-owned businesses eventually "graduate" from set-aside programs, ensuring that set-asides are a boost, not a permanent condition for businesses. Set-asides for minority businesses can be likened to the set-asides or preferences that some cities have for local businesses. Whether past discrimination is an issue or not, doesn't it make sense to encourage the development of minority-owned businesses?

The issues are also different when we consider higher education. Some schools accept minorities with lower standardized test scores in the name of affirmative action, leading opponents to holler "unqualified." But when standardized tests are involved one always has to ask what they measure. Do they measure intelligence? Likelihood of college completion? Or simply the ability to take multiple-choice tests? Do they incorporate race and gender biases? As long as there are questions about admissions standards, I think it reasonable to relax them in some instances, especially in the case of public universities where minority tax dollars help support the very elite institutions that exclude them with inappropriate admissions standards.

In all three areas—employment, business contracting, and education — African Americans and Latinos are especially underrepresented. In some cities with set-aside programs, minority-owned businesses get fewer than 3 percent of the construction contracts. The Minority Business Legal Defense and Education Fund, founded by former Congressman Parren Mitchell, has documented inequalities in the contracting process that remain, despite set-aside programs that exist in many areas. Similar gaps exist in employment and in education.

Those who want to dismantle affirmative action argue that these are the 1990s, not the 1960s and that race doesn't matter as much as it once did. It matters more than it should, though; it matters so much that college-educated African Americans earn just 70 percent of what their white counterparts earn. Until race really doesn't matter, affirmative action continues to be important.

King Features Syndicate, January 20, 1995

THE MYTH OF EDUCATIONAL EQUIVALENCY, OR WHEN A BLACK WOMAN'S MASTER'S DEGREE EQUALS A WHITE WOMAN'S BACHELOR'S DEGREE
BY JULIANNE MALVEAUX

The Black Leadership Forum, an organization that includes the NAACP Legal Defense and Education Fund, the National Urban League, the National Council of Negro Women, and others, deflected energy from the controversial *Taxman v. Piscataway* case that the Supreme Court had committed to hear this year. They agreed to finance 70 percent of the nearly $450,000 settlement that Taxman and her lawyers will receive from the Piscataway School Board. Sharon Taxman was the white business education teacher who was laid off in a downsizing while Debra Williams, an African American business education teacher, was retained. Since the two women were hired the same day and deemed "equally" qualified, the school board justified retaining Williams on the basis of "diversity." Faster than she could spell "diverse" (if she could, frankly, either spell it or understand it), Taxman was filing a lawsuit. Her quest for "equality" was affirmed by every court up to the Supreme Court, which agreed to hear her case. Civil rights activists thought this was the wrong one to take to the nation's highest court, and so they bought Taxman out.

I am not sure how I feel about the buyout. It seems like postponing the bad medicine of antipathy that comes from this Supreme Court not only for diversity but also for equality. But I am convinced that there are at least two villains in this story, and one of them is the Piscataway School Board. Come again? To some these guys seem like the good guys. They retained an African American teacher and laid off a white one, upholding "diversity." At the same time, though, they tragically argued that two workers were "equally" qualified when one held a master's degree while the other had a lesser education.

If I were Debra Williams I'd be fuming through the ears. The myth that hard work and the quest for education would give you a leg up was busted in her case. Rather than the school board affirming her superior education (or at least attempting to balance it by other differences—differences in evaluations, effectiveness, or other compensable factors), they told her that her master's degree was worth little or nothing, not enough to get her more than equally qualified over a lesser qualified (I almost typed inferior, but that is the oppressor's game) colleague.

A careful examination of what happened in Piscataway explains why affirmative action has become America's whipping post. Instead of white folks telling white folks that they aren't competitive, they tell them that a job was assigned or retained because of "affirmative action." That's not affirmative action, that's the lazy dishonesty that fuels the myth of white superiority.

Consider Proposition 209. We all know that it was championed by Republicans Pete Wilson and Ward Connerly, but the early poster boys were two white men who presented themselves as academics and said they could not find jobs in the California State University system, despite their "qualifications." To be sure, these men both had Ph.D. degrees, but neither had earned academic distinction. They'd not published. Nor had they, it turns out, thanks to an incendiary report from investigative journalists, ever actually applied for jobs in the California state system.

Nonetheless, one of these men said he could not find a job as a philosophy teacher in California. In the year he said he looked, five philosophers were hired, and three were white men, but he didn't take them on. There was an eminently qualified white woman hired, and he didn't take her on either. An African American woman, also hired, was not the target of his ire. She should not have been since she could have written or talked circles around him. Where was this inferior product of our nation's system of higher education supposed to get a job? It didn't matter. In his warped mind, some mythical black person was out there holding his job and, by golly, he was going to make affirmative action beneficiaries pay. Thus Proposition 209.

Enter the second villain. Sharon Taxman must have her head in the sand, her mind on the blink. Hasn't she ever heard that people lose their jobs? Spit happens, and the best thing to do with spit is to wash it off and move on with life. She put her life on hold, apparently, because she could not stand the notion that some black woman should get a job she thought she should have. Never mind that the black woman, her colleague, had more education. Never mind that her colleague was the better teacher. Sharon Taxman is white and she has wrapped herself in the privilege of whiteness. Thus, her lawsuit.

The Supreme Court wouldn't see that because they are mostly white, too. Those who opposed Taxman would have had to overcome both the Court's distaste for affirmative action (and their pejorative description of such policies as "race-based preferences") and their own fealty to whiteness. The civil rights community bought Taxman off because they understood that the Piscataway School Board improperly packaged this case, choosing affirmative action and diversity as the wrong reasons to let an inferior teacher go. If the school board had looked more carefully at the two women and their qualifications, this case might not have come to court.

That's the rub. Spit happens. Downsizing takes place. What the Taxman case has said so far is that when downsizing doesn't fall on black people's shoulders, white people are ready to go to court. Or when all else is supposedly equal, white folks are supposed to prevail. This is a premise that deserves challenge, but then there are others, such as the premise that a white woman's bachelor's degree is the equivalent of a black woman's master's. That's only the case in a racist society.

Black Issues in Higher Education, December 1997

DOUBLE STANDARD ON SPORTSMANSHIP
BY JULIANNE MALVEAUX

Poor sports usually get bad raps from sports journalists. Such wasn't the case a week or so ago, though, when Irina Spirlea made it clear that she deliberately bumped into U.S. Open finalist Venus Williams "to see if she would turn." Spirlea deliberately attempted to provoke a confrontation with the body slam that she admitted to initiating, but too many sportswriters laid the blame on Venus Williams or took no position on the collision.

I'd understand the sportswriters soft-pedaling the incident if it were clearly an accident. People do, after all, bump into each other. But Spirlea was clear that her body slam was intentional. She further clarified her ill will by using an obscenity to describe Venus Williams. She was only tepidly taken to task by the same sportswriters who have more than enough to say about other poor sports. One wonders why they were so silent, and whether it suggests that some sportswriters have an antipathy to Venus Williams.

Some of the commentators did not hide their mixed feelings. A CBS commentator sourly noted that the only thing "rattling" in one of Venus Williams' early matches was her beads. (Actually the only empty rattle was coming from that commentator's mouth.) Another openly whined that she had not "gotten to know" Venus Williams and complained that she was "close" to her family. Were young Williams not close to her family, these same commentators would have carped about distance in her family. There seemed to be tangible negative bias in the way Venus Williams was covered.

Some said Williams was braggadocian, her bravado off-putting. Others said she wasn't friendly, forgetting that friendly is a two-way street. We learned that a hyper-sensitive young tennis player said she smiled at Venus and Williams didn't smile back. Perhaps Venus Williams didn't see the smiler! Still, her actions, real or imagined, were characterized as unfriendly. Williams engaged in neither trash-talk nor body-slamming. Instead this young, precocious woman with no Grand Stand tournament experience was simply psyching herself up when she spoke of the strength of her game. As I bristled at the unfair commentary accompanying Williams' matches, I found myself thinking of Maya Angelou's saucy words, "You can write me down in history with your dirty, filthy lies . . . but still like dust I rise." And rise she did, beating the brash, rude and untalented Spirlea and performing credibly against the much more experienced Martina Hingis.

Was Richard Williams right to bring up race in this context? Perhaps not. But he simply said what millions of African Americans were thinking. Even if the bump were not racial, the way the press handled it certainly seemed to be. They seemed to almost support Spirlea in her arrogant rudeness, even in her use of obscenity. Otherwise, where were the columns about foul language in the genteel sport of tennis? Where were the commentators excoriating Spirlea? If Venus Williams could get negative reviews simply because of the braids she wears, shouldn't Spirlea (who, frankly, behaved like the very "big, tall, ugly, white turkey" she was described as by Richard Williams) be excoriated because of her language? Mind you, some of the very reporters soft-pedaling Spirlea's behavior are the ones who rush to chide others for unsportsmanlike conduct. This time around, they were silent.

The bump and its aftermath aren't, in the scheme of things, especially important. Venus Williams shrugged it off, saying she wasn't hurt by "that little bump." She came off looking as if she has more class in her little finger than Spirlea and some of the commentators have in their whole bodies. Still, the bump is perhaps symbolic of the way the majority press too often treats African Americans they don't know, don't understand, and can't get next to. If Venus Williams smiled more, schmoozed more, and spent less time on her game and more time trying to charm a hostile media, she might have gotten better press treatment. Then again, if she spent her time doing that, she might not have become a finalist at the U.S. Open.

Irina Spirlea said she bumped into Venus Williams because she wanted to see if she would turn. She used an obscenity when she learned that Venus would not lose focus in the face of her hostility. Those sportswriters who pride themselves on dealing with matters of gamesmanship ought to write about the brilliance of a young woman whose eyes on the prize would not be averted by the petty nonsense of a loser like Spirlea.

King Features Syndicate, September 10, 1997

ADVANTAGE, WHITE
BY JULIANNE MALVEAUX

Long-time readers of this column will not be surprised to learn that I *still* am not a sports fan. I can go for a little hometown loyalty (which means I'll be challenged on Monday when I see the 49ers and the Redskins—who should not be called the Redskins — at play), always enjoy a live game, and enjoy rooting for our "firsts" and "exceptionals," like the outstanding Williams tennis sisters, Venus and Serena. But I don't get into the details, won't argue the fine points, and think too much public money goes into building stadiums and sports complexes, creating corporate subsidies on the backs of ordinary people. Indeed, the last time I went to a ball game, at Baltimore's Camden Yards, I blanched at the cost of the tickets ($35 each), chafed at the cost of a hot dog (about $5), and wondered how often an "average" American family with an income of about $40,000 a year can get out to a ball game.

Sports is in the news these days, though. St. Louis Cardinals batter Mark McGwire made baseball history on September 8 when he broke Roger Maris' record for 61 home runs in a season. With a dozen more games to go, McGwire may establish an even more lofty record of 63, 64, or even 66 runs. Hot on his heels is Chicago Cubs hitter Sammy Sosa, a man who hails from the Dominican Republic and seems to be truly enjoying the competition. Indeed, these two men have offered an exemplary model of collegial competition and mutual support; they almost persuade me that there are some life lessons that one can extrapolate from the playing field. And while some fans have been eager to contrast McGwire and Sosa and read racial implications into their race, the two men have simply smiled, played ball, and broken records. It's all good.

Except I could not help but wish the cheers and well wishes Mark McGwire enjoyed on Tuesday night could be transferred to another playing field. I speak specifically of the U.S. Open and the fan response to Venus and Serena Williams. On Monday, Venus beat Mary Pierce, an uptight, smug Frenchwoman, in two sets, with a tiebreaker, and some outstanding play. But Venus beat Mary Pierce at the U.S. Open, where U.S. fans cheered the Frenchwoman, not their countrywoman. The crowd didn't have her back, and that had to have hurt.

Why did a U.S. crowd turn against Venus Williams? Did skin color trump national origin as far as they were concerned? Did they react badly to Williams' amazingly rapid rise through the tennis ranks? Last year this time she was ranked 66 and making headlines when another European piece of work, the Romanian Irina Spirlea was trying to "do the bump" with her. Again, U.S. fans and commentators seemed solidly against Williams, even as Spirlea admitted she had purposely set up a confrontation with her. Venus was focused — "I'm not going to let that bump bother me" — but you would have thought that she was from someplace other than the United States by the support she generated. In a year, her world tennis ranking has zoomed from 66 to 5, but U.S. fans have hardly matured in their perception of Venus Williams' play.

This matter interests me because not a week passes when some disgruntled reader sends me a letter or an e-mail asking me why I persist in describing myself as "African American." "You are being separatist," a reader from upstate New York writes. "You were born in America, you are a U.S. citizen, therefore you are an AMERICAN." The reader capitalizes the "American" throughout as if the capital letters will have such an impact that they will change my mind. An hour watching Venus Williams beat Mary Pierce from France, and listening to Americans cheer an American woman's opponent, is enough to permanently secure the African in front of my American. It is notice that I understand the rules of the game, which in this case seem to be "advantage, white."

Sports isn't the only realm where the rules of the game are "advantage, white." The labor market still generates different results for African Americans than for white workers, beginning with higher unemployment rates (9 percent for African Americans and 4 percent for whites), going on to lower wages. (The 1997 average hourly wage for white women was $10.02, compared to $8.49 for African American women. White men earned $18.20 an hour, compared to the $12.92 that African American men earned.) While the nation celebrates historically low unemployment rates, my thought is "advantage, white" because if overall unemployment rates were as high as rates among African Americans, there'd be a whole lot of shouting going on right about now.

Mark McGwire and Sammy Sosa achieve with the help of supportive fans whose cheers maintain their motivation and bolster their achievement. Venus Williams achieves despite, not because, of the U.S. Open fans, whose embrace of her opponent is not only a repudiation and a challenge, but also confirmation of the separate realities that African Americans too often experience.

San Francisco Sun Reporter, September 11, 1998

DENNY'S SETTLEMENT — REMORSE OR SIMPLE PRAGMATISM?
BY JULIANNE MALVEAUX

Why did the Flagstar Corporation decide to spend about $60 million settling discrimination lawsuits against its Denny's subsidiary? Was the discriminatory treatment some African Americans experienced "worth" a sum that amounts to more than 1.5 percent of sales? And given the size of the settlement, why has CEO Jerome J. Richardson continued to insist that the settlement is, according to his letter to analysts and investors, "not an admission that Denny's or Flagstar had or has a policy or practice of discrimination?"

From where I sit, Denny's deserves any bad press it has garnered in the past year or so. Two years ago, a California Denny's eatery denied a black girl a free birthday meal. A San Jose location asked black students to pay a cover charge to enter the store, and to pay for their food in advance. On April 1, 1993, after a lawsuit was filed, publicity generated, and a settlement agreed upon, an Annapolis, Maryland Denny's restaurant spurned six black Secret Service officers accompanying President Clinton, serving white officers while their black colleagues waited more than an hour for an order taker.

Shortly after the Annapolis incident, the Flagstar Corporation entered into a "fair share" agreement with the NAACP, promising to expand minority ownership of Denny's franchises. A year later, no African American owns a Denny's franchise, but Flagstar owns a coveted NFL franchise in South Carolina. Some say the NAACP's agreement with Flagstar muted concerns many had about the company's discriminatory policies and helped it compete against other contenders for the NFL franchise.

Denny's and its discriminatory behavior had receded from the news until this recent settlement. Alternately reported as a $46 or $54 million settlement, the total sum that Flagstar spends settling claims, communicating about claims, and battling its bad rap will exceed $60 million. In addition to $45.7 million in settlement to named plaintiffs and others in California and Maryland, settlement that will net individuals as much as $35,000 each, Flagstar will pay $8.7 million in attorney fees, and millions more in related costs.

Flagstar is spending at least a million dollars advertising the settlement and encouraging people who have been discriminated against to come forward with claims, using Caroline Jones Advertising, a black-owned, New York-based agency to coordinate this advertising. Millions more will be spent on the hiring of a civil rights monitor, the testing of restaurants, and training programs for employees. Richardson told analysts and investors that these costs might total $6 million.

Flagstar will also settle a 1993 complaint filed by a children's choir that was denied service at a Virginia Denny's restaurant. Denny's says they turned the choir away because they could not serve 132 people late at night, but they've still agreed to make cash payments to the choir members, to establish a trust to benefit the choir, and to make "substantial" contributions to a series of civil rights organizations in settlement of the choir's complaint.

Jerome J. Richardson says the settlements close a painful chapter in Flagstar's history. In defiantly noting that Flagstar may have won discrimination claims, but chose not to pursue them because "the cost of litigating would be unacceptably high, not only in terms of attorney's fees, but also in terms of continuing public perception of an adverse relationship between Denny's and its African American customers," Richardson fails to take responsibility for the incidents that took place on Flagstar property. In suggesting that the settlement was offered because perceptions tarnish Flagstar's reputation, Richardson is being disingenuous. Here's a 411 to Mr. Richardson—It's not the litigation that tarnishes Flagstar's reputation, it's the discrimination.

The Flagstar settlement might be viewed positively except for the equivocations in Richardson's statements to investors and his measured apologies. These fits and starts, despite the settlement, suggest that the Denny's bias suits would not have been settled without the involvement of the civil rights division of the Justice Department. The Flagstar settlement signals that discrimination costs, but Richardson's weak statements signal a tacit acceptance of the discrimination that whites often characterize as "unintentional."

King Features Syndicate, May 26, 1994

DAYS OF ABSENCE?
BY JULIANNE MALVEAUX

Two years ago, perhaps a million African American men came to Washington, D.C. at the behest of Nation of Islam minister Louis Farrakhan. They came, he said, to "atone" for their transgressions, in what he described as a "non-political" show of support for an array of family values. Two years after the March, the notion that men should atone has been ripped off by the equally popular Promise Keepers, and demographers are still trying to figure out if the Million Man March ever made a difference.

For many men, the difference was a difference in spirit. While I opposed the march, I was sensitive to the concerns of men who felt that they, as black men, experienced some epiphany from their gathering in Washington, D.C. Too many men that I know and respect said their spirits were buoyed by rubbing shoulders with their brothers and others who responded to the call, however flawed it was. Many said their presence had nothing to do with NOI minister Louis Farrakhan, but more with the notion that they wanted to be wherever another million black men were. Much as I appreciated their energy, I chafed at the sexism of a march that encouraged the men to "march and lead" while black women, according to Farrakhan, were to stay home to "teach and pray."

The Million Man March happened two years ago, and we might all say "been there, done that" were it not for Louis Farrakhan's perpetual quest for immortality. Rather than let the march write its own history, the Muslim leader persists in putting his own spin on the events of October 1995. He sees the march as transformative, but he can't say what the march has transformed. Nor, frankly, can he produce the audit that was promised weeks after the march took place. It is a curious inconsistency that organizers of the march insist on saying there were more than a million men present, but so few dollars collected that the activity lost money and imperiled the vitality of many of the black-owned businesses the march promised to support.

Even that might be forgotten, but for the fact that Minister Farrakhan would like to commemorate the second anniversary of the Million Man March by calling for a "day of absence" on the part of African American workers, a day designed to remind white people that they can't take black folk for granted.

Excuse me, but one of the key results of the contemporary labor market transformation is that any worker can be taken for granted. Temporary and part-time workers are in more demand (but more indistinguishable) than full-time workers. People are afraid to ask for wage increases. Despite the UPS strike victory, workers who rely on collective bargaining for salary increases have their struggles laid out for them. While the economy has expanded like crazy in the past six years, the level of economic insecurity has also increased. What is the purpose of a Farrakhan-called day of absence?

From where I sit, a day of absence does little more than illustrate how superfluous are the labor market efforts of some workers. What if black people didn't show up to drive the bus? Standing right behind them would be some more black folks, or whites or Latinos or Asian Americans, all willing to drive the same bus for the same amount of money. What if black people failed to report to their jobs as teachers, nurses, and social workers, all occupations where African American women are disproportionately employed? To be sure, there would be a pause, but jobs would quickly be filled by others who have the skills.

It was, perhaps, feasible to call for a day of absence in the early 1960s, when African American service workers held the life and comfort of white workers in their hands. That was a generation ago. Now, an upper-middle-class white couple is more dependent on a delicatessen than on food-serving Delilah. Black folks can cause whites some discomfort, but not through an employee day of absence.

African American people had $373 billion in earned income in 1995. What if, instead of being missing in action, we simply decided to be missing at the cash register. What if African American people agreed not to spend money on white folks' clothes, cars, and entertainment. That would be an action of absence, one that both preserved income (by failing to spend) and increased wealth (by working).

Black people cannot make a difference with an ill-advised day of absence. We can make a difference when we target our spending toward our sociopolitical goals. We make headlines with threats to stay home, but we make profits or losses with targeted buying decisions.

King Features Syndicate, October 16, 1997

WE ARE ALL MULTIRACIAL
BY JULIANNE MALVEAUX

When I was in the second or third grade at Immaculate Conception Elementary School in San Francisco, the teacher made a novel assignment. Pulling a map of Europe down from the wall, she asked each student to write an essay on his or her European roots. If my recollection is correct (and it might be skewed by the content and context of the anecdote), she was one of those preening teachers who sets some students on edge. I vaguely remember this woman walking through the aisles and telling Maria to write about Italy, Ian to write about England, and Patrick to write about Ireland. Then she turned to me and looked at me and said, "Julianne, you won't have to do any homework this evening since none of your ancestors are from Europe."

At seven or eight years old, I didn't get it. I thought I'd been let off the hook. Then I got home and told my mom that I had no homework because I had no European roots. Somehow, my mother mustered her righteous rage and made her way back to the school to tell the simpering teacher that "Malveaux" is a name with French origins, and that slave women often had slave children because of European participation. Indeed, before the day was out, I learned (much to my chagrin) that there is French and Irish and Native American and maybe even a little German in me. I say I learned to my chagrin because as far as I am concerned I am simply a woman of African descent whose parents are people of African descent, whose lives have been defined by that African descent. End, I'd like to think, of story.

Enter the United States Census. For years, a panel has been mulling over the proposition that people of mixed-race backgrounds be allowed to describe themselves as members of more than one race. They have considered, and rejected, the proposal that people be allowed to select a "multiracial" category, but have suggested that people be allowed to check more than one box when racial identity is concerned. I think they are right in eschewing the multiracial category for a number of reasons, but mostly because my third-grade experience reminds me that we are all multiracial. There are few pure Africans in America, few pure Caucasians. Many of us have mixed bloodlines, but as Itabari Njeri writes in her book *The Last Plantation*, America subscribes to the "little dab will do ya'" school of racial identity. In other words, in the one-drop school of race, Mr. Plessy, in *Plessy v. Ferguson*, was lighter than many of those who would have persecuted him.

A multiracial census category confounds, not clarifies, contemporary race matters. Do people who are the product of a black-white relationship find some common ground with those who are the product of white-Latino relationships? To be sure, we have tenuous ties as "people of color," but beyond that, is there any concept of community?

Too many people have used Tiger Woods and his misguided remarks about being "Cablinasian" to guide their thinking in this matter. But Fuzzy Zoeller didn't ask Tiger not to serve pad thai or chow mein, he asked him not to serve fried chicken. The lesson: no matter how mixed, how multicultural you are, just a little dab will do ya'. In other words, according to the one-drop rule, much of America sees Tiger Woods (and the rest of those multiracial folks) as black.

Does race matter? Absolutely. It matters in the composition of our political and economic elite. It shows up in terms of who weighs in and who is excluded. We can be as mixed race as we want to be, but Tiger Woods could not have played at most of our nation's golf courses a generation ago. The signs didn't say "white" and "multiracial." They said "white" and "colored."

No one is asking any "multiracial" person to shrug off part of her heritage, or to choose one set of grandparents over another. Racial classification in the United States has been about closing gaps, preserving access, and moving to a more race-neutral place. That movement, though, is predicated on a set of realities. The overall unemployment rate this month was 5 percent, the black unemployment rate 11 percent. Why the difference? Race matters. It is this difference we want to measure.

It is inevitable that, in these changing times, the most passionate civil rights advocates have to grapple with issues of change. Our lens on "multiracialism" may be one of those issues we struggle around. There is a difference between allowing people to check more than one box to describe racial and ethnic heritage, and picking an "all of the above" box called "multiracial." The Census panel drew a fine, and perhaps an appropriate line. It is too soon to assert the existence of a multiracial community, and it is perhaps too late to remind our nation that we are all multiracial people, even when we are African American.

San Francisco Sun Reporter, July 9, 1997

A NATIONAL CONVERSATION OR A SHAM?
BY JULIANNE MALVEAUX

Every year, on the Fourth of July, I read the Frederick Douglass 1852 speech, "The Meaning of the Fourth of July for the Negro." In his brilliant dissection of America's broken promises to slaves, Douglass absolutely rages about our nation's hypocrisy around issues of race, and calls the Fourth of July "not a celebration but a sham." Some friends think my insistence at reading Douglass' speech is like picking a scab on a wound, a way of heightening my own racial rage. I don't need Frederick Douglass to fuel my anger. All I need to do is to flip through those statistics that describe economic inequality, to ponder the overrepresentation of African American men in the criminal "just us" system, or shop someplace where my skin color automatically earns me a shadow in the form of store security.

Now, President William Jefferson Clinton is talking about healing our nation's racial scab or at least talking about it. In his speech at the University of California at San Diego on June 14, he asked if "we can become one America by the 21st century." "Can we be one America," the President queried, "respecting, even celebrating our differences, but embracing even more what we have in common? Can we define what it means to be an American, not just in terms of the hyphens showing our ethnic origins, but in terms of our primary allegiance to the values America stands for?" Even as he called for conversation, he acknowledged, "If we do nothing more than talk, it will be interesting, but it won't be enough."

The President's speech had two key weaknesses. The first is its economic optimism. Mr. Clinton relies too much on our "strong and growing economy" as an "antidote to envy, despair, and racism." To be sure, the unemployment rate is now lower than it has been in 23 years, but that 4.8 percent unemployment rate translates into 10.3 percent for African Americans. And wealth is more concentrated in our country than ever. Stock market records and low unemployment rates don't translate to economic well-being for working people, especially when the growth in temporary and part-time jobs is faster than the growth in permanent jobs, when a growing number of Americans have no health insurance, and when most are covered by HMOs that quibble over providing some forms of care.

Race and economics are inextricably connected, and the President's economic myopia threatens to sabotage his race conversation at the outset. As Dr. Martin Luther King, Jr. noted in his posthumously published essay, "A Testament of Hope": "The black revolution is much more than a struggle for the rights of Negroes. It is forcing America to face all its interrelated flaws — racism, poverty, and militarism. It is exposing the evils that are rooted deeply in the whole structure of our society. It reveals systematic rather than superficial flaws and suggests that radical reconstruction of society itself is the real issue to be faced."

Another flaw in the President's speech was the unacknowledged issue of an apology for slavery that was raised when a bipartisan group of Congressional representatives broached the issue. In an interview that was recorded before the President's speech, Mr. Clinton tepidly said he would "consider" an apology, but he made no reference to an apology, or to the Congressional effort in his speech. As a result, folks like Newt Gingrich were able to scoff at the possibility of an apology, and the media focus shifted, somewhat, from the President's speech to Newt's ludicrous remarks.

An apology is only a first step toward racial healing, but it is a step. A second step might be to authorize construction of a Slavery Museum and Monument in our nation's capital, something that commemorates the contributions that slave labor made to this country, and reminds us, much as the Holocaust Museum does, of the consequences of indifference to humanity. Another step might be to work on the closing of economic gaps between African American people and others. And, since an apology is likely to increase discussion of reparations, a final step might be to deal with the "uncashed check" that Dr. Martin Luther King referred to in our "national conversation."

The unfinished work of our time, said President Clinton, "is to lift the burden of race and redeem the promise of America." We've been talking at least since Frederick Douglass called our notion of one nation "a sham." Action is the necessary next step.

King Features Syndicate, July 20, 1997

THE FOURTH OF YOU LIE
BY JULIANNE MALVEAUX

The item was buried in the corner of a newspaper full of urgent items. It indicated that a textbook had been rejected by a school board not because there was too little multicultural content in the book, but because there was too much. Too much! I wondered if the book had been written by Afrocentrist Molefe Asante, by historian Dr. John Hope Franklin, or by *Ebony* magazine writer Lerone Bennett, Jr. Instead, the books that were being rejected had been written by a team of historians, and had been controversial in some school districts because they did not include enough multicultural content.

Too many mainstream historians have decried the tendency to point out hypocrisy in American history, to find every holiday and cause for celebration tainted. But the fact is that our nation is so far from its ideals that it is pathetic. And every holiday has some taint, some stain, because the ideals we celebrate as universal often only applied to some people.

Historian Howard Zinn reminds us of this when he writes about America's working class history. For the longest time the poor did not have the right to vote, a right that was restricted to white, male, property holders. Before the signs said "white" or "colored," they said "No Irish Need Apply." These realities are swallowed by our idealism in celebrating freedom, justice and so-called equality.

Columbus did not discover America, and Columbus Day ought to be called Indigenous People's Day. President Abe Lincoln was not a moralist who freed the slaves. He used African people as a pawn in a regional battle, and embraced the concept of unequal pay for those black soldiers who equally risked their lives in the Civil War. Thomas Jefferson, that great philosopher, was also a slaver, and so his declarations of freedom are contaminated by his hypocrisy. And perhaps the most poignant indictment of American history is Frederick Douglass' stinging speech, "The Meaning of the Fourth of July for the Negro." Douglass asks what liberty we are talking about when we talk about life, liberty and the pursuit of happiness. He is fiery, angry, pained. A century after Douglass asked his questions, there is still a gulf between the way many Americans view history. Much of the gulf has to do with the history we celebrate and the history we are silent about.

In Washington, D.C., malls, monuments and museums speak to our rich history. There is a museum for air and space, a monument to President Lincoln, and to President George Washington. There is a Holocaust Museum that details the history of oppression that happened on another shore, but there is no nod to the horrible legacy that slavery left in this country. If we can walk through simulated concentration camps to experience the horror of twentieth-century brutality, why can't we walk through simulated plantations to experience the horror and blood on which our nation's profits rest?

To walk through the nation's malls and monuments is to understand the profundity of America's lie and the resistance that some people feel to exploring dimensions of the lie. How can a textbook have "too much" multicultural content? How can we resist "too much" truth? The cliché says that to know history is to avoid repeating it, yet when we experience church burnings, political setbacks, and racist beatings of African American "suspects," there is a sense of déjà vu.

The Fourth of July is supposed to be Independence Day. Too many people are unwittingly using it to celebrate their independence from, and ignorance of, our sordid past. It is not the Fourth of July, but the Fourth of You Lie, the institutionalization of the lies that are the foundation of this tainted nation. So as some parade and barbecue, others simmer at the irony of official lies that some people call history. Those who lived the part that has been obliterated by allegations of "too much" multiculturalism know American history as self-serving fiction.

King Features Syndicate, June 29, 1996

MUMIA IS A MIRROR ON DEATH PENALTY ATTITUDES
BY JULIANNE MALVEAUX

The case of Philadelphia journalist Mumia Abu-Jamal mirrors many of the imperfections in our nation's criminal justice system. Convicted in 1982 of the murder of a police officer, Jamal has consistently maintained his innocence. Trial records suggest that there were errors in the way the trial was conducted, the jury selected, and evidence collected, presented, and interpreted. How was a mostly white (10 of 12) jury seated in a city that is 40 percent African American? Why did the prosecution fail to provide the defense with the names and addresses of eyewitnesses to the incident in which the Philadelphia police officer died? More than 125 people witnessed the incident, but only a handful, with poor physical descriptions and conflicting testimony, were heard by the court.

Mumia Abu-Jamal was shot in the alley where he stopped to prevent his brother's beating at the hands of a police officer. It took two hours to get the bullet out of his back. While at the hospital, according to some witnesses, he was beaten. But his hands were never treated with the paraffin that would have revealed whether he had handled a weapon.

The most egregious miscarriage of justice in Mumia Abu-Jamal's case is the use of his political beliefs to lead to a conviction. Because much was made of Jamal's adolescent membership in the Black Panther Party, the prosecution was able to extrapolate that anyone who would utter the "revolutionary" words "power to the people" (isn't that what Newt Gingrich and his allies are telling the American middle class?) would also kill a police officer.

Mumia Abu-Jamal has written about criminal justice and injustice and his own life in prison in a collection of columns and essays that was released last month. In *Live from Death Row*, he writes of his own case and the lives of many others, placing pathos in the larger context of criminal justice contradictions. One of the most moving essays is about his then five-year-old daughter visiting him in prison, about her tiny fists banging against the Plexiglas that separated her from her father. "Over five years have passed since that visit," Mumia Abu-Jamal wrote in 1994, "but I remember it like it was an hour ago: the slams of her tiny fists against that ugly barrier, her instinctual rage against it—the state-made blockade raised under the rubric of security, her hot tears."

Many are hoping that the collective rage against the death penalty will be muted by "law and order" concerns. So Pennsylvania Governor Tom Ridge has signed Mumia Abu-Jamal's death warrant. Unless a stay of execution or a new trial is won, Jamal is scheduled to die on August 17, 1995. People all over the world are protesting, people in Philadelphia, Los Angeles, Boston, Chicago, Atlanta, New York, San Francisco, Oakland, Seattle, Washington, D.C., Minneapolis, Lansing, Vancouver, Toronto, Kingston, Amsterdam, Frankfurt, Berlin, Gütersloh, Karlsruhe, Rome and London are showing their support for Mumia Abu-Jamal and fighting his execution warrant. The mainstream media has ignored the protests, which have been thousands-strong in some cities.

It is ironic that our government affirms the death penalty at a time when the few holdouts in the world community, like South Africa, reject it. The irony is compounded when limits on death penalty appeals are buried in federal anti-terrorism legislation. Will Mumia Abu-Jamal die because of our collective desire for law and order? Or will the thousands that rally for him have an impact on his fate? Mumia has written of his daughter's tiny fists trying to shatter Plexiglas. What will it take for concerned people to shatter the notion that the death penalty is criminal "justice"?

King Features Syndicate, June 9, 1995

BAD BLACK AND THE FARRAKHAN PHENOMENON
BY JULIANNE MALVEAUX

When Louis Farrakhan speaks, America listens. Whether he is asserting the need for black economic development or accusing Jewish people of a media conspiracy against him, he has the power to pull worshipful cameras into his orbit, the power to take his words from the periphery of African American thought to center stage.

And he has the power to move black people. According to a *Time/CNN* poll, nearly three-quarters of all African Americans are familiar with Farrakhan, and more than 60 percent of those familiar with him view him in a positive light. Sixty-two percent say he is good for the black community, 63 percent say he speaks the truth, and 67 percent say he is an effective leader. Many see him as the most effective black leader on the scene.

Why? I don't think it is because African Americans buy into Louis Farrakhan's anti-Semitic rhetoric (only 20 percent in the poll found him anti-Semitic). Instead, I think Louis Farrakhan's in-your-face discourse touches a nerve among those African Americans who are forced to swallow the bitter bile of race conflict. The best way to view Farrakhan, I think, is to view him in the context of reading Ellis Cose's book on black middle-class angst, *The Rage of a Privileged Class*. Some African Americans respond to Farrakhan because they can't respond to the discrimination and pain they experience each day. And white America would be well advised to deal with the roots of that discrimination and disparate treatment, not with Farrakhan.

Louis Farrakhan carries the historical mantle of "bad black," the black man who was defiant, angry, and confrontive with white America. He is the late-

20th-century incarnation of upstarts like Gabriel Trotter and Denmark Vesey, of Marcus Garvey and Malcolm X when Malcolm was Nation of Islam spokesperson. Indeed, the parallel between Farrakhan and Malcolm is ironic since Malcolm mentored Farrakhan, and since Farrakhan's role in Malcolm's assassination has never been determined. But the two men are admired for much the same reasons— because they are up-front, in-your-face angry and articulate, and because beneath the confrontive nature of their anger there is the redemptive nature of their mission—black empowerment and economic development.

If our economy generated more equal results, Farrakhan's fire might fizzle. If those who want to start businesses could get loans, then the alternative model of involvement with the Nation of Islam might look empty and unfulfilling. But, truth be told, many adherents to the Nation's philosophy have had doors slammed in their faces before. They've given American free enterprise a chance and they retreated to the Nation under the weight of broken promises. Farrakhan's rhetoric about the "white man" and the "Jew" strikes a chord in those who find the system unfair. Those who chafe at Farrakhan's rhetoric ought to peel back the onion to get to its roots—the current social and economic condition of African Americans.

Farrakhan and the Fruit of Islam offer an image of African American manhood that contrasts sharply with the image that gets the most media exposure. While national news focuses on the extent to which black men are unemployed, criminal, careless, and marginal, the disciplined and bow-tied Fruit appear to be their antithesis. They stand at attention when Muslim officials enter a building. They circle their leaders in tight, silent webs and jostle anyone — reporters, officials, women—who moves counter to their unspoken rules. Their mystery is riveting, hostile, peculiar. And it is so counter to the way white America works that it attracts the support of black America.

The difference between the way white folk and black folk feel about the American dream and its outcome is at the crux of black acceptance of Louis Farrakhan. Flawed interpretation of history aside, he tells a truth so awful that most white Americans turn away. He says there are no clean hands in the slave foundations of our nation's history. That means no Irish-American hands, no Italian-American hands, no Brahmin hands, no Jewish hands. The seeds of slavery are the roots of our nation's contemporary inequality. Our avoidance of those issues makes Farrakhan's raw rhetoric appealing to a nation that has room for a Holocaust Museum but no Slave Monument, for a *Schindler's List* but no true depiction (like Howard University professor Haile Germina's film *Sankofa*) of slave realities.

When viewed from a historical prism, Louis Farrakhan isn't America's only bad black. His appeal is as real as that of Nat Turner, Marcus Garvey, or others who spit in the wind at the American dream. The challenge is not to rail at the spitting, but at the source of the anger. When the American dream is not a nightmare for so many African Americans, then Louis Farrakhan's rhetoric will twist, not spit, at the wind.

King Features Syndicate, February 21, 1994

FEAR OF CRIME OR FEAR OF COLOR: BERNHARD GOETZ REDUX
BY JULIANNE MALVEAUX

Bernhard Goetz shot four black men in a subway on December 22, 1984 because one of them asked him for five dollars. At the time there was mixed sympathy, much of it for Goetz because people believed New York City was so dangerous, so violent that it was necessary for a white man to carry a gun on the subway to protect him from all the teeming forces of color that threatened safety, law, and order.

Now a different story comes out, thanks to Daryl Caby's lawsuit against Goetz. Now it turns out that Goetz was under the influence of drugs and that he shot Caby not because of any perceived threat, but because Caby smiled and had a "glint in his eye." What if Caby had frowned?

Goetz was acquitted of criminal assault and attempted-murder charges by a white jury in Manhattan. He served a little time for unlawful possession of a weapon, but, quite frankly, he ought to have been convicted of both attempted murder and unlawful possession of an arsenal. For a time Goetz was the hero of the folks we now call the "angry white men," a model for the protagonist in the movie *Falling Down*, a real-life "make my day" Clint Eastwood. Now, Caby is suing Goetz for $50 million in a civil lawsuit that is populated by a jury of color. The civil lawsuit is giving the world a closer look at Bernhard Goetz, and the picture is far less flattering than is imaginable.

Ronald Kuby, the lawyer for the defense, has been able to elicit much information about Bernhard Goetz's views. They make him seem more at home with Montana's freemen than in comfort on the streets of Manhattan. Goetz has said that Caby's mother should have had an abortion. He has said the streets could be cleaned by getting rid of "spics and n———rs." He's prided himself on pulling a gun on people who have merely challenged him verbally, and his murderous assault was just one of a series of his confrontations with the people he thinks the streets should be cleansed of. He has said that the killing of a verbally abusive youth might "make the world a better place."

Goetz is absolutely unrepentant for his actions, and for the damage they caused. He seems also incapable of understanding the danger of carrying a weapon onto a crowded subway, and about the possible damage stray bullets may have inflicted on innocent bystanders. Goetz seems self-righteous, self-serving, and self-aggrandizing. But he was also found innocent by a jury of his peers, white New Yorkers whose fear of crime exceeded their respect for human life. If people went around shooting everyone who asked them for a handout, what kind of society would we have?

Fortunately, Goetz has not been asked to ponder society, simply his actions. From news accounts, Ronald Kuby (the late William Kunstler's law partner) has been aggressive in his questioning of Goetz, making it clear that Goetz was looking for trouble, not safety, when he got into a subway with a gun. Each of Kuby's efforts to elicit remorse or an apology from Goetz for the shootings has been rebuffed, making Goetz look all the more absurd. For example, when challenged to say something to Daryl Caby, the man he paralyzed, he offered little, advising Caby to become a vegetarian. If Goetz is a vegetarian, health considerations aside, that is a rationale for the universe to run out and devour pigs and cows. That's just a joke. Vegetarians are sometimes noted for their passivity, but all the vogues in the world can't calm the ire of a raging racist like Bernhard Goetz, who gives even vegetarians a bad name.

More than a decade after Goetz tried to slaughter four black men, he is having his day of reckoning, an opportunity for Caby to get satisfaction, and for society to show its disapproval of Bernhard Goetz's actions. Yet, in many ways our so-called judicial system has responded favorably to Goetz, with the random vigilantism and extreme punitiveness that characterize our legal system. Young men with as little as $50 worth of crack cocaine can be sentenced to jail time under new drug laws. And while three strikes you're out is somewhat preferable to the Goetz system of one strike and you're dead, it seems that the same fear of crime that propelled Goetz has propelled the structure of our justice system.

But Ronald Kuby is illustrating that Goetz wasn't at all afraid of crime, using it as an excuse to justify his recklessness. If the analogy holds, our nation isn't so afraid of crime, either. Our fear of crime is a proxy for other fears and our need to exert control and dominance over certain populations. Would that Kuby could question our legislators with the same zeal that he is questioning Goetz. He might find as much evidence of dishonesty in our legal system as he has found in Goetz's rationalizations for his pistol packing.

San Francisco Sun Reporter, April 16, 1996

TIMOTHY MCVEIGH: CHARMING UNTIL PROVEN GUILTY?
BY JULIANNE MALVEAUX

Like every other person charged with a crime, Timothy McVeigh must be considered innocent until proven guilty. Yet there seems to be a preponderance of evidence that he is the person who blew up the Murrah Building in Oklahoma City, the awful bombing that left 168 people, including dozens of children, dead. Days after the Murrah Building was reduced to rubble, days after theories were floated that "foreign" influences were responsible for the bombing, after perhaps hundreds of Arab Americans were hassled by the police, Timothy McVeigh was arrested. Since then, it seems, there has been a quest to put Timothy McVeigh in context, to portray him as the intense but relatively harmless (white) boy next door. Too many have described him in accessible terms, as charming, good-looking, pleasant. Too many seem to have forgotten what he is accused of and the likelihood that he is guilty.

Just a few days ago, on television's top-rated morning show, the *Today* show, *Spin* magazine's Jonathan Franklin was the featured guest. In his discussion with Matt Lauer, Franklin described McVeigh as "the kind of guy who would shovel your driveway in the snow," a pleasant and engaging man. Franklin spent more than an hour with McVeigh and received letters from him, but his interview was conducted on the condition that he only speak of McVeigh's time as a soldier in the Gulf War. While the Gulf War experiences are interesting in understanding McVeigh, equally interesting is the extent to which Franklin stretches to place McVeigh in some kind of context. McVeigh, writes Franklin, "looks like a job applicant," he speaks "eloquently," he is "gangly and good-natured." Sounds like someone you'd enjoy meeting, until you remember the Murrah Building crumbling around 168 people.

McVeigh has been "so cooperative" with the prison guards that they don't bother to shackle him for the interview. On television, Franklin describes the easy rapport that McVeigh has with the guards, the fact that the guards feel comfortable with him. And I begin to gag, not only because of the crimes that McVeigh is alleged to have committed, but also because of the clearly differential treatment that he has received as a federal prisoner.

Consider, for example, the case of Mumia Abu-Jamal, the Philadelphia journalist who is accused of murdering a single police officer. Rarely has Abu-Jamal been seen without his shackles. His relations with prison guards have been tense. A dread locked black man has as much of a chance of having easy rapport with prison guards as the proverbial snowball has of surviving in hell. But Abu-Jamal is accused of killing one person; McVeigh is accused of killing 168. Are his military service, his "gangly, good-natured" ways, his whiteness and boy-next-door vibe going to be the lens through which his crimes are viewed? Why are so many people taking the time to attempt to humanize and understand Timothy McVeigh?

Certainly, McVeigh deserves to be placed in some kind of context, but so do hundreds of others who are accused of horrible crimes. If they are African American, male, and from the inner city, though, there is no context, just the set of facts that suggest that black men are predisposed to crime. Few have taken the time to get inside the heads of gang members who kill each other for glancing the wrong way. Few have written of the things that make them tick. When arrested, these youngsters have as much of a chance of finding congenial prison guards as they do of getting justice from our nation's courts. They are guilty until proven innocent, while McVeigh is not only innocent, but in the eyes of some, also charming, until he is proven guilty.

The image of Timothy McVeigh as "Mr. Clean" is likely to be tarnished as he continues to giggle and behave inappropriately through jury selection, as the magnitude of the Murrah Building bombing is recounted for jury review. Still, I am offended by the guards who feel comfortable enough with McVeigh to laugh and joke with him, offended by the writers who see him as "good-natured" and clean-cut. They seem willing to suspend their knowledge of the crimes he is accused of to explore his humanity, but unwilling to get past their disdain and horror for the more mundane accused. I wonder why.

King Features Syndicate, April 4, 1997

SHOULD RACE MATTER ON SEINFELD?

BY JULIANNE MALVEAUX

It has been almost a year since President Clinton appointed his Advisory Commission on Race, almost a year since he launched the discussion that is supposed to lead our nation to racial reconciliation. Well-meaning Americans all over the country have taken the Clinton challenge far more seriously than he has, tackling issues more complicated than "Can we all get along?" In some communities, town hall meetings have been the basis for dialogue and debate, but after debate there is always the question "Where do we go from here?" Too often, people go from a bristling and bustling multicultural conversation back home to turn on a television and tune in to a view of a segregated America.

During the question period after a recent speech on race relations in our society, I was engaged in conversation by a young white man who asked a series of thought-provoking questions. I couldn't help but notice his pile of books and their titles, as well as the magazine cover that featured actors from the NBC *Seinfeld* comedy. "It's one of my favorite shows," the young man told me, and I couldn't help wonder how someone who had been so fully engaged in a conversation about diversity could turn into a couch potato sucking in the lives of the whiney white *Seinfeld* actors.

Whether you are a fan of *Seinfeld* or not, you'd have to live on another planet not to know that the top-rated show will air its last episode in a couple of weeks. There has been tremendous hype leading up to the fact that this nine-year phenomenon has come to an end, with newspaper features, magazine covers, and prime-time interviews all exploring what will become of the actors who play a quartet of neurotic New Yorkers whose most profound thought is "yada yada." While the actors may well be very talented, and Jerry Seinfeld himself may well be very funny, I'm not sorry to see a show that depicts such a narrow slice of life go off the air.

While the show is set in New York City, you get little sense of New York's diversity in *Seinfeld*. The *Seinfeld* central characters—Jerry, Elaine, George and Kramer—are four self-absorbed New Yorkers who are capable of obsessing over life's minutiae ad nauseum. While I'm not a regular viewer of the show, I don't recall any episodes focusing on these people getting so far out of themselves that they volunteer or give to charity. Except for a show in which one of the characters realized he had no African American friends and so went to seek out "a black guy," race doesn't matter in Jerry Seinfeld's New York. Talk about a slice out of fantasy life!

Even that city's richest and most self-absorbed white folks have to confront issues of diversity occasionally.

Unfortunately, the world that Seinfeld created may look much like the world some Americans fantasize about. The most perplexing dilemmas these people ever have to deal with revolve around the etiquette of the soup line, their sexual peccadilloes, and New York City parking. They don't have to worry about more complex issues like taxes, employment, or schools. They aren't alone. There are dozens of other shows with whiney white self-absorbed casts. *Friends* and *Party of Five* stand out as special examples of that. And then there are integrated shows where race never comes up, even though it might. In the ever-popular *Ally McBeal*, for example, producers go out on a limb by giving the title character an appealing, smart, African American roommate. Then, even when the two women engage in a romantic competition for an African American man, race doesn't come up. Duh.

There's a flip side to this—situation comedies that purport to be slices of African American life seem to feature stupid and stereotypical African Americans. The whites that venture onto these shows are almost uniformly insensitive and ignorant, straw men who are the butt of jokes about rhythm and race knowledge. These bumbling black broadcasts, direct descendants of the Amos and Andy comedies of the 1950s, are almost as insulting as *Seinfeld's* race-myopic episodes.

While it would become a bit monotonous if every television comedy dealt with complex sociological issues, it is extremely myopic for shows like *Seinfeld* to act as if race doesn't matter in New York City. And it seems paradoxical that people who are engaged in race debate haven't more frequently wondered how *Seinfeld's* world got to be so whiney and white.

King Features Syndicate, May 1, 1998

OSCAR IS A WHITE BOY WITH AN ATTITUDE
BY JULIANNE MALVEAUX

I didn't watch the Academy Awards on Monday night, didn't deal either with the notion of 70 years of excellence in movies. Why? 'Cause "excellence" is a term that has been coined to calibrate white superiority and African American exclusion. Why else relegate black people, in 1998, to just a few nominations despite our astounding excellence in film. Why ignore the brilliant writing, directing and acting of Kasi Lemmons' *Eve's Bayou* except to decide that the kaleidoscopic confidence of African American life is unworthy of the Academy's attention.

Oscar. Robin Williams called the tarnished statue "The Dude." I'd say Oscar is a white boy with attitude, the total exemplification of the notion that white is not only right but superior, and that black has to be kicked to the curb. Otherwise, why ignore Spike Lee's outstanding *Four Little Girls* to offer an award to a much more flawed documentary experience. Oscar. The "best" in film, depending on whose definition of "best" you are speaking of. Does best mean the best performances, or the most sentimentally inclined? Isn't it sobering to note that while the Academy celebrated 70 years of exclusion, it took a whole eleven years before Hattie McDaniel was nominated for anything in 1939. Then it was another decade before Ethel Waters won a nomination. Nine years passed before Sidney Poitier garnered a nomination.

Though black folks are our nation's entertainers, we don't get nominated for Academy Awards every year, and certainly not in every category. Great films like *Eve's Bayou* don't get a nod, and good films like *Amistad* and *Jackie Brown* are only lifted up in the name of the white actors who support them. Pam Grier acted the part of her life, but the only nod *Jackie Brown* gets is best supporting actor? A bazillion Africans survived the *Amistad* middle passage and its aftermath, but all praises go to the actor who plays a former President. Sounds to me like Oscar is a white boy with an attitude, a white boy who has so unbalanced the playing field that black folks can look but not touch.

When we look, we see the way our stories become cannon fodder for white writers. When we look we see the way our stories become the selective salvation of white Oscar judges. How could anybody in *Jackie Brown* not play off Pam Grier? How could a supporting actor be "best" without giving due praises to the best actress? I suppose it was a *Titanic* thing. Some non-melanin-infused folks have the option of spending $200 million or so on a movie. Other folks scramble to get a Hollywood "green light" for outstanding films like *Soul Food* or *Eve's Bayou*.

Let's be clear. If *Soul Food* were done in whiteface it would have garnered several nominations and at least one win (if, for nothing else, the music). If *Eve's Bayou* were a white film, eliciting stellar performances out of white children (consider, for example, *The Piano*), there would be nominations bouncing off the walls. Instead, this movie gets two thumbs up from Siskel and Ebert and thumbs down from the Academy. But moviemakers who are African American need not set their sights on their industry's highest honors. Oscar is, after all, nothing more than a bronzed-over white boy with an attitude.

Here's the attitude. We'll watch them cutting, shooting, stabbing, driving by and getting high. We'll watch them snoring, whoring, scoring, watch them even when they are boring. But we won't watch them stretch, we won't watch them bend, we won't watch them try to be our friends. We won't watch them unless the stereotype portends. And we won't let them be our standard-bearers. The standard is held up, I suppose, in a movie like the emotion-washed *Titanic*. Some are so myopic as to find no standard in the same set of universal emotions, less acknowledged because black folks are feeling love and loss and conflict (never mind the fact that *Soul Food* never flooded and the creek didn't really rise in *Eve's Bayou*).

The Academy's bias is obvious to all but those who fondle Oscar. Absent ways to influence the Academy, though, there is little African Americans can do. We can't influence biased judges to see quality, not skin color. We can't make people see excellence when they are dedicated to keeping their heads in the sand. But we can lift up those talented African Americans who make films.

So cheers to Debbie Allen and the cast of *Amistad*, though the film had its flaws. Delicious kudos to Kasi Lemmons and the outstanding cast of *Eve's Bayou*. And then there are others who have brought black life to the screen in ways that are not stereotypical—like John Singleton, director of *Rosewood*, Theodore Witcher, the writer/director of *Love Jones*, and Tracey and Kenneth "Babyface" Edmonds with *Soul Food*. They remind us that you don't have to cut it up and shoot it up to film it up. But they won't get Oscar, the white boy with attitude.

Since Oscar is the highest acclamation that those in the Hollywood business can earn, it is no consolation to the black folks who do movies that they are loved and appreciated. They have earned our love, but not the Oscar, our appreciation, not the elevation that comes from white boy with attitude. Is that a curse or a blessing or a combination of the two? Just asking.

King Features Syndicate, March 24, 1998

CHAPTER 6

THE FUTURE OF WORK

While the stock market soars, 75 percent of all Americans over 16 work, and most rely on their wages for survival. The status of workers and the future of work are of key importance in our society. We keep hearing that we need more people to focus on science and technology in their education, but demographics suggest that we will need more people to care for our elderly and children. Yet, the average home health worker earns about $250 a week. If I earned $250 a week, I'd have an attitude. Why do we want people with attitudes taking care of our mothers and grandmothers? When we don't pay people well, it speaks not only to our indifference to them, but also to hypocrisy in statements we make about our children and elderly.

Two trends will shape the workplace of the future—globalism and technology. We are woefully underprepared for both. From an international perspective, we are mired in a protectionism that ignores the role of trade in our own national growth. In terms of technology, too many Americans are sidelined as the vehicles on the information superhighway speed by. Furthermore, our visions of the workplace are skewed by a popular culture that allows us to forget that 10 million workers earn the minimum wage and that unions improve the status of organized workers.

While the future of work is unscripted, it is likely to be as bifurcated as the future of our society. Some workers will have benefits; others will not. Some can expect secure workplace futures; others cannot. Public policy will address the status of some; others will be ignored. And while the economy grows and unemployment rates remain low, some workers will grapple with unemployment.

Meanwhile, workers are under attack. Legislation and regulation make organizing more difficult than it has been in the past. Uneven employment growth dictates the fate of millions. Yet workers are the backbone of our economy and society, something we forget when we ignore the concept of a living wage!

JOB GROWTH CONCENTRATED IN LOW-WAGE AREAS
BY JULIANNE MALVEAUX

Vice President Al Gore has made much of the fact that our nation will need some 375,000 computer programmers in the next decade or so. Part of the need for new programmers is driven by a problem that drives many who use computers, the Year 2000 (often called the Y2K) problem. Millions of computers have not been properly programmed to move from 1999 to 2000, and it is likely that some chaos will ensue when we move from December 31, 1999 to January 1, 2000.

Gore is right to raise questions about the shortage of computer programmers. But the greater dilemmas in the labor market of the future deal with some of the lowest paying jobs in the occupational spectrum, as well as some of the jobs that are most affected by the way our health care system is organized. Some of the most rapidly growing jobs, to be sure, are spurred by technology, with computer engineers and systems analysts among those rapidly growing jobs. According to the Labor Department's publication, *Occupational Outlook*, the greatest numerical job growth by the year 2005 will be among cashiers, a job that is typically female and now pays $248 per week, or less than $13,000 per year for full-time workers. Six hundred thousand more cashiers will be needed by 2005.

The second largest absolute demand for new workers will be among janitors and cleaners, the third largest amount among salespersons, and the fourth largest demand is among waiters and waitresses. These jobs are relatively low-paying service jobs, not high-paying, high-tech jobs. Much of the conversation about the workforce of the future, then, is only a partial lens about the future demands of work. Along with rapidly growing demand for technology workers, there is persistent and significant demand for low-paid service workers.

Another key demand in the next decade is for workers in health. The health sector is growing twice as rapidly as the overall economy, and one in five new jobs will be jobs in that sector. Those won't all be high-paying jobs, either. Many will be among home health aides and nursing aides, low-wage workers, mostly women. The status of these workers will largely depend on the way health service delivery is organized. Already, health maintenance organizations have introduced service inefficiencies that cause difficulties for some patients. As elderly sick people are shifted from hospitals to nursing homes and private facilities, it is likely that their helpers will have fewer skills and command less pay. From where I sit, Al Gore's brave new world will yield the same old poverty for too many working women. Women need not be victims in the workplace of the future. The fate of those in service and health jobs will depend on their tenacity and ability to organize. As the AFL-CIO's executive committee gathered in Las Vegas this week to strategize for the future, the organization's women's department convened a couple of hundred organizers to talk about ways to organize working women. Buoyed by organizing victories and strike settlements at the MGM and Frontier Hotels in Vegas, the AFL-CIO'S women's department was prepared to explore strategies for reaching out to unorganized women.

There are significant challenges. The workplace of the future will be more decentralized, and organizers are likely to have to go door-to-door to make persuasive cases to potential union members. Where these workers are women, organizers will have to combat the sense so many workers have of being overwhelmed by both work and family responsibilities. This feeling of too much to do and too little time is often associated with high earners, but is likely to be much more common among those whose earnings and options are limited. Too, there is a hostility to organized labor that is perhaps best illustrated by California's Proposition 226, a measure that would prevent unions from involvement in political action.

But as women inch up their share of the labor force from 46 percent now to 48 percent by the year 2005, the challenges that working women face are likely to multiply. If unions can help them meet these challenges they have a shot at improving the number of women they can organize. The data on the labor market of the future suggest that organized labor has a shot at working women, especially those at the bottom. These are the women who most desperately need to improve their wage options. They are the women who are most willing to consider organization as a solution to their problems. And these are the women who understand that for all the growth in technology jobs, someone will have to empty the bedpans.

King Features Syndicate, March 19, 1998

UNEMPLOYMENT AND UNCERTAINTY
BY JULIANNE MALVEAUX

When the March unemployment rate was released on April 7, policy makers breathed a sigh of relief. That the rate ticked up from 5.4 to 5.5 percent was seen as a sign that the economy is moving toward "steady growth." A further drop would have suggested inflationary pressure on the economy, according to the conventional wisdom. Few members of the Joint Economic Committee bothered to show up to question Commissioner of Labor Statistics Katharine Abraham. The discussion of the unemployment rate lasted less than an hour.

This suggests that our nation should be satisfied with nearly 8 million officially unemployed people, and the others that experience some kind of labor market disadvantage—the part-time workers who want to work full time, those who have dropped out of the labor market, the underemployed who work in jobs below their skill level. Though Labor Secretary Robert Reich has talked about the importance of job training and what needs to happen in the labor market, he seems to talk to himself on these matters. Jobs was one of the issues that was blatantly ignored in the Contract on America.

When placed in the context of this entire decade, the unemployment rate is not very high. But the 5.5 percent that we measure today is a different 5.5 percent than the one we measured a decade ago. It fails to capture the uncertainty that so many workers feel, not because they are unemployed, but because they are under-employed, because they are working in temporary jobs, or because they fear that their company will, like many others, "downsize" them out of a job. It is this uncertainty that policy makers need to focus on when they deal with the labor market. It is this uncertainty that has been, in large part, ignored.

But on his recent trip to California, President Clinton gave a nod to economic uncertainty, albeit to the uncertainty that just one population group feels. He talked about the "feelings" white men have in economically troubling times. White men aren't the only ones who experience uncertainty. Most others experience even more. White men have lower unemployment rates and higher income levels than every other population group. They hold more of the "best" jobs, the upper management jobs in Fortune 1000 companies, than anyone else. The Glass Ceiling Commission report said that 95 percent of the executive suite was male, and 97 percent of those males were white. What about the "feelings" of those locked out of the best jobs? Don't they have to be considered?

Still, the President's focus on white males makes an important point. When there are enough jobs to go around, affirmative action is not a societal burden. It isn't, then, a tragedy of "us versus them," a tale of economic competition gone awry. When job markets are tight, sharing gets tense. Thus, part of the affirmative action backlash is coming from the top down, from the Senate, Congress and unfortunately from the White House where the President has seen fit to acknowledge the feelings of white men while ignoring the reality that others experience.

The Joint Economic Committee needs to ask questions about labor market policy when they hear unemployment rate data. They need to ask if our nation can live with 8 million officially unemployed people, and whether government should play a role in generating jobs for these people and those who don't show up in the statistics. President Clinton recognized the anxious white men who chafe at affirmative action, but he failed to discuss those anxious others who have unemployment and underemployment as a reality. Anxious white men share uncertainty with others in the labor market. And affirmative action, while opening doors, does little to relieve that uncertainty.

King Features Syndicate, April 14, 1995

FAMILY AND MEDICAL LEAVE WORKS FOR SOME
BY JULIANNE MALVEAUX

The first law that President William Jefferson Clinton signed after he took office was the Family and Medical Leave Act. The legislation had languished for eight years, from its introduction in 1985 by Congresswoman Patricia Schroeder, to its signing by President Clinton in 1993. The long process to passage reflects the mixed feelings that many had about the legislation.

Those who introduced the legislation saw it as an important way to provide workers who must attend to family needs with some job security. When the legislation was introduced, only a handful of states had laws that protected women who took time off from work because of pregnancy. As the legislation was developed, it became clear that pregnancy was not the only "family" reason people needed time off from work. Time to care for elderly parents, or to adjust for an adoption were among the other reasons a worker might ask for family and medical leave. Two years after Family and Medical Leave became law, Donna Lenhoff, Director of Work and Family Programs for the Women's Legal Defense Fund, notes that "a number of businesses have welcomed this law for providing uniformity and a level playing field, along with a minimum labor standard that employees need." Some employers have found that family and medical leave provisions increase employee loyalty.

For all the accolades that family and medical leave has attracted, there are also those who say that family and medical leave distorts labor market options.

In the debate that preceded the President's signing of the Family and Medical Leave Act, it was alleged that family and medical leave would cost profits, reduce productivity, cause layoffs, threaten economic growth, and increase discrimination against women. A Labor Policy Association Survey notes that most Fortune 500 companies say that the Family and Medical Leave Act has had either no impact or a positive impact on productivity, and that most managers have little or no difficulty in complying with intermittent leave programs. A survey for the Conference Board said that most found it easy to comply with the Family and Medical Leave Act, and that nearly half felt it improved employees' ability to deal with family needs.

The controversy over whether family and medical leave works is muted by the concern that it only works for some. The legislation only offered family and medical leave to those workers who were employed by firms with more than 50 workers. That leaves out half of all workers, who are increasingly employed by small and medium-sized businesses. Part-time workers are also excluded from family and medical leave coverage. Like many of the perks that are provided by federal legislation, family and medical leave protects those who have good jobs in good companies, those who have some job security. It leaves too many out.

Even those with job security raise questions about family and medical leave. The exact provisions of the law provide unpaid leave for 12 weeks for those who qualify. People who live from paycheck to paycheck are unlikely to take advantage of family and medical leave, since their unfunded leave may intensify the financial hardship that their families face. While the principle of family and medical leave is inclusive, the reality is much less so. If only those who can afford to be unpaid for three months take advantage of family and medical leave, then too many get no relief from this legislation.

As important as family and medical leave is, the concerns of those who insist on inclusion are also important. Two years after President Clinton signed this vital legislation, concerns about inclusion plague any analysis of the bill's impact. There is some Republican hostility to family and medical leave and Senate Majority Leader Bob Dole has described the Family and Medical Leave Act as "a disincentive to jobs and opportunity." But there is also some indifference to family and medical leave because the legislation simply doesn't trickle down far enough. Family and medical leave works for some workers. What will it take to make it work for everyone?

King Features Syndicate, August 4, 1995

CELEBRATE WORKERS
ON LABOR DAY
BY JULIANNE MALVEAUX

For most Americans, Labor Day means picnics, parties and parades, barbecues and back-to-school bashes. In the middle of the celebrations, though, it makes sense to take a moment and commemorate the real meaning of Labor Day, which ought to be a celebration of workers. Even though most of us work for a living, though, we fail to appreciate the way that the labor of others enables and supports the way we live.

From the early-morning thwack of the newspaper on my doorstep to the late-night nuking of a frozen dinner, my life is supported by the work of others. The man who delivers the paper, the writers whose words I devour in the paper, the people who manufacture the toiletries that make it possible for me to present myself to the world, bus and taxi drivers who transport me from one place to another, the waiters and waitresses that serve the food I eat at restaurants, the hands that plant and harvest the food they produce and serve, these working hands make my life, and all of our lives, possible. But workers have been the last to gain from the much-touted economic expansion that we've experienced in the past four years—indeed, while corporate profits have risen, worker pay as a percentage of national income has declined four years in a row, from 1993 to 1996. Our Congress reluctantly increased the minimum wage from $4.35 to $5.15 an hour, an increase that did not keep up with the pace of inflation since the last minimum wage increase. We rely on people's work to manage our lives, but we don't reward most work with the appropriate pay increases.

Despite the good economic news, too many workers struggle to make ends meet. While headlines blare the news that home prices are rising, a lower portion of Americans own homes now than in 1980. Fewer Americans, too, can afford to buy new vehicles. Fewer companies provide the comprehensive range of benefits, like health care, that were once provided; and even at firms that provide health care, workers wait longer to have benefits available to them. The number of Americans who hold more than one job has risen, and more than a quarter of a million Americans hold two full-time jobs. There are myriad reasons why three-quarters of us are worse off wage-wise than a decade ago, but one of the reasons is that corporations, government, and non-profit organizations find it easier to cut labor costs than others.

In celebrating Labor Day, we have to ask ourselves hard questions about labor and the future of work. Should people have more job security? Should wages be higher? How can workers push corporations to provide higher wages? Our Labor Day celebrations are tainted, in part, by the struggle that so many workers have to make ends meet and the insecurity that so many feel about the future of work.

USA Today, October 21, 1997

WORK, WORTH, AND POPULAR CULTURE
BY JULIANNE MALVEAUX

Although work is the central factor in the lives of most Americans, popular culture tends to depict work in ways so unrealistic that the naive cannot be blamed for getting the wrong impression. A television romp through workplace-centered programs would lead one to believe that we all work in hospitals, as lawyers or police officers, or in the media, as professionals with a fair amount of discretion over our time and our surroundings. While this is true for some workers, many dance to the beat of their bosses' drummer. This is why I had to smirk when I read about Arlie Hochschild's new book, *The Time Bind* (Metropolitan Press, forthcoming) which asserts that many parents are so pressed for time that they find the office a refuge, a place to "goof off."

No doubt, Ms. Hochschild is writing the reality for well-paid professional and managerial workers who, seeped in the culture of "quality circles" and "bonding," spend more face time with their subordinates than with their children (and, perhaps, enjoy it more). The reality for clerical, service, and other workers is likely to be quite the opposite. Who will voluntarily work unpaid overtime to more closely "bond" with a typewriter or word processor, to serve just a few more burgers, or to empty just a few more bedpans (although at the rate some hospitals are going, patients are going to be charged with emptying those themselves)?

The gulf between professionals/managers and clerical/service workers is not so much a gulf in workplace orientation as it is a gulf in pay. There are 27 million full-time managers and professional specialty workers in the workplace, earning a median weekly wage of $718 per week. That sum ranges from a median high of around $1100 for lawyers, engineers, and physicians, to a median low of around $500 for food service managers, social workers, and clergy. In contrast, there are 26 million full-time technical, sales and administrative support workers, at a median weekly wage of $474. Clerical workers have a median wage of $405 per week, while some technical workers have wages that are much higher.

Guess whose world you are more likely to be introduced to in a television sitcom? Guess whose world more closely fits with the one Arlie Hochschild depicts in *The Time Bind*? To be sure, the challenges that professionals face are no less pressing than those that clerical workers face. Still, with so many women, especially, juggling household, family, and low wages (about 80 percent of all women earn less than $25,000 per year), our notion of workplace reality is somewhat skewed if we suggest these women are piddling around at the office because their lives are too busy at home.

Further, the issue of juggling is a challenge, at best, for families where both parents are present. What about single-parent families, those more likely to be headed by someone with a modest income? How does *The Time Bind* reflect their world?

I am concerned about work and popular culture because so many policy makers have had so little exposure to the world of real work. They seem to think that public assistance recipients, for example, can be effortlessly integrated into productive workplaces without any consequences. They seem to think that workers so crave flexibility that they will shrug off hard-earned overtime for it. Arlie Hochschild's book presents a vision of the office as such a delightful place that some prefer it to the home. Some workers have the luxury of such preferences, and the support system to back them up. Others have neither luxury nor support. The sewing machine operator who makes $254 per week (there are more than half a million such workers), the assembler that makes $378 (1.1 million workers in this category), the janitors that earn $301 per week (nearly 1.5 million of these workers), or the typists that earn $395 per week (half a million of these) aren't often depicted in popular culture, aren't often considered in the policy context. These are the workers, though, that often make it possible for professional and managerial workers to find their offices such safe havens from the rest of their responsibilities.

King Features Syndicate, April 24, 1997

TELEVISION FICTION, WORKPLACE REALITY
BY JULIANNE MALVEAUX

Popular culture has managed to seep into the curriculum at many universities. Using the lens of television, movies, billboards, and the other media methods that sell us dreams and nightmares and distort our realities, some professors are able to lead students through study and discussion about values, politics, economics, and social issues in our culture. The syllabus for one of these "popular culture" classes moved me to consider the ways we view income through a popular lens. There is a great gulf between the popular portrayal of income, work, and occupational status and the reality.

To be sure, prime-time television is hardly a barometer of the socioeconomic status of American workers; it is illustrative to review prime-time programs from a propaganda perspective. In pursuit of drama, or even humor, what kind of characters are used to make a point? Are they contemporary or historical, physicians or nurses? Who are the people who occupy the fantasies and leisure time of millions of our fellow citizens? What does a writer's selection of these people, these fantasies, say about the distance between popular images and our reality?

I am confronted by these questions as I look at the income data released in a recent Census report. The September 1997 release of *Money Income in the United States: 1996* (P60-197,U.S. Government Printing Office, Washington, D.C.) reported a 1.2 percent increase in household income between 1995 and 1996, good news given the wage stagnation that so many workers have experienced in the past year. (Of course this good news might be contrasted with the 24 percent growth in the stock market in 1996; even after the late October "adjustment" in the Dow Jones Industrial Average in 1997, stock prices had risen 11 percent, while wage increases still falter.) Indeed, much was made of the fact that per capita income grew for almost all of the race/ethnic origin groups the Census classifies. White income grew by 1.8 percent, African American income by 5.2 percent, and Hispanic income 4.9 percent. Less was made of the fact that white per capita income, at $19,181, is almost double that of Blacks ($11,899) and Hispanics ($10,048).

Prime-time television seems oblivious to these income differences, or to matters of income, in general. While more prime-time programs are set in the workplace, these are workplaces that contrast sharply with the reality. Workers wander in and out of the workplace, mill around their desks and in and out of conversations, have time to conduct affairs during work hours, and seem to have scant concerns about money. The hardest work seems to be done by physicians, nurses, and health support staff, attorneys, and police officers, a group that is hardly typical of the overall work force.

Too many television characters have an easy opulence about them. Although it is rarely spoken, they imply that money simply doesn't matter. Perhaps I'm quibbling in the name of reality—prime-time television would be a dreary reality if fantasy focused on balancing checkbooks, finding child care, and extending the life of a broken-down car. Still it is illustrative to note how few of our nation's full-time workers earn enough to have access to the lifestyles often portrayed on television.

Of our nation's 90 million full-time, full-year workers, just 3.2 million (or 3.5 percent) earned more than $100,000 per year. Of those 3.2 million workers, 2.5 million, or 79.3 percent, are white male; 383,000, or 11.9 percent, are white female; 70,000, or 2.2 percent, are African American males; 29,000, or 0.9 percent, are African American females; 68,000 (2.1 percent) are Hispanic males; and 17,000 (0.5 percent) are Hispanic females. For all of television's depiction of progress by race and gender, the numbers tell quite a different story. Just a handful of Americans earn top incomes, and women and people of color are woefully underrepresented among them.

In contrast, too many earners have low and moderate incomes. The majority (53 percent) of women who work full-time, for example, have incomes under $25,000. Among African-American women, 60 percent have incomes below $25,000, and among Hispanic women that number rises to 70 percent. Many of these women are household heads and their earnings are the sole support of their families. The concerns of these workers aren't as attractive to prime-time fantasy writers as are the lifestyles of the rich and famous.

Contemporary prime-time television more closely reflects the nation's economic reality than it did just a decade ago, when popular prime-time programs focused on tycoons and oil barons, not doctors and lawyers. The expansion of the top-three network hegemony of ABC, NBC, and CBS to include Fox and UPN has given a younger, "cooler" and more diverse spin to prime-time. Further, the popularity of blue-collar protagonists like Roseanne Barr has made the factory or diner a more acceptable setting for a sitcom.

When the Fox and UPN networks are excluded, though, the portrayal of African Americans in the workplace and as earners is skewed and distorted. I'm not necessarily advocating taking the 28 percent of the African American population that is poor and making them the fodder for situation comedies. But I'm thinking that shows like the excellent but short-lived *Frank's Place* (produced by Tim Reid) showed both the diversity and the reality of the African American experience.

Still, if one spends an evening or a week consuming prime-time fare, one walks away with the sense that almost everybody is earning a cushy living and money doesn't matter. The data, however, tell a very different story.

King Features Syndicate, October 29, 1997

LEGISLATION FOR A LIVING WAGE
BY JULIANNE MALVEAUX

While some members of Congress have been concerned with creating tax breaks for those who earn incomes up to $250,000, others have been crafting legislation to help those whose incomes are on the bottom. Congressman Ronald V. Dellums has sponsored HR 1050, A Living Wage for All Act. It is cosponsored by Representatives David Bonior (D-Mich.), John Conyers (D-Mich.), Alcee Hastings (D-Fla.), Cynthia McKinney (D-Ga.), Eleanor Holmes Norton (D-D.C.), Donald Payne (D-N.J.), Nancy Pelosi (D-Calif.), Bernie Sanders (I-Vt.), Nydia Velasquez (D-N.Y.) among others.

The legislation would codify the rights that President Franklin Roosevelt stated in the Economic Bill of Rights of January 11, 1944, including the right to earn a living and the right to adequate medical services. HR 1050 also sets forth rights not declared in the 1944 Declaration, including the right to organize, environmental rights, and the right to private security. The legislation requires a re-examination of contemporary economic policy, specifically forbidding the use of recession, stagnation, or unemployment to reduce wages, salaries or inflation.

This progressive legislation is partly the result of years of work from the San Francisco-based Jobs for All Coalition, and two community activists, Barbara Arms and Wade Hudson. Years of research, community meetings, and political organizing have gone into HR 1050. Professor Bertram Gross, a man who once advised President Roosevelt on the 1944 legislation, has worked closely with the Jobs for All Coalition. Now Dellums, Pelosi, Gross and others will hold a November meeting in San Francisco to develop more support for the legislation.

HR 1050 is a legislative snowball unlikely to pass the Congressional hell that the 104th has become for bills sponsored by Democrats. But recent reports that economic expansion continues (with a 3.5 percent growth rate in the third quarter) while wages remain stagnant ought to provide some mobilizing impetus for HR 1050. So might some of the ill-considered statements of some members of Congress regarding middle incomes. One member said he thought $80,000 was "lower middle class" and that it took $250,000 to $750,000 to attain a middle class lifestyle. Talk about hiding your head in the sand! The average family has an income just over $40,000 a year, which suggests that according to some Republican leaders, most of us have less than "lower middle class" incomes.

Whether it passes or not in the 104th Congress, HR 1050's stated purposes, "to establish a living wage, jobs for all policy for the United States, in order to reduce poverty, inequality, and the undue concentration of income, wealth and power in the United States" will spark important discussions about the way that current economic policy maintains poverty and generates inequality. It focuses its attention on the 8 million or so people who earn the minimum wage, and the millions who work, illegally, in below-minimum-wage jobs. It looks at the Federal Reserve Board's policy of stimulating the economy and containing inflation by keeping the unemployment rate high. And it asks whether it is good economic policy to pay such a high price for expansion without prosperity.

Berkeley Congressman Ron Dellums describes HR 1050 as a "call to our historical sense of justice and fairness; a call to the richness of FDR's vision and the hopes and aspirations of a generation which had known the Great Depression." As the levels of child poverty have risen in our country, and as issues of economic insecurity confront an increasing number of people who are frightened by the prospects of layoffs and downsizing, an economic bill of rights is long overdue. But HR 1050's prospects are bleak in a 104th Congress determined to penalize the poor for their poverty, eliminating programs like the Earned Income Tax Credit to fund giveaways to the wealthy. Perhaps HR 1050 can be an antidote to the 104th Congress's approach to the economy. If the upcoming meeting in San Francisco is any indication, it can be a way to mobilize citizens and taxpayers around issues of economic fairness.

King Features Syndicate, November 2, 1995

DOES PROPOSITION 226 PROTECT
PAYCHECKS OR CORPORATIONS?
BY JULIANNE MALVEAUX

Proposition 226 was introduced, theoretically, to protect worker paychecks from unwanted deductions, especially from unions. Heavily supported by California Governor Pete Wilson, who serves as the measure's chairman, Proposition 226 purports to provide people, in Wilson's words, "the right to free choice with their own money." He says that when unions and others are able to automatically deduct dues from paychecks it amounts to "a massive shakedown."

Few agree with Wilson. From the American Cancer Society to the California Public Employees' Retirement System Board of Administration, to the Sierra Club, to the California Association of Nonprofits, the measure has been widely opposed. Why? Because payroll deduction is an easier way to collect money from people than to ask them for it directly. Because workers frequently prefer the convenience of payroll deduction to the process of writing regular checks to causes they support. Because payments from union dues to medical premiums, to support for social services, come from payroll deductions that would be illegal if Proposition 226 passes.

Indeed Proposition 226 will cost between $1.4 million and $4.2 million for implementation of new regulations, and about $2 million to maintain compliance just for state employees. Non-profit organizations and others would pay part of this cost, as would some of the businesses that are involved in payroll deduction. The paperwork could be so staggering that it would discourage workplace giving plans.

Proposition 226 is no simple accounting matter, no bad example of micromanagement through initiative. Its genesis is purely political. Corporations that have attempted to influence public policy through lobbying and advocacy would like their input in the policy arena to go unopposed. Thus, they want to hamper unions, who have also been involved in the lobbying and advocacy process. When Congress proposes minimum wage increase legislation, you can almost always count on the corporate community to oppose such legislation, but you can almost always count on unions to support it. But if unions don't have the funds to engage in advocacy on behalf of their members, they'll be silenced.

Traditionally, unions have been a progressive force fighting for the rights of workers on the job. They have worked to improve the terms and conditions of work, to make sure there is not only fair pay, but also a fair work environment. In contrast, in a low-unemployment environment where wages have risen only slightly, many corporations have fought for their rights to have work done "their way," with flexible time, less overtime, and few worker protections. To muzzle labor is to change the delicate balance between a corporation's right to maximize profits and a worker's right to earn a living wage.

This issue, then, is less about protecting workers than about an ideological attack on a union movement that has been invigorated since John Sweeny, Richard Trumka and Linda Chavez-Thompson took leadership at the AFL-CIO. The partisanship is evident when one considers the very sharp tone that Pete Wilson took when he compared police officers and firefighters to "fascists" because of their opposition to Proposition 226. The six-figure grant from an Indiana insurance tycoon, J. Patrick Rooney, to fight Proposition 226 also draws clear lines about whose interests are served if this measure fails. Nearly half a million dollars has come from Grover Norquist's Americans for Tax Reform. Yet Norquist was hardly likely to do what he'd like unions to do — check with each of his contributors to find out if his intrusion into California politics is an acceptable use of their money. Indeed, the corporate equivalent of Proposition 226 would be that publicly traded firms would have to clear advertising, lobbying, and other expenditures with each shareholder.

The adage that often shapes American politics still holds true, "as goes California, so goes the nation." Initiatives similar to Proposition 226 may be on ballots in Oregon, Florida and Nevada. Legislatures in Arizona, Alaska, Maryland, Minnesota, Mississippi, Missouri, Pennsylvania, Vermont and Wisconsin are also considering laws to curtail union contributions. Congress, too, has entered into the fray of "paycheck protection" all the while pocketing six-figure soft-money contributions from corporate America.

Is this paycheck protection or corporate protection? If we "follow the money" back to Pete Wilson, Grover Norquist, and J. Patrick Rooney, the answer is obvious.

King Features Syndicate, May 28, 1998

CHAPTER 7

FOREIGN POLICY IN A BORDERLESS ECONOMY

Is it the new world order or the same old stuff? The United States has held out on its payment of UN dues for more than six years, yet we try to play world leader in offering moral leadership and support for world democracy. We also offer trade and aid, although in fluctuating sums, and based on the perceived strategic importance of our trading partners. How important is the African continent perceived to be? Whatever happened to Haiti? And can we make foreign policy by referendum or town hall meeting?

The new world order actually turns out to be the same old conundrum of contradictions. We rely on trade to support economic growth in the United States, but we've ignored the fact that when the international economy falters, we too must share the burden. What goes up must come down, including the value of the dollar, the ruble and the yen. We can't expect constant growth, yet we bristle when it doesn't happen.

We talk about human rights violations at home; we ignore them abroad. Or, we ignore them when it's to our advantage. Otherwise we are rude and sanctimonious in our judgments of others. We should check ourselves before we wreck ourselves, because the borderless economy is actual, not optional, and we will constantly be challenged on issues that address our terms of trade.

FOREIGN AID IN THE NEW WORLD ORDER
BY JULIANNE MALVEAUX

Like every other form of government spending, foreign aid is on the chopping block. We spent $13.57 billion in foreign aid in fiscal year 1994, and have appropriated $13.68 billion to spend in FY 1995, though Congress may cut some of that amount in the next few months. In December, Senator Mitch McConnell (R-Ky.) submitted a proposal that would cut foreign aid further, to about $11 billion in FY 1996. The cuts would be accomplished by moving the Agency for International Development (AID) and the Peace Corps into the State Department, and by eliminating budget allocations for Africa, for population, for the InterAmerican Development Fund and the Africa Development Foundation. Also eliminated would be the InterAmerican Development Bank, the African Development Bank, and the Asian Development Bank. United Nations agencies, including UNICEF, would also get smaller appropriations.

Senator McConnell is among those who would terminate aid to developing countries where U.S. assistance has "shown no results." Instead, foreign aid would be awarded on a competitive basis for countries whose growth rates are high and whose incomes are on the rise. Among those countries affected would be the African countries, both because their low growth rates contrast poorly with the double-digit growth rates of places like Thailand, and because those countries have been depicted as those where U.S. assistance has "shown no results."

The move to place the Peace Corps in the State Department also has implications for the African continent, where nearly a third of all Peace Corps volunteers work. Internationally, the Peace Corps is seen as a "do good" agency with little, if any, political agenda. The State Department, on the other hand, has a clear political agenda, and is sometimes perceived as a hotbed of covert action. Peace Corps volunteers that are filtered through the State Department might be seen as less benign than current Peace Corps volunteers.

Senator McConnell's proposals are full of contradictions. He would remove the earmark to Africa (which is about $800 million), but would create an earmark for new Eastern European countries. He would maintain the level of military aid to Israel and Egypt at some $5 billion, which would constitute nearly half of the total foreign aid budget. Nearly a billion dollars would be spent on trade and export promotion, giving our foreign aid, if you want to call it that, a distinctly commercial cast. We'll be involved in countries if there are strong lobbies to force our involvement (like the Israel lobby), or if our involvement pays off.

African Americans, among others, have rallied around the elimination of the Africa appropriation. The Constituency for Africa, an umbrella group of some 150 African American organizations, mobilized hundreds of people to an early February meeting where Ambassador Andrew Young, Congressional Black Caucus Chairman Donald Payne, and others talked about the importance of aid to Africa, especially in terms of the continent's economic development. Responding to allegations that money spent on Africa to date has "shown no results," CFA President Melvin Foote noted that money spent before the end of the cold war was strategically spent in response to the Soviet presence in Africa. That money was less for development than for countering the Soviet presence, and it should be viewed as such, Foote reminded me.

Jesse Helms and Mitch McConnell have public opinion on their side, though. Most people question our foreign aid expenditures, even though they think we spend much more than we do on foreign aid. Polls show that people think we spend 20 cents out of every federal dollar on foreign aid, but we actually spend just one cent of every dollar on assistance to other countries. Some argue that even that one cent is too much if the spending doesn't relate to this country's bottom line.

The challenge in the "new world order" is to make a case for aid to countries in Africa, and to suggest that the market-driven approach to foreign aid isn't necessarily the most effective one. The isolationist tendency in Congress, reflected in ways we would reduce our participation in the United Nations, seems to demand a new rationale for our international involvement. Those who come together to protest cuts to African aid have to do more than appeal to the conscience of an isolationist Congress. They have to talk about a "new world order" approach to foreign aid that views every part of the world as worthy of assistance. And they have to talk about assistance in terms of investment, about development as the return on investment.

King Features Syndicate, February 10, 1995

WHO IS KILLING AFRICA?
BY JULIANNE MALVEAUX

I generally don't expect much from the *New Republic*, a magazine whose long-gone liberal leanings have been replaced by neoconservative attacks on

African Americans, feminists, and anyone else with a brain. One of *NR*'s more disgraceful articles was an inaccurate and poorly constructed attack on Harvard Professor Charles Ogletree; another was a weak attack on the black reporters of the *Washington Post*. In both cases, unattributed whining quotes by whites clearly envious of black folk were featured parts of the essays. Well, I don't expect much from the *New Republic*.

Still, so little Western press commentary is focused on Africa that I had to pick up (not buy, you understand, just pick up at the U.S. Air Shuttle where all kinds of magazines are free) the issue titled "Africa is Dying." The photograph on the cover of the magazine is a riveting picture of a tiny child and a larger child, or perhaps parent, wrapped in a sheet, with a pot on her head, and a bundle of belongings on her back. The set of articles includes nostalgia from Henry Louis Gates, scolding from the self-hating Keith Richberg (a *Washington Post* reporter whose book, *Out of Africa*, confesses a warped gratitude for slavery), and other writing. The *New Republic*'s Africa writing is tied together by a condemnation of African politics as they currently exist, and by an acceptance of the economic inequality imposed by a colonizing West and unaddressed to this day.

I agree with the *New Republic* writers on some of the African politics matters, but I fault them for ignoring the origins of corrupt African politics. Mobutu fled Zaire with his fortune intact, but who installed Mobutu and propped him up as long as it was convenient? As long as the African continent was a pawn in the power game between the United States and the former Soviet Union, dictators were well supported, their oppressive regimes protected by their status on the chessboard. Now that the stakes are different, and neither the United States nor the former Soviet Union wants to play chess, some are looking at Africa as a lost and dying continent. The *New Republic* has asserted that Africa is dying. They avoid the question, though, of who is killing Africa.

Take Nigeria as an example. There are no excuses to be made about the awful human rights violations in Nigeria, the brutal hanging of Ken Saro-Wiwa, the illegal incarceration of President Abiola, and the failure of the Abacha regime to call for elections. Wole Sonyika has been among those who have written about the travesty that Nigeria has become. The unwritten part of the story, though, is the role that Shell Oil has played in all of this. The rape of Ogoniland by Shell is at the root of the hanging of Ken Saro-Wiwa, but Shell was there before independence, a guest of the Brits. Shell was there, and Britain collected oil royalties for years, and after they collected royalties they chose despots to collect royalties. Much of the conflict in Nigeria has been about oil extraction, its costs and benefits. If Nigeria has become a travesty, Shell Oil and Great Britain have blood on their hands.

To be sure, Shell Oil did not make anyone hang Ken Saro-Wiwa. Shell Oil simply demanded certain conditions so that they could continue to extract oil and pay off despots. The people of Nigeria have realized little, and the Ogoni people, whose living conditions have deteriorated because of the oil extraction taking place on their land, have realized even less. It amazes me that the *New Republic* can devote an issue to Africa dying without dealing with some of the structural economic issues contributing to the "death."

The economy is directly addressed in an article on South Africa. Here, Peter Beinart writes that there is no revolutionary transformation in South Africa. Instead, he asserts, there has been an acceptance of economic inequality. If Cape Town, South Africa is successful in getting the 2004 Olympic Games, Beinart says, this represents a victory for the white elite in South Africa, the elite who is likely to profit directly from the Olympic Games. They'll be the vendors and the hoteliers, while black South Africans will be as locked out of the process of Olympic economic development as they have been locked out of the "revolution" that Beinart says didn't happen.

As distasteful as Beinart's conclusions are, they are at the crux of the current Western perception of the African continent. Many think black Africans will have to accept second-class status, brokering natural resources and natural infrastructures to get the cooperation of capitalists who have less interest in social development than they do in profit. They point to the very corrupt politics, the instability, the violence, and the refugee problems that come from this, as one of the reasons the African continent is dying. Even if a few countries do well economically, it is asserted, those gains are likely to be attenuated when neighboring countries experience instability and refugee populations cross borders.

One of the problems with this perspective, though, is the assumption that there will be no interventions in the current state of affairs. This assumption is troubling when it is considered in the context of the 50th anniversary of the Marshall Plan, the multibillion dollar welfare program that the United States designed for Western Europe in the wake of World War II. Without the Marshall Plan, we might well have been reading articles about the demise of Europe, but we were determined to make sure Europe not only survived, but thrived. Now, the countries we once restored are our key economic competitors. Is this why there has been no Marshall Plan for Africa, just the World Bank interference in African affairs, and the structural adjustment programs that have contributed to the erosion of the stock of African resources?

An African Marshall plan should certainly not enrich the continent's scoundrels, the Mobutus and Abachas that have extracted both money and pain from their people. But a Marshall plan might help move Africa to the 21st century. The United States and the former Soviet Union are not the only ones who need to contribute to this Marshall plan. Every European country with colonial ties to the African continent ought provide reparations for the suffering they have caused. If Africa is dying, the murderers are colonialists who struck a set of fatal blows some 30 years ago, then sat back to watch a continent writhe in the pain imposed by imperialism.

When the former G-7 meets in Denver on June 20 to talk about Africa, they need to talk about their role in destroying a mighty continent, and about the development of an African Marshall plan, not just trade relations. And they need to talk about African participation at their meeting. Otherwise, the so-called Summit of 8 (the G-7 plus Russia) is no better than that cabal of colonialists, a century or so ago, who met in Europe to divide the African continent up for their own exploitation.

San Francisco Sun Reporter, June 3, 1997

THE GLOBAL ECONOMY THROUGH BRAZILIAN EYES
BY JULIANNE MALVEAUX

President Clinton won Congressional approval for NAFTA four years ago by alternately cajoling and strong-arming individual members of Congress for their votes. He pulled NAFTA off with a narrow vote, and after nearly giving away the company store. Last week, though, he learned that the company store was not enough to give, and that strong-arm tactics don't always work. By describing "fast track" as a "no-brainer" he offended so many members of his own party that only 50 were willing to support him. In the end, the fast-track legislation didn't come up for a vote because the President wasn't willing to risk public defeat. Meanwhile, though, he made major concessions on the way the 2000 Census will be counted, and on other pieces of legislation.

Labor was among those to see the fast-track defeat as a victory, but labor wasn't the only faction that fought fast track. Environmentalists, protectionists, and others were reluctant to give the President the authority to negotiate trade treaties that they could only vote up or down, without having the opportunity to have input on those details that the President has been so oblivious to, details like environmental safety, fair and safe labor standards, and other key issues. One of the people who opposed the fast track to increased poverty was Brazilian Senator Benedita da Silva. In the United States to promote her new book, *Benedita da Silva: An Afro-Brazilian Woman's Story of Politics and Love* (Food First Books, 1997), this first Afro-Brazilian woman to become a Senator in that nation's Congress offered scathing observations about the globalization of the economy. She sees some of the international monetary authorities as mere handmaidens to the interests of developed countries to keep developing countries as colonies. The International Monetary Fund and the World Bank, says da Silva, tell poor countries that they must follow a set of "open" policies to get loans. "It is an economic model that reverses the efforts made by many Third World nations in the 1960s and 1970s to create domestic industries," she writes.

I had the privilege of meeting Benedita da Silva when she traveled to Washington, D.C. this week to talk about the struggle for the rights of Brazil's disenfranchised communities, about poverty, race, and gender in her country. A product of the favelas of Rio de Janeiro, da Silva made political history with her role in founding the Workers' Party, her election as the nation's first black city councilwoman, and her election as Senator. Her legislative thrust has been to improve the status of those at the periphery, especially farmers and domestic workers. Thanks to her, the lowest-paid workers in Brazil now enjoy minimum wages, paid vacation, maternity leave, and retirement benefits.

Because she is a "voice for the voiceless," da Silva has become astute about ways the global economic system has the potential to put workers at a disadvantage. "I don't believe in total globalization," she told me. "With growth, governments must also implement projects that address people's needs." Her opposition to fast-track legislation was rooted in her concern for working people and the damage they might experience with trade agreements that ignore their interests.

Her concerns are based on some trade realities. "Brazil has been trying to build a high-tech sector—computers, satellites, biotechnology, optics—but it has been under pressure from the United States for years to stop protecting its high-tech industry and open up to U.S. exports. Meanwhile the U.S. government has heavily subsidized its own high-tech industry by providing billions in research. In the 1990s Brazil caved in to U.S. pressure to stop protecting its computer industry and since then the imports have flooded in. When the rich countries tell us to open our markets, they are saying 'do as I say, not as I do.' From my point of view what they really want is open access to our markets and resources so they can continue to profit at our expense."

Da Silva has a point. We export more to Brazil than they export to us. We sent $11.9 billion worth of goods and services to Brazil in 1996, while we bought $9.3 billion of their exports. Mostly we bought manufactured goods, like refrigerator and auto parts and components. We cut our labor costs down by buying these goods and services in Brazil, and in exchange we constrain them from developing local industries so that they can export fully manufactured products to us and to other countries.

Benedita da Silva has written an autobiography with compelling economic content. Once a worker and a domestic, she has emerged as an advocate for the rights of workers. Her journey from the favela to the Brazilian Congress has given her a unique perspective on the global economy. She advocates forming regional trading blocs (such as the Mercosur between Brazil, Argentina, Uruguay and Paraguay), and renegotiating the foreign debt. But most importantly, she advocates protecting the interest of workers and of the poor. Bill Clinton could take a lesson from Benedita da Silva.

King Features Syndicate, November 14, 1997

FASTING FOR JUSTICE IN HAITI
BY JULIANNE MALVEAUX

Randall Robinson ought to be in South Africa right now. Executive Director of the foreign policy advocacy and lobbying organization TransAfrica, Robinson has worked closely with Nelson Mandela and African National Congress leaders. One of the first to be arrested outside the South African embassy in Washington, D.C., Robinson was also pivotal in bringing groups of African Americans to South Africa to observe conditions there. By any account Robinson ought to be celebrating a hard-won victory in the South African vote.

Instead, as black South Africans went to vote, Robinson entered the third week of his fast to protest our country's policy toward Haiti. He says he will fast "as long as refugee policy is what it is." "The policy of automatic repatriation is both cruel and racist," Robinson said. "The administration has to pay attention to the tide of public opinion, to the notion of morality." The day after Robinson spoke of morality, President William Jefferson Clinton was carousing at the White House correspondents' dinner, making jokes about his Whitewater fiasco. Is there a bell up there, and how does one ring it? How does a nation signal our President that carousing while another man is starving for his convictions is somehow inappropriate? Who will signal that the treatment of Haitians is something central, not peripheral? Randall Robinson has taken that challenge with his fast, and yet it will take more than a fast to move our President and public policy in the right direction.

When Haitians attempt to come to the United States they are spurned at our borders, automatically repatriated. Sending them home is like conspiring in their death, punishing their audacity with sanctions. Says Robinson, "The Clinton administration is on the wrong side of this matter. They are complicit in the killing of Haitian people."

Since six members of the Congress got arrested to protest the administration's Haiti policy, the Clinton administration says it is "re-thinking" its policy toward Haiti. This isn't the first time there has been a reconsideration. In the months since he took office Clinton has wavered, waffled and wondered aloud about what to do about Haiti. And while he has done nothing, hundreds of Haitian refugees have been interdicted by the Coast Guard. Since the September 1991 coup, more than 42,000 Haitians fled the island by boat and were interdicted by the Navy. The flow of refugees dropped in 1993, perhaps because Haitians hoped that President Aristide would be restored to power. Still, more than 2,300 Haitians were interdicted last year. People are still risking their lives because of repressive conditions in Haiti.

Contrast the treatment of Haitians with the treatment of Cubans. Haitians are turned back, while Cuban refugees are granted a hearing to see if they have a "well-founded fear of persecution." If such fear is established, they are provided with safe haven. Randall Robinson notes, "There is no accounting for the difference in treatment. No accounting for it, except they are black. If the policy is not racist in intent, it is racist in effect."

It's not just about the refugees. It is also about the democratic situation in Haiti. When Aristide was in power, there were fewer people fleeing the country (only 1,100 were interdicted in 1991). They were committed to their democracy, they had exercised it, and despite economic hardships, they were committed to living in Haiti. Those who brave the high seas now do so because of the repressive environment in the island republic. People are wantonly killed because of their politics, their bodies left on the streets to be, in Robinson's words, "devoured by pigs." The United States and the United Nations say they are helpless to stop the carnage. Whatever happened to sanctions, to the freezing of assets? Or the embargo that many believe will dismantle the military?

A decade ago, when the anti-apartheid movement was at high pitch, skeptics said divestment wouldn't speed elections along. Now, the same arguments are being made about embargoes and Haiti. In risking a hunger strike, Randall Robinson reminds us of the power of conviction. It worked in South Africa, and it can work in Haiti.

King Features Syndicate, April 28, 1994

CUBAN EMBARGO HURTS U.S. BUSINESS
BY JULIANNE MALVEAUX

How can the United States normalize relationships with Vietnam, but continue our long-term embargo against Cuba? How can we ignore human rights violations in China and still offer it most favored nation status, but take a hard line against Cuba? We've partly justified our trade relationships with Vietnam and China because of the size of their markets and the economic benefits that trade brings to the United States. But the Association for Free Trade with Cuba points out that 11 million Cubans in our own hemisphere also represent a marketing and trade opportunity for United States businesses.

If the trade embargo were lifted, trade between the United States and Cuba could range between $2 and $6 billion. United States companies could capture all or part of the $400 million Cuban grain market, supply all or part of Cuba's $150 million in fertilizer needs, sell Cuba $90 million in medical supplies, and become a player in the $500 million tourist industry that attracted half a million tourists in 1993. Before two planes piloted by Brothers to the Rescue were shot down, relations between the United States and Cuba seemed ready to thaw. Many analysts had noted that Cuba is no security threat to the United States, and that the embargo simply makes life harder for the Cuban people. But the Helms-Burton Bill, passed in the wake of international outrage about the deaths of Brothers to the Rescue pilots, tightened the terms of the embargo and made it unlikely that U.S. businesses will trade with Cuba anytime soon.

The Helms-Burton Bill hopes to put so much pressure on the Cuban economy that there will be a social collapse, driving Fidel Castro from power. Part of the reason for the legislation is that at least one United States Senator, still smarting from the Bay of Pigs debacle, sees red at the mere mention of Fidel Castro's name. The Association for Free Trade with Cuba's Tom Miller says the embargo has "rubber teeth biting our own backside" because our harsh actions against Cuba are likely to backfire in the international community. Some provisions of the Helms-Burton Bill would allow lawsuits that impede business relations in Cuba and treating the executives of companies doing business with Cuba as felons. If these provisions are enforced they are likely to draw international ire.

While the United States tightens its embargo against Cuba, businesses in other countries are eager to do business with Cuba. The embargo that was tightened to bring pressure on Cuba will also eliminate opportunities for U.S. businesses. Indeed, because international trade is so pervasive, U.S. products are sometimes available in Cuba, but at higher prices. According to Tom Miller, on the same day that the Helms-Burton legislation passed, Apple computers were made available in Havana by an Italian who identified himself only as "Captain Mac."

The United States may have overreacted to the tragedy of the Brothers to the Rescue pilots. Our petulant refusal to normalize economic relations with Cuba sends a signal and places some pressure on Fidel Castro, but it also cuts United States businesses out of an 11 million person market that has billions of dollars of consumer potential.

King Features Syndicate, March 23, 1996

WHEN WILL WE PAY OUR UN DUES?
BY JULIANNE MALVEAUX

President Clinton has threatened to veto one of the appropriations bills if it cuts our country's ability to provide assistance to developing countries. It's about time someone in leadership began to look at our international role and obligations, to assert that a country as rich as the United States ought not begrudge that small part of GDP that is used to provide international aid. Though most of us think we spend as much as 10 percent of our GDP on foreign aid, just a fraction of 1 percent of GDP is spent for those purposes.

Our antipathy to our foreign citizenship can be seen in our multi-year failure to pay our dues to the United Nations. We have owed the United Nations money since 1982, with our accumulated back dues amounting to over a billion dollars. The situation is so dire that while the UN celebrates its 50th anniversary, it has also placed a freeze on travel for its employees. If the U.S. and other countries who owe back dues don't pay, it is possible that the UN might shut down.

Why don't we pay our UN dues? We stopped paying when Ronald Reagan was President, angered by the anti-U.S. statements that have come from so many developing countries. We linked our non-payment to concern about UN expenditures, and demanded that an independent Inspector General be appointed. The UN responded to our concern by appointing an independent financial authority, though several years after the U.S. initially made the request. UN compliance with the U.S. request has not quickened the dues payment, though. Years after the Inspector General's office was established, our dues are still in arrears.

President George Bush was an Ambassador to the United Nations, but he was not able to persuade Congress to release the money that we owe the United Nations. President Clinton has preached against the isolationism that plagues our country and our Congress, but the matter of UN dues was not a priority in the first two years of his administration. Now he must depend on a hostile Congress to authorize payment of our UN dues, but with Medicare and Medicaid under attack, with education and training funds being cut, is there space in the debate for our UN dues?

There should be. The United Nations does more than provide peacekeeping missions in places like Somalia and Bosnia. The UN also provides literacy training, inoculations and other health services, wells and access to clean water, and an array of other services. This year the United Nations Children's Fund celebrates its 45th year of "Trick or Treat" fundraising in the United States, a program that raises money to provide medicine, vaccines, sanitation, food and basic education for millions of children. As many as 2.5 million children are protected from malnutrition and disease because of UNICEF programs.

On October 23 and 24, nearly 170 heads of state will converge in New York to culminate a year's worth of celebration of the United Nations Fiftieth Anniversary. President Clinton will kick off the commemoration, no doubt talking about world peace, the world community, and the importance of the United Nations. If I were President Clinton, I'd have to squirm a bit upon facing my peers and offering greetings, knowing that my country believes in a world community enough to participate in it, but not strongly enough to help support the world organization that facilitates community.

To be sure, the United States has differences with the United Nations. Are our differences so substantive that we want to see the organization strangled by financial hardship? If our country is sincere about the importance of world community, we ought to pay our delinquent dues to the United Nations.

King Features Syndicate, October 12, 1995

SPOTLIGHT ON AFRICAN GROWTH AND TRADE
BY JULIANNE MALVEAUX

In the international trade arena, the spotlight has been focused on the Pacific Rim, with special attention on the most favored nation (MFN) trading status that China currently enjoys. Buoyed by revelations that prison labor has been used to produce a number of China's exports, a coalition of lawmakers and labor, religious and conservative groups has joined forces to oppose the renewal of that country's MFN status. The coalition joins the left and the right, focusing on China's policies on human rights, labor rights, religious rights, trade and abortion. The issue of MFN status is important because the ability to export goods to the United States on favored terms has a positive impact on China's economic development.

While the issue of China's status remains unresolved, some legislators have suggested that we shift the spotlight to the African continents, where economic development needs are as critical as in China, if not more so. This week several members of Congress announced their support for HR 1432, the African Growth and Opportunity Act, which creates an American policy that helps qualified sub-Saharan African countries move from development assistance to economic self-reliance. Nations who benefit from HR 1432 must be committed to economic growth, political reform, market incentives, and private sector growth. The legislation has bipartisan support, and the sponsorship of 31 members of Congress, including 19 members of the Congressional Black Caucus.

This was a good week for Congress to talk about African trade. In Harare, Zimbabwe, 600 business leaders and 110 policy makers met during the regional South African Economic Summit to talk about ways countries can work together to compete in the world market. Leaders of the 12-nation South African Development Community (SADC) have agreed to develop a free trade zone and to move toward regional economic integration. The SADC is chaired by South African President Nelson Mandela, and includes participation from Angola, Botswana, Mozambique, Namibia, Tanzania, Zambia, and Zimbabwe.

At the Harare conference, the International Monetary Fund indicated the progress Africa has made toward economic stability. Growth has risen from a scant 1 percent in 1992, to a healthy 5.5 percent in 1996, and inflation levels have been falling in most sub-Saharan African countries. Both trends are expected to continue, as is the extent to which African countries have reduced their account deficit. Sponsors of HR 1432 have been mindful of these trends. Congressman Charles

Rangel (D-N.Y.) noted that Africa's potential may be as great as that of China. "The United States needs the whole world" with which to trade, Rangel noted at a May press conference.

Growth rates have been cited as one of the reasons that our country has been interested in trade with China. Now, growth on the African continent exceeds that in the United States. Thus, the HR 1432 push to end quotas on textiles from parts of Africa, to develop a free trade area, and to establish a U.S.-Africa Economic Forum are timely.

The G-7 countries, plus Russia, will meet in Denver, Colorado on June 20-22 to discuss, among other things, trade relations with Africa. Unfortunately, the "Summit of Eight" excludes participation by African trade and economic ministers, such as South Africa's Trevor Manuel. Africa will be on the agenda, then, but not at the table. Denver Mayor Wellington Webb is ensuring that there will be some dialogue from those who have Africa as a primary interest with a "Town Hall Meeting on Africa" that he is convening a week before the Summit of Eight. Cosponsored by the University of Denver and the Constituency for Africa, the meeting will examine aspects of HR 1432, and also explore themes that the Summit of Eight must consider if they are serious about African trade.

HR 1432 represents a shift in the way members of Congress are viewing the African continent. Motivated, perhaps, by the First Lady's recent visit, and further impelled by positive developments in the African economy, this legislation represents an understanding of those current legislative realities that focus on self-sufficiency instead of traditionally granted foreign aid. While this economically motivated approach is appropriate for these times, structural deficiencies in the African economy evidenced by low savings rates and dependence on foreign aid also merit our attention. If African development had as high a priority as the development of the former Soviet Union, then HR 1432 would be a very different piece of legislation, and an African leader would be seated with former G-7, which perhaps ought to be the Summit of Nine.

King Features Syndicate, May 12, 1997

WILL HISTORIC JOURNEY HAVE A LEGACY?

BY JULIANNE MALVEAUX

I have been amazed at the paucity of commentary on President Clinton's historic twelve-day trip to the African continent. Instead of conversation and analysis on the substance of the trip, we have seen a recalcitrant bevy of white male pundits whine that the President has done too much apologizing for racism, for slavery, for the unequal treatment of Africa in the world policy market. The fact is that the President has never apologized, merely expressed regrets for untenable situations. But the broader fact is that fixation on the trivia of an almost apology has sidetracked more serious analysis of the implications of this trip to Africa.

From where I sit, our nation's attempt to embrace the theme of "trade not aid" is an international version of our domestic "welfare reform." You will work for your economic relationship with the United States, authors like Congressman Philip Crane (R-Ill.) are telling African countries. There is no free lunch.

Many African countries support the "trade not aid" focus, figuring aid hasn't exactly been forthcoming anyway. Since the Republican "Contract on America," aid to the African continent has dropped from more than $800 million to just about $700 million. (Meanwhile, aid to Israel has grown and is more than $4 billion.) For some African leaders, HR 1432 is the only train leaving the station. Accustomed to being sidelined by the United States and ignored in both foreign diplomatic and economic policy, many feel that even the paternalistic attention that comes from this legislation is better than no attention at all. Others feel that the "conditionals" that are imposed in HR 1432 are inevitable nudges toward "free market" economic organization (as well as conditions sometimes imposed by international monetary groups like the World Bank and the International Monetary Fund) and that they might as well go with the flow.

But South Africa has not been enthusiastic about HR 1432, nor especially flattered by our country's attention. Some South Africans might argue they have been the focus of our nation's attention long enough, with the policy of "constructive engagement" unnecessarily prolonging the grip that the apartheid regime had on South Africa. In any case, an interesting feature of the President's trip has been South Africa's insistence on a peer relationship, something that leaders in other countries had neither the political nor economic autonomy to insist on.

There is another aspect of the Clinton trip that many have ignored. The cornerstone of this President's domestic economic policy is international trade.

American expansion depends on our ability to sell goods and services to other countries. "Trade not aid" is a mantra for us as much as it is for Africa. To the extent that African economies improve, we benefit because rising per capita GDP on the African continent means an increased demand for goods and services exported by the United States.

Currently, the United States sells $10.6 billion worth of goods and services to countries on the African continent. We buy $18.7 billion worth of goods and services from Africa. Our balance of trade with Africa is an $8.1 billion deficit. When African countries have greater means to purchase our goods and services, that deficit narrows and we gain from African trade. That's why it is in the United States' interest to build infrastructure, to develop the telecommunications industry, and to attempt to move Africa toward "currency normalization" and "free markets."

The countries most likely to purchase U.S. goods are those which are both most industrialized and with highest per capita GDP levels—Egypt, South Africa, Nigeria, Algeria, and Morocco. The goods most frequently purchased are cereals, industrial machinery, aircraft and ships, arms, and road vehicles. Africa sends oil, metals, clothing, spices, minerals and gems to the United States. While U.S. trade with Africa is a mere 2 percent of all of its trade, some of our imports from Africa make a key difference in our economic vitality.

Economic focus notwithstanding, this Africa trip has enormous symbolic and cultural significance. That is why, perhaps, the President has such a large delegation accompanying him. Three cabinet secretaries, several assistant secretaries, more than a dozen members of Congress, a coterie of corporate executives, and others, including Rev. Jesse Jackson and NAACP President Kweisi Mfume, have all joined the President not only because this trip has economic significance, but because this is the first time a President of the United States has taken the time and focused such attention on Africa. At the same time, we need to understand, this is not just about apologies and cultural significance, but also about economics. This historic trip will leave no legacy if all we remember are the speeches, not the way that economic relationships will be altered.

King Features Syndicate, April 1, 1998

CHAPTER 8

FUTURE, FEAR, UNCHARTED FRONTIER: CHILDREN, YOUTH AND EDUCATION

Do you know the song, "The Greatest Love of All"? The song is sappy and allows a singer to show off her vocal cords. Whether it is Al Jarreau or Whitney Houston crooning, the words "I believe that children are the future" resonate. They are rhetoric!

We keep saying we believe that children are our future, but do we really believe that? At home and abroad, we abuse children in the labor market, ignore them in the classroom, attack them because of their music. Are we frightened of our children? Of the technology they master more easily than we do? Of their language? Do we act out our fear, and what do our actions mean for our own futures?

Some call our youngsters "the lost generation," but who lost them, and how? Aren't they, instead, a reflection of our own confusion and chaos? And can't we gain inspiration from the most resilient of our youngsters, those who thrive despite horrific pasts?

If there are lost children, did we lose them in our indifference to providing quality education for every child? Instead of committing ourselves to the notion that every child can learn, too many who make policy would categorize children as either worthy or unworthy. Frighteningly, the children we now categorize will support us in our old age. What if they have the right to categorize us as deserving or not, worthy or not, able to access resources or not?

CHILD LABOR ABUSE AT HOME AND ABROAD
BY JULIANNE MALVEAUX

International child labor horrors made headlines when television talk-show diva Kathie Lee Gifford was accused of using sweatshop labor in Honduras and New York City to produce a line of Wal-Mart clothing that featured her name. A tearful Gifford said that the last thing she would ever do is harm children, and bashed the media for making the matter a big news item. Her tears were scant balm for the horrors that child workers endure while producing her clothing, but Gifford is partly right in taking the media on. If writers are concerned with child labor abuses, they need not leave our nation's borders to catalog the violations. In the United States, children work in sweatshops, factories and fields. Youngsters who ought to be in school are pressed into service, sometimes being maimed or killed as a result of their work.

To be sure, the United States is no developing country. Worldwide more than 73 million 10-to-14-year-old children work full-time in mines, glass factories and other dangerous places. In this country, child labor laws protect most but not all children. Immigrant children are most frequently unprotected, working in fields and in sweatshops despite laws that restrict the number of hours and the conditions of work for youngsters under 16. The other form of flagrant violation is the long hours of teen workers in the United States. Despite laws that restrict the number of hours that teens can work, many hold full-time jobs and their schoolwork suffers for it. Sometimes fatigue and overwork mean that their bodies suffer as well.

The National Institute for Occupational Safety and Health (NIOSH) estimates that, in 1993, working youth sustained 21,620 injuries and illnesses serious enough to result in time off the job; 64,000 were so seriously injured that they had to be treated in hospital emergency rooms. Experts estimate that more than three times as many youth as were seen in emergency rooms were hurt on the job. This means that as many as 200,000 youngsters are hurt in the workplace annually! Young workers had higher injury rates than their adult counterparts, and 68 died from workplace injuries in 1994.

How are young people hurt at work? NIOSH says most are hurt working in or around motor vehicles, operating tractors or other heavy equipment, working near electrical hazards, falling from roofs, ladders, or other structures, cooking and working around cooking appliances, and lifting heavy weights. Although the law explicitly prevents youth involvement in some of these enterprises, employers often disregard the law, sometimes with fatal consequences.

Domestic child labor abuses are hardly as titillating as international child labor abuses. It is much more interesting and outrageous to read of the 8-year-old employed in a glass factory, the 10-year-old weaving rugs, or the 12-year-old doing piecework than to learn about the 15-year-old whose incapacitating third-degree burn happened at a local eatery. But if we say we care so much about child labor abuses that some are considering a boycott of international imports produced with child labor, then we ought to care enough to take a long, hard look at our own backyard.

Taking stock at home doesn't let celebrities like Kathie Lee Gifford and Michael Jordan off the hook. Both pleaded ignorance when they learned that clothes bearing their names were manufactured by youngsters. Next time around, these celebrities and others will know enough to ask about the terms and conditions of work for the people who earn cents an hour to help them make millions. Gifford, Jordan, and others can redeem themselves, though, by making the point that child labor abuses don't just happen in Honduras. The abuse may be as close to home as your last fast-food sandwich.

King Features Syndicate, June 14, 1998

THE ANXIOUS OPTIMISTS
BY JULIANNE MALVEAUX

Whatever. The word is like a gauntlet thrown down between my generation and theirs, a word that embodies all of their ambivalence of their situation. Whatever. I don't know, don't care, don't want to find out. It is what is. Whatever.

I first encountered the whatever generation (also known as Generation X) when one of them came to work for me. She was self-directed, bright, and with a chip on her shoulder the size of a tree. She had the job that she would do in mind, no matter the description, a map of boundaries set, no matter the requirements. She wielded no ax when you crossed her line, only that shrug and utterly distancing word. Whatever.

For the longest time I thought this young gifted and black woman was some kind of an anomaly. But a recent poll suggests she is typical of her generation.

Supremely self-confident, but also cognizant of the world and all its flaws. Prepared to do better than her parents, but by climbing a ladder that lacks some of the traditional rungs. Prepared to tackle the world, but not through politics or civic affairs. Instead, through a self-defined involvement that challenges conventional civic activity.

Youth Voices is a project of the Washington, D.C.-based Center for Policy Alternatives. Through focus groups and polling, CPA hopes to identify the common dreams and concerns of those 18-to-24-year-olds who vote at half the rate of the general population and communicate more cynicism at the political process than the most grizzled pundit. More than a thousand youth were sampled nationwide, and they responded to questions with a shrug and that whatever word, a word that communicates indifference, concern and ambivalence, optimism and pessimism, and the confidence that their voice is important, misunderstood, and yet vital. Indeed, three-quarters of the "whatevers" who responded to the Youth Voices poll said they felt both misunderstood and underestimated. Yet their unwillingness to engage in traditional political expressions (just 13 percent volunteered for a political candidate or party, compared to 87 percent who worked through a church or religious organization) compounds their underestimation.

Youth voices echo American voices when they focus on economic security, health care, and employment. They are wiser than our majority voices when they acknowledge the strains that racism and discrimination place on our society. They are more cautious than the rest of us when they bring issues of personal security home, voicing opinions about crime and punishment that are, frankly, unyielding and conservative. They are ahead of the curve when they focus on issues of business ownership as a way to balance that precocious optimism with national economic realities.

As I read the results of the Youth Voices poll, I was startled at the image that I had of a young person, determined to make her way despite the odds. My image was of a young person who knew which cards to hold and which to fold, which images to trust and which to discard. The Youth voice seems aware of every hurdle one will need to clear, and undaunted by the prospect of that clearing. These youth say they trust government to provide education, economic security, and other perquisites, but while they trust they do not rely. So they straddle the fence between anxiety and optimism, wondering which way the wind will blow for them. The Center for Policy Alternatives has captured the ambivalence of this youth voice with their poll, the bravado of young people who say they can fly, combined with the sober reality of accepting clipped wings.

These anxious optimists are the children of Labor Secretary Robert Reich's anxious class. Uncertain. Unsure. Hopeful. Whatever.

King Features Syndicate, May 10, 1996

CHRISTOPHER WALLACE: R.I.P.
BY JULIANNE MALVEAUX

Christopher Wallace was twenty-four years old when he was gunned down in a drive-by shooting in Los Angeles. It didn't have to happen in Los Angeles, it could have happened in Detroit or San Francisco, in Atlanta or Washington, D.C. Unfortunately, too many young African American men are locked in a fatal embrace with death, an embrace that has roots in the braggadocian flirtation that idealizes street life and street death as the essence of cool.

If Christopher Wallace were anybody other than "the Notorious B.I.G.," also known as Biggie Smalls, his death would be a minor tragedy with limited ripple effects. His family and friends would weep and moan at an emotion-charged funeral that focused on the shortness of his life. His preacher would pull out a set of well-worn platitudes that might have no relationship to the life that the deceased led and talk about the ways that everything happens for a reason. Unless Christopher Wallace had distinguished himself in some way, his death, like that of thousands of other young black men, might merit no more public attention than a line or two in the obituary section of his local newspaper.

But Biggie Smalls' death merits headlines because he was a noted entertainer who may have been part of a fatal bicoastal feud that claimed his rival, Tupac Shakur, scant months ago. His death has sparked a flurry of commentary about the fast life and craven images that many of the "gangsta" rappers have worshiped, the way these young men seem so uncannily to predict their own deaths. The tragedy is that the lives squandered in the headlines and on screen are an eerie reflection of equally valuable but unheralded lives, squandered in the streets. The tragedy here is that this "rap feud," if it is indeed that, is the most pernicious form of black-on-black crime. Whatever its cause, the outcomes are tragic.

I don't understand this thing about young men and machismo, about the "dissing" that can earn one a death sentence, and the "colors" that can cause a crisis. I wonder if the embracing of street life is, perhaps, a reaction to the fact that young black men are often unwelcome in other avenues of life, that when they find doors shut to them in classrooms and corporate settings, they revert to the familiar "hood" with all its limitations. I am also reminded that the majority of young black men are not gangsta rappers, and that many who get caught by drive-by bullets weren't villains, but victims, young brothers who simply got caught in the wrong place at the wrong time.

Biggie Smalls may have danced a slow drag with death, but Christopher Wallace could have had a life. The headlines that speak to "Biggie's" death treat it as an inevitability. What interventions might it have taken to save Christopher's life?

USA Today, March 13, 1997

TECHNOLOGY: NECESSARY, NOT SUFFICIENT FOR PARITY
BY JULIANNE MALVEAUX

It is five in the morning and night is fading into dawn. I am in my favorite place at my favorite time, hunched over my computer before day in the morning, stringing together sentences in the same way that a child string beads on thread, trying to make sense and create resonance from words. I could do this, I suppose, with a pen and a yellow pad. Indeed, twenty years ago, I did. Now, my fingers bend to the keyboard and resist writing more than a few paragraphs by pen. Technology has set me free from scraps of paper and ink-stained fingers, but it has also yoked me to a laptop and electronic adapter that I carry almost everywhere.

Technology has transformed the way we write, think, communicate, and learn. We've speeded up communications, have access to more information, and depend on precious microchips that, like so many other resources in our society, are unevenly distributed. There is a racial technology gap that has momentous implications for educational attainment and workplace readiness in the future.

A 1995 report of the Department of Education indicated that black and brown children are 30 percent less likely than white children to have Internet access computers in their classrooms. Even when computers are available in schools, the ratio of students to computers is nearly twice as high in inner-city schools than in suburbs, where some classrooms may have as many as a dozen computers. Further, black and brown students are also only a third as likely as white students to have computers at home. At the periphery of the computer revolution, both at home and at school, where are these young people likely to be in the 21st-century workplace?

If computer literacy will be as necessary as basic literacy in the future, what kind of futures will those without computer access have? While some Americans are speeding down the superhighway with modems that connect to the Internet at faster and faster rates, others are traveling on an unpaved side road in broken-down jalopies, or even on foot, as far removed from the superhighway as they will be from the workforce of the future. But it is important to ask if computers are a necessary condition to productive workforce futures. I believe that the technology gap will dictate part, but not all, of the educational and workforce future for disadvantaged youth.

In other words, computers are not a panacea. There's much educational content, but also lots of junk, on the Internet. Some of the youngsters who have computers at home use them to enhance their schoolwork, while others are busy in chat rooms or game rooms, engaged in a sophisticated form of leisure. Computer access is key, but basic skills and literacy are equally important. The inner-city schools that lack Internet access computers need the same resources as computer-wired suburban schools have. But every school needs skilled and committed teachers to teach basic literacy and mathematics. Every school needs a writing program that helps youngsters express themselves concisely. Students need to learn history and civics, in addition to reading, writing, and arithmetic, and their schools need the resources to teach these subjects.

There aren't enough books to go around in some inner-city schools, and teachers are copying pages for each day's lesson to compensate for that. There aren't enough teachers to go around in schools that crowd more than 30 to a classroom. Safety is as pressing an issue on some high school campuses as computer access. Because schools are funded with property taxes, inner-city schools spend fewer dollars per pupil than suburban schools do. Some say that throwing money at educational problems is an ineffective way of closing gaps, but a few more dollars would go a long way toward closing the resource gap.

The Congressional Black Caucus has made access to technology a priority, not only for students but also for a community that experiences the technology gap. Imagine the access that many will gain if there are storefront computer centers, computers in libraries, and in other places. Imagine how the lives of homeless people or those without telephones are improved with an e-mail address! There are many reasons that technology must be made more accessible and available to a wider audience.

Teachers, too, have found ways to use technology to enhance teaching, teamwork, and learning. Although it seems counterintuitive, some researchers have suggested that computers can even be a tool in cooperative and collaborative learning. For example, one education researcher, Simon Hooper, assistant professor of education at the University of Minnesota, has found that cooperative grouping actually improves computer-based learning. Students can work effectively together around computers in small groups, he found, enhancing both interpersonal and group skills as well as computer skills. Those who study the impact of technology on education have found a range of other benefits from the use of computers in the classroom.

My point—computers and technology can certainly improve most students' skills. Computer literacy is often a workplace requirement. But closing the technology gap will not close the educational, employment, and economic gap. Technology is a necessary but not sufficient tool for parity.

We still need committed and competent teachers. We still need adequate classroom materials, including those rudimentary antiques like books, paper, pens, and laboratory equipment. Inner-city schools need the same extracurricular programs that other schools have. And inner-city students need to get off the campus with field trips to museums and other community resources.

Our focus on technology should not blind us to the other inequities that so many African American students experience in the educational process. Even as we struggle to close the technology gap, we should understand that the gap is a symptom of a broader set of societal inequalities.

Black Issues in Higher Education, May 9, 1997

MARCH MADNESS DISTORTS CLASSROOM REALITY
BY JULIANNE MALVEAUX

When people start talking about "March Madness," spring is clearly in the air. If not the fresh scent of new flowers, the stench of old gym socks is evidence that the seasons are changing. Sixty-four college basketball teams were selected to compete their way to the "Final Four" tournament to be held this year in Charlotte, North Carolina. For most, March Madness is nothing but an overdose of basketball. For me, the madness is not basketball, but the incongruity that so many black male collegians can represent their universities as athletes. If as many, proportionately, starred in the classroom as on the basketball court, the notion that black men are an "endangered species" might easily be countered.

I don't use that "endangered species" language because it strikes me as exaggerated, unreal and passive. To describe black men as a species different from the rest of the human species seems to rob us all of our essential humanity. If the black man is endangered, so are the rest of us. And it isn't about species, it's about politics. Endangered species suggests a passivity, as if the plight of the black man is "in the air" somewhere. Rodney King lay down and was hit by 56 blows that were unconnected to human hands. Black male matriculation rates simply "went down," unconnected to poverty, joblessness, and uneven law enforcement. Black men can slam-dunk basketballs but not SAT scores because the stench of gym socks, not number 2 pencils, is in the air. Isn't there something wrong with these assertions?

Let's look at differences between the basketball court and the classroom. At the University of Arizona, African Americans are just 2 percent of total enrollment, but 62 percent of the basketball team. The University of Arkansas team is 87 percent African American; just 6 percent of those who matriculate at that campus are African American. At Boston College, my alma mater, 67 percent of the Sweet Sixteen team is black, compared to just 4 percent of the students enrolled. Michigan, Duke, Missouri, Syracuse, Purdue and Tulsa all reflect the same pattern. Fewer than 10 percent of the students enrolled are African American, but more than half of those on winning teams are black. In a couple of cases—University of Louisville (12 percent) and University of Maryland (11 percent)—black enrollment is more than 10 percent. In a couple other cases—Indiana University (33 percent) and University of Kansas (43 percent)—the basketball team is less than half black. Even in these cases, the ratio between black participation on the basketball court and in the classroom is more than 8 to 1. At Arkansas and Connecticut, the ratio is as high as 15 to 1.

Is it easier to find hoopsters than scholars? Or do coaches simply have more resources than college recruiters? What kinds of compromises can be worked out for ballplayers that don't apply for regular students? And does the issue of basketball revenue play a role in the way hoopsters (instead of scholars) are treated?

Whatever the case, a simple look at the composition of NCAA teams suggests that campuses like Arizona, Florida, Louisville, and Marquette are hospitable environments for black students. One might even use the teams as video recruiters for the schools. But a student accepted at the University of Florida or Purdue is in for a rude awakening if he thinks the campus looks anything like the basketball team. At Florida, only 6 percent of those enrolled are African American; at Purdue, the number is only 8 percent.

A recent report from the American Council on Education reflects the fact that classroom happenings are very different from those on the basketball courts. Of the million-plus bachelor's degrees that were granted in 1991, just 24,300 went to African American men, a few hundred less than the 24,500 degrees granted in 1981. Black men earned fewer master's and doctoral degrees in 1991 than 1981, as well. Dominant in sports, black men have a tenuous toehold in the classroom.

March Madness offers the public a skewed slice of campus life. The NCAA games show black men in starring roles that they aren't often able to assume in the classroom or in university administration. If those who recruit can find starring players, one might ask why they can't find faculty, administrators, and students to star in other kinds of campus drama. Perhaps that's the difference between an active and a passive search for participants.

King Features Syndicate, February 24, 1994

AT WAR WITH OUR YOUTH
BY JULIANNE MALVEAUX

I don't want to be called a bitch or a ho any more than any other woman does. Nor do I appreciate the pulsating repetitiveness of so-called "gangsta rap" and the misogyny implicit in that music. But I must say I've been puzzled at the National Political Congress of Black Women and the war it has been waging on gangsta rap in general and Tupac Shakur in particular.

First the NPCBW picketed a music store in Washington, D.C. because it sells gangsta rap. Why picket the store, not a concert? The store sells more than rap, and no one puts a gun to anyone's head to make them buy it. Several of NPCBW's leaders, including its chair C. Delores Tucker, were arrested. They paid a $50 fine, and the District of Columbia was a few dollars richer, but they probably didn't reach the rappers with their protest!

Now, NPCBW is fussing because Tupac Shakur has been nominated to receive an NAACP Image Award. Just a day before the awards ceremony was to be taped, leaders asked that Shakur's nomination be withdrawn. Why did it take them that long to figure out that the same Shakur who was nominated for the award is the young man whose livid language peppers gangsta rap music? Why did it take them so long to note that this is the same youngster (Shakur is all of 22) who seems to be out to get arrested in every major city in this country, with charges ranging from assault on an undercover police officer to attempted rape? While I think it entirely appropriate for NPCBW to raise questions about whether Tupac Shakur should receive an Image Award, I wonder why it took them so long to make the point, and whether this outcry is a function of a desire for publicity, and little more.

I don't have a lot of sympathy for gangsta rappers, and would rather not hear their offensive sounds again in life. That's why I generally turn the radio off when that mess comes on. But I think gangsta rappers are easy targets. They are young, black, outrageous, often vulgar, sometimes violent. But they are the products, not the architects, of a violent society. Focusing our ire on them, and not on the forces that produce them (or the record companies that produce their music), puts us in the position of going to war against our own children. If we black women are outraged about gangsta rap, we ought not buy it and we ought to tell our sons and daughters not to buy it. We ought to tell radio stations not to play it, and support those stations, like New York's WBLS, that have pulled the plug on rap music.

But I'm not sure that we ought to join the masses in focusing on this easy target. I don't like the image of black women picketing our own youngsters, and I don't like the notion that the only time black women's protests get attention is when they are focused on young black men. Black women who care about political issues need to focus on the way violence is codified in our political process, in a budget that can afford prisons but not jobs, "defense" but not education. The gangsta rappers, obnoxious as they are, are symptoms, not causes, of our violent society.

In the past two years, when we black women have collectively raised our voices, we've brought clarity to situations that had been murky before. When African American Women in Defense of Ourselves gathered in support of Anita Hill, we noted that sexual harassment was not a race thing. When NPCBW worked on Presidential appointments in 1992, they made the point that gender interest and racial interest doesn't always coincide. But in picketing stores that sell rap music and focusing our ire on an individual rapper, we don't clarify issues, we confuse them.

What happened to innocent until proven guilty? What happened to using our economic power to signal the music we don't like? Black women can oppose violence and woman-bashing without going to war against our children. Instead of picketing a record store, we probably ought to tune out and turn off the rappers, and picket the Pentagon instead.

King Features Syndicate, January 5, 1994

HISTRIONICS ABOUT EBONICS
BY JULIANNE MALVEAUX

To let the commentators tell it, educators in the city of Oakland have gone mad. They are teaching black English as a second language and seeking federal funds to do so, and depending on which "black leader" you quote, this is a "bad joke" or a "cruel hoax" on the African American community. Coming a few days before Christmas, and a few weeks after affirmative action stumbled with the passage of Proposition 209, all one could say was "bah humbug."

The real comment is "bah homework." If those who are commenting would do as much reading as the children they want to protect are asked to, they'd know that Oakland never said it would teach black English to youngsters. Indeed, on December 18, the Oakland Unified School District Board of Education approved a policy affirming standard American English language development for all students. In other words, they aren't suggesting that "we be teaching dis and dat and dese and dose." (The quote marks appear because I don't ever, ever, ever want to be accused of an inability to deal with the so-called King's English.)

It seems that without a lot of information, key African American leaders are condemning the Oakland approach to teaching standard English. But then if you believe everything you read, you'd have to doubt the Oakland approach, too. After all, it seems that conventionally educated African Americans are asking that their children and grandchildren get something different than a conventional education. But then, isn't this what the school choice, school chance, school circumstance advocates are saying? Students aren't like T-shirts. One size, one schedule, one curriculum simply does not fit all. Oakland actually ought to be commended for seven years of experimentation in a Standard English Proficiency Program that has demonstrated success in retention, achievement, and graduation. It requires understanding, though, in order to commend them.

Oakland is trying to balance two concepts, language deficiency and English proficiency. Too many African American students in Oakland are viewed as "language deficient" because they don't speak the King's English. They "be tripping and be trying," but the command of the English language is highly correlated with family income, education, and exposure. Too many students in Oakland come from families where there is unemployment, poverty, and a sidetrack, not the mainstream. Should these students be welcomed into classrooms, or shunned? Should they be judged deficient, or offered a bridge to proficiency? The focus on Ebonics is an Oakland School District focus on teachers, not students. It teaches teachers sensitivity, understanding, and a way to build a bridge. Only a combination of press ignorance and raw cynicism would turn an effort to increase sensitivity into an effort to glorify non-standard English.

English proficiency has always been the goal of the Oakland Board of Education. But when they asked each other how to get to proficiency they found that little discussion had taken place about the teaching and treatment of African American students in the classroom. Toni Cook, former Chairman of the Oakland Board of Education, and a current member, said she saw the key issue as the education of the black child. She noted that 71 percent of those in Oakland's special education courses are African American, and 64 percent of those held back are African American, both numbers out of proportion with the 53 percent representation of African Americans in Oakland's schools. How can we fix it? Cook fretted, wearing her hat as a former college professor and motivator. The data show that one way to fix it is to use Ebonics as a bridge to standard English.

By now, though, the discussion has been skewed by reporters who find fun and fury in Oakland's decision. The discussion has been fractured by those African American leaders who have used their prestige to suggest that the Oakland decision is wrong. The discussion about learning has been sidetracked by the pundocracy, the people who get paid to say what they think no matter how much or how little they know. Bah, homework.

Let me be clear about my biases. My skin crawls when I hear the word "ax" instead of "ask," and it takes all my worldly self-control to sit still when someone says "I 'likes-es' greens." I am less repelled by the language of the streets, seeing in it a perverse bilinguality that speaks to the street in all of us. In other words, I've been hanging with my homies in the hoopdie, or I've been spending time with my friends in their less than traditionally maintained car. That's kinda fun, but not the commercially viable language that I take to editorial meetings and business deals. Or if I do, believe me, it is not for lack of knowing better.

Black people have always had to be bilingual, but we have also always known the space, place and context of our bilinguality. When there is no context, when commercially viable workplaces lock us out, our children end up monolingual, and only marginally so. Should our schools lock them out or pull them in? Can teachers take the language used and turn it into standard English proficiency? The Oakland Board of Education says yes. But their position has been "dissed" (or disrespected) by a drive-by analysis that reacts to headlines and nothing more. Now they have to explain themselves with press releases, web site information kits, and bibliographies that try to tell the whole story.

The Ebonics controversy is a study in race, media distortion, plantation politics, and black ethics. It is also a study in how one misses the forest for the trees, how one manages to lose the goal, the education of black children, in the midst of all the hoopla. A chronology of the controversy says a lot about pack journalism, about a breakdown in analysis, and about the ways that too many people have built a soapbox on the backs of black children who, when all the analysis is over with, still have to learn.

Oakland should not be on the defensive, but on the offensive, about issues of African American education. Based on their experience, the Oakland School Board ought to be the ones to bring educational leaders together to discuss key issues around the education of African American youngsters. Are educational challenges the same, or different, from those of the majority culture? And as long as we accept the notion that different children have different needs, why can't African American youngsters be accommodated? Too often, in African American History Month, there is talk about visionaries of the past. But by opening a can of worms about learning styles and Ebonics, the Oakland School Board might be described as the visionaries of the future. Let's get the facts straight on the Ebonics controversy, and celebrate the educators who said their goal was, no matter how, to teach black children standard English proficiency.

Black Issues in Higher Education, December 30, 1996

THE POLITICS OF EDUCATION
BY JULIANNE MALVEAUX

One of the key differences between Democrats and Republicans was illustrated during August's conventions. While there were about 300 members of the National Education Association registered as delegates at the Democratic convention, Republican Presidential candidate Bob Dole used his convention acceptance speech as an occasion to attack teachers and teacher unions. And while Democrats talked about the importance of education, Republicans used their convention as an opportunity to talk about home schooling.

The actions of the 104th Congress further speak to these differences. This summer, the House voted to cut education funding by $395 million when HR 3755 passed in July. That's on top of about a billion dollars' worth of cuts since January 1995. Teacher training and the "Safe and Drug-Free School Program" are special victims of these cuts, which come when public school enrollment is rising, perhaps by 3 million students in the next six years. The Department of Education says we need more teachers, schools, and maintenance funds to accommodate these new students. The Congress says there ought to be less.

This is a political ploy as transparent as the Republican ploy to close government down to see if we would miss it or not. Too many of the "Irreligious Wrong" (also known as the Religious Right) want to capture our nation's thinking by dealing with educational issues. Thus, the Parental Rights and Responsibilities Act (Senate Bill 984/House Bill 1946) would allow every parent to sue in federal court to challenge public school curricula, health guidelines, library policies, or any laws or policies that affect children. Further, the focus on home schooling and voucher programs is really a focus on the devolution of our nation's educational system.

Too many people have focused on the problems in education without looking at the positives that our structural school system has to offer. And too many have suggested that students just aren't learning because there is too much multiculturalism, too much focus on those issues outside reading, writing, and 'rithmetic. But education has always been more than a reading and writing thing. From laws that require school attendance to skirmishes over the curriculum, politics is part of education. And the battles, now, over education are implicitly political.

The rightward drift in our nation's politics is reflected in a rightward educational drift. Not only has the so-called Christian Coalition attempted to play a key role in educational issues, but they have attempted to capture school board seats as a way of dictating the educational agenda. This ought to be sobering to the left, since more than 40 percent of the last class of Congressional inductees are former school board members. If school boards are the path to political power, then why aren't more people with a progressive agenda attempting to capture school board seats?

Students are returning to school right about now, and as they return, threats to education continue. The Clinton administration and the Department of Education have put together an upbeat set of materials on school partnerships, and a number of others have focused on the Congressional attacks on the current educational system. But few people are looking behind the headlines to understand why these educational skirmishes are really manifestations of conflicts in popular values and culture.

Too many people have used our school systems as a political soapbox. If they didn't, Bob Dole would have ignored teachers' unions when he made his acceptance speech in San Diego. The twenty-first century dictates that we cater to the best and the brightest of our students, not those who best fit into a political agenda. But as millions throng back to school, both Clinton and Dole seem to have forgotten that these youngsters are our futures, our hopes, and our dreams.

King Features Syndicate, September 13, 1996

ON THEIR OWN—FOSTER CHILDREN AT 18

BY JULIANNE MALVEAUX

Richard was a bubbly, energetic 20-year-old college junior when I met him three years ago. Well-spoken and even better mannered, he worked my nerves by constantly referring to me as "ma'am." A political science major and computer science minor, the young African American man told me his sights were set on graduate school and, later, college teaching. He had both the drive and intelligence to meet his goals, and was juggling a better than B average with several student leadership positions. "Your parents must be very proud of you," I told Richard at the end of my visit to his campus. "Ma'am," he sighed, "I don't have any parents." In his 20 years he had been raised by more than 11 sets of foster parents, with his last placement before high school graduation lasting just two years.

I was stunned that this mature, focused young man lacked the parental support and guidance that so many young people depend on as they make the transition between adolescence and adulthood, but even further shocked to learn that each year, about 25,000 students like Richard leave foster care because the state will no longer reimburse their foster parents for expenses after they turn 18. That means they are, literally, on their own. They must earn their own living, provide their own food and housing, and make their own decisions. Though a few states have "transition programs" that support independent living for youths between 18 and 21 years of age, most of the foster children who turn 18 find themselves completely without resources.

To be sure, these young people represent just one-tenth of one percent of the 2.5 million youngsters who will graduate from high school this fall. If they are bright and have "worked the system well," they are likely to be headed for college or vocational school after high school. Others will be aided by our tight labor market in their search for employment. But the "emancipated" foster children can't count on parents and extended family to surround them with love and advice. They can't count on public assistance, which has withdrawn aid from single people unless they have children. According to Kathy Barbell, Foster Care Director for the Child Welfare League of America, "Most males find themselves in homeless shelters, on drugs, or in jail."

The 25,000 that are annually emancipated are at the tip of the foster care iceberg. There are half a million children in foster care, an increase of 61 percent from a decade ago. These young people are disproportionately black and brown (40 percent are African American, 12 percent Latino, and 4 percent from other ethnic groups), and a third of them are teenagers whose difficult foster care situation is compounded by the vulnerability and volatility of adolescence. While many foster care agencies and foster parents are dedicated to the young people they serve, many see foster children as income-producing cash cows. When they cease to produce income, economic reality pushes them out of their foster homes and into the world.

If they have beat all the odds and are college students, like Richard, they have food and shelter during the academic year, but must bunk with friends or acquaintances during summers or periods when campus housing is closed. Their belongings are shuffled from one commercial storage locker to another, and they often find themselves surviving because of the kindness of strangers. The fact of their survival is an amazing testament to human resilience, but it is an indictment of a foster care system that simply slaps 18-year-olds upside the head and sends them reeling into adulthood instead of providing them with much-needed transition assistance.

The transition could be as simple as that offered in Texas, which provides free college tuition to state colleges for foster children. Idaho provides subsidized vocational training. As many as one in six foster children receive some form of employment or career-training assessment. But after that, they are on their own.

For many teens the weighty sounds of the high school graduation march "Pomp and Circumstance" mark their transition from adolescence to adulthood. For others, the family trip to the college dormitory is a signal of transition. But at least 25,000 18-year-olds must concern themselves with survival, not year-end rituals. Young people like Richard make it clear that survival is certainly possible. But they also remind us that 18-year-olds aren't always prepared to cope with adult responsibilities. Often, they need help in making the successful transition from adolescence to adulthood.

King Features Syndicate, May 15, 1998

PROPOSITION 227 IS BAD EDUCATIONAL POLICY
BY JULIANNE MALVEAUX

Should educational policy be set by referendum? Can people, based on a ballot measure, decide that they won't have special education, gifted and talented programs, or special classes for those who are mathematically challenged? Of course they can't, but Californians were able to decide on Tuesday that there should be no more bilingual education in California. Instead, the 1.4 million students who are not proficient in English will have a year to sink or swim in a one-year English immersion program. After that, unless special (the law actually says "exceptional") conditions are met, students whose first language is not English will be out of luck.

Never mind educational theory and the years of study that have gone into setting up bilingual education programs. Never mind what is best for students. Sixty-one percent of California voters said they don't want bilingual education anymore, so now Proposition 227 has become law. It is interesting to ask, though, whether these voters are rejecting bilingual education or the people who speak it. This is the state, after all, that passed Proposition 187, a piece of legislation that was decidedly anti-immigrant. Californians passed Proposition 209 two years ago, an anti-affirmative action measure that sent African American and Latino enrollment rates at the University of California on a downward spiral. Now instead of closing borders and slamming doors in higher education, they are shutting the doors to Latinos at the elementary school level. And they are sending hostile signals that are at odds with the notion of our global, borderless economy.

Think about it. NAFTA seeks trade with Mexico, but Proposition 227 seems to say the terms of trade have to be spelled out in English. Conversation about "cooperation" values our neighbors, no matter what language they speak. Proposition 227 is an unnecessary English-only chest-thumping kind of law. Why can't teachers, principals, and those who know educational policy make decisions about bilingual education? Because this isn't about education, this is racism and politics. And it stinks.

Consider this — while only 37 percent of Hispanic voters supported Proposition 227, 67 percent of white voters favored the measure. According to the *New York Times*, 57 percent of Asian voters and 48 percent of African American voters supported the elimination of bilingual education. Proposition 227 is little more than a wounded white bid for supremacy. Companion measures are likely to be introduced in other parts of the United States, as well as in Congress, where Frank

Riggs (R-Calif.) has introduced a measure that would limit federal funding of bilingual education.

This legislation flies in the face of our nation's current economic strategy, which is to trade all over the world. Why should anyone trade with a country that has such antipathy for people who speak other languages? The Latin American market is a growing one, but plenty of young Californians will be losing their native language ability as they are forced to immerse in English. Still, Californians have had their emotional release, their tantrum against the inevitable reality that their state will soon be majority minority. They can go to the ballot box to work out their frustration and anger, but they can't lower the birthrate or stop legal immigration. They have simply succeeded in making life more difficult for their fellow citizens.

Thankfully, minority rights advocates have filed suit in Federal District Court challenging the legality of Proposition 227. They say the ballot measure violates the principle of equal protection because it would fail to provide adequate education for those citizens whose native language is not English. They've got a point — what do those who put this measure on the ballot think will happen to those who can't learn English in a year? Will they be held behind? How many times? How will this affect their access to college or employment? Could the proponents of Proposition 227 have possibly thought they were doing anyone a favor with this legislation? Or were they simply asserting the dominance of English?

The bottom-line question is a simple one, though. We'd react with derision to a ballot measure that stopped educational programs for gifted children, and with annoyance to a ballot measure that attempted to eliminate the teaching of mathematics or science. We leave those key decisions to teachers. Why not leave the bilingual education decision to those who make educational policy?

King Features Syndicate, June 5, 1998

CHAPTER 9

MOVING FORWARD, STANDING STILL: PERSPECTIVES ON THE STATUS OF WOMEN

Describing the status of women is like describing the way that colors shift in a kaleidoscope. There is progress and regress, a narrowing wage and income gap and still a clinging to attitudes of the past. Thus, capable contemporary women idolize a fairy-tale princess who grew up before our eyes, and corporate wives still have to get down and dirty to get their fair share of a divorce settlement. Yes, the real deal is economic—it's wages, and pensions, and the roots of the gender gap.

Isn't it amazing, though, the way we get away from the economic bottom line? Women work, not because we want to, but because we have to. Women work, and our work makes a difference in the quality of our family lives. Women would work better in a society that was woman friendly, a society where there was really a village available for mothers and children. And ain't I a woman? I describe myself, often, as "black, feminist, outspoken, and unintimidated." Sounds like a wolf ticket? I can cash it. Sounds like a prideful boast? I can back it up. Seriously, while African American women don't always sing from the same hymnal or march to the same beat (indeed, some of us don't march at all), we all bask in the proud legacy of those who went before, women whose legacy of sisterhood, scholarship, and service always inspires.

What do we do with these models of sisterhood and service in an era that rewards neither? And can feminists and womanists dare demand lockstep conformity as we challenge pervasive patriarchy? Hardly. Instead, we oscillate, strangled by contradictions and conflicting interpretations of the status of women. In my opinion, it's not difficult to assess women's status when women earn 74 percent of what men do. The real deal, always, is economic.

ARE WOMEN THE NEW PROVIDERS?
BY JULIANNE MALVEAUX

A recent survey by the Whirlpool Foundation and the New York-based Families and Work Institute indicated that working women provide about half of their household income. Nearly half of all married women say they provide half or more of family income. The survey reflects the notion that it takes two incomes to support a household, and that with the stagnant growth in male incomes, more and more families rely on women. The women who see themselves as "new providers" embrace both the economic and the nurturing components of their roles. According to the study, 56 percent of the women surveyed enjoy the role-juggling that they do and would not have it any other way.

That's, of course, unless money were no object. If finances did not have to be considered, a third of the women in the Family and Work Institute survey would work part-time, 20 percent would do volunteer work, 31 percent would take care of their families full-time, and just 15 percent would work full-time. And even the women who say they enjoy role-juggling admit that their families get more financial security from their husband's jobs than from their own.

It is interesting to see the ways surveys like this are played in the press. The headlines read that women are bringing home half of the family bacon and like doing so. Between the lines, though, we read that women would organize their lives differently if they could, if money didn't matter so much. Although the headlines scream that women are moving toward equal provider status, the fine print says that while women are a key source of family income, women earned more than men in just 23 percent of married-couple families where both spouses worked. Two-thirds of the women say their spouse's jobs offer more financial security, better benefits, or pensions.

To be sure, this survey challenges the notion that women's wages are supplemental to family income, and makes clear that families need women's incomes to survive. So when people talk about family values, they also need to talk about women's incomes and ways to enable women to work. For example, child care access is important to women's ability to earn.

Labor Secretary Robert Reich and Women's Bureau director Karen Nussbaum are traveling the country to talk about child care issues, especially for women who work "non-standard" hours. More than 7 million mothers, with more than 11 million children under age 15, worked outside the 9-to-5 hours, and had more difficulty finding child care than other women. The Labor Department report

"Care Around the Clock: Developing Child Care Resources Before Nine and After Five" was released at a child care center near the San Francisco Airport that operates up to 24 hours a day. Child care facilities like San Francisco's Palcare are more the exception than the rule, but their existence speaks to the need to develop support services for working women.

Both the study on child care and the survey on work make it clear that single mothers who work have an even greater burden. If it takes two incomes to raise a family, what odds do families with just one earner face? And if child care is difficult to find for those who have a partner to fall back on, what about those who are raising children on their own?

Some would solve single mothers' problems by talking about marriage and family values. But if we acknowledge women's importance in contributing to household support, the greatest family value of all is fair pay for women's work. The survey that suggests that women are contributing much to family income also suggests that differences between men's pay and women's pay remain.

King Features Syndicate, May 12, 1995

ECONOMIC ROOTS OF THE GENDER GAP
BY JULIANNE MALVEAUX

Do men and women view government differently? If they do, might this difference explain the gender gap that determined President Clinton's victory in this month's election? While pundits are still shaking their heads about the gender gap and the way both parties appealed to so-called soccer moms, researchers at the Washington, D.C.-based Center for Policy Alternatives can point to their August Women's Voices poll and say, "I told you so."

Riveting when it was released in the early fall, the Women's Voices poll now provides some guidelines for the second term of the Clinton administration. Unfortunately, though, the President seems too committed to holding a centrist, budget-balancing, government-reducing position to pay attention to the women whose votes he courted scant weeks ago. The crux of the difference between men and women, as defined by the Women's Voices poll, is the role that women hope government will take in moving us to the twenty-first century. While men see government as part of the problem, women see it as part of the solution, and hope that government will increase the level of security that Americans experience in our society.

Security? Women think government can help keep children safe, keep health care secure, keep retirement secure. Women think government can help improve the economy and see connections between economic pressures and the lack of time many feel because of heavy workloads. Women don't see government as an omnipotent "big daddy," but instead see government as part of a community. They see business as part of that community, too, and want their employers to be better partners. Unlike men, who seem to zoom right in to profit as the bottom line, women seem willing to make demands on businesses that may reduce bottom line but increase the well-being of workers.

According to Women's Voices, men were more concerned about jobs, taxes, and spending than women. Women were more concerned about education, moral decline, crime and violence, and retirement. To interpret the results, it seems that men are concerned about direct economic issues while women are concerned with those issues that affect the quality of life as well as the economy. Women seem willing to put their money where their concerns are, too. Most women would contribute one percent of their paycheck to pay for child care, an emergency leave fund, or additional education. Fewer men are willing to make such contributions.

Perhaps because they have so many questions about business operations, four in ten women would like to own their own businesses. Even those who are not interested in owning businesses want to see government do more to help get businesses started. According to Women's Voices, African American women and younger women are most interested in owning businesses.

Age is a stealth issue for women, and it seems to concern them more than it concerns men. Women worry about retirement, but also about their ability to take care of older relatives. Women are also concerned about pensions, a reasonable concern given the fact that women are likely to receive lower pensions than men based on employment and related histories.

If President Clinton studies the Women's Voices results carefully, he will stop crowing about economic expansion, and start viewing issues of security that weaken the strength of the expanding economy. If he understands the economic roots of the gender gap, he will pay less attention to balancing the budget, and more attention to children, education, and Social Security. Reflecting the concerns that women have, the President would see government as part of the solution, not part of the problem. The Women's Voices poll might well provide Mr. Clinton with a checklist for his January State of the Union address.

King Features Syndicate, November 22, 1996

MIXED MESSAGES ON WOMEN'S WORK
BY JULIANNE MALVEAUX

This week working women lost a voice of pluck and humor when Erma Bombeck died. Bombeck wrote a humorous column about everyday life for more than 30 years. She poked fun at dust balls and pro bowls, at family life and daily strife. She started writing her column because, she said, she was "too old for a paper route, too young for social security, and too tired for an affair." For baby boom career women like me, she is an unlikely heroine, her droll remarks about cleaning refrigerators and slicing vegetables a generation away from my reality. But the fact is that Erma Bombeck wrote about the women's work that few women want to talk about, the housework that many of us do whether we have spouses or not, children or not. Most of the research on the intersection between housework and family suggests that women, even when working full-time, do the bulk of the household maintenance, putting more hours into the matter of household management than spouses, children, or even similarly situated single men do.

Erma Bombeck was part of the "bridge generation" of working women who raised families and then, at the cusp of the women's movement, sought work because traditional women's roles were unrewarding to them. Bombeck wrote about that which she knew best, and found an audience because women on both sides of the bridge could identify with her. But during the week of her death, two women's events remind us that there are women on both sides of the bridge she crossed, some still defined in terms of traditional roles, others trying to break stereotypes and attracting criticism for it.

On one hand, April 24 was National Secretary's Day. Millions of bosses around the country treated their secretaries, administrative assistants, and other clerical helpers to roses and refreshments, instead of raises and respect. The very notion of National Secretary's Day bothers me. We don't, after all, have National Electrician's Day or National Auto Assembly Worker's Day. That's because electricians and auto assembly workers are paid for their clearly defined work, and don't need roses by rote or lunches in lock step to convey any intangible appreciation that their bosses have for their work. Instead, in some cases, these workers get bonuses when they exceed production guidelines, time and a half when they work overtime, and a piece of the profits as well as praise when companies are especially productive.

But 26.8 million workers, mostly women, work in secretarial and clerical jobs, earning an average of $19,500 a year. With the downsizing that has affected much of the corporate world, 42 percent of the Fortune 500 companies say they have reduced support staff. Thus, today's secretaries work for multiple bosses, have an array of skills, and often watch their jobs disappear as some clerical tasks are outsourced. National Secretary's Day, for all its good intentions, strikes me as some sort of anachronism, a blast from a sexist past when a national appreciation day was an acceptable substitute for economic empowerment.

If some people have their way, Take Our Daughters to Work Day, which follows National Secretary's Day, will also soon be a thing of the past. In the fourth year since the Ms. Foundation for Women instituted the day that focuses on girls and their career aspirations, critics now say that boys are left out and need, also, to be included in this career day. Many of these critics ignore labor market realities— that women are drastically underrepresented at the pinnacle of many professions, the irony of their point captured in a Ms. Foundation remark that "people who live with glass ceilings shouldn't throw stones."

It seems incongruous to me that people who note National Secretary's Day can't make room for Take Our Daughters to Work. It seems incongruous that those who genuflect to the gender stereotypes that crowded so many women into the pink-collar ghetto of clerical work can't see the need to get past those stereotypes with an enlightenment like Take Our Daughters to Work. In some ways National Secretary's Day is at one end of the bridge Erma Bombeck crossed, Take Our Daughters to Work Day at the other. And in the middle there are the ties that bind— the fact that in the past and in the future, housework plays a major role in women's lives, and the fact that even after someone said we'd come a long way baby, society sends mixed signals of women's work.

King Features Syndicate, May 25, 1996

CORPORATE WIFE OR CORPORATE PARTNER: FAMILY ECONOMICS
BY JULIANNE MALVEAUX

Lorna and Gary Wendt's divorce ought to be a private matter. But Gary Wendt is chief executive of General Electric's Capital Unit, and his wife of 32 years says she was a partner in his success. And what success—when Lorna and Gary Wendt married in 1965, they had $2500 between them. Now, they are fighting over an estate worth as much as $43 million.

Lorna Wendt's work clearly set Gary Wendt's star on an upward trajectory. Her labor financed his attainment of an advanced degree, and she managed the family, the entertaining, and the moving that supplemented his career. No wonder she was both stunned and stung when he offered a scant $8 million of his estate as a settlement. Though Lorna Wendt didn't get half of the family estate from Connecticut Superior Court Judge Kevin Tierney, she increased her settlement by more than 50 percent by taking her case to court. Further, she lifted up the cause of many women who seek a more equitable share of marital property in non-community property states.

There are not many women who fall into the ranks of "corporate spouses." After all, fewer than 2.8 million men (and just half a million women) earn more than $100,000 a year. Not too many people are engaging in multi-million dollar battles over marital estates. At the same time, some of the issues that Lorna Wendt tackled are issues that affect "every woman." When one spouse worked in the formal labor market, and the other worked at home, should pensions be split, and how? How are the contributions of a partner who has never been remunerated in the formal labor force to be valued? Is it fair for someone to depend on housework, support, and marital stability on one hand, and then disparage it on the other? Should corporate wives (or husbands) also be considered corporate partners?

The public accounts of the Wendt debacle reflected more than a little bit of mean-spiritedness. One report said that Gary Wendt said that hard work, not housekeeping, was his ticket to the top. Given GE's corporate culture, though, one would have to wonder if he would have had a ticket to ride were he single, or shoddily attended to. In some corporations, even now, family life is one of a number of things that are evaluated for success. Dismissing Lorna Wendt's contribution to his career seemed to spur Mrs. Wendt on to get her share. She maintained that she should get half of everything from the cash value of stock options to membership in country clubs.

There are two things about the Wendt divorce that bear further examination. The first is the way that stock options are divided and the notion that stock options should be valued as property. Stock options are often offered as an incentive to corporate officers, but they are often golden shackles that tie executives closer to a corporate entity and distort their mobility decision in favor of future rewards. If stock options are seen as part of a marital estate (or any other estate for that matter) and control of these options might easily pass from a principal worker to his or her heirs or claimants, corporations may lose their ability to control the source of their ownership. Imagine, for example, a settlement that allowed Lorna Wendt to exercise some fraction of Gary Wendt's stock options. What might that have meant to GE?

The question is also raised because some executives bargain for stock options in lieu of bargaining for better salaries. While stock options represent a participatory risk, salary represents a tangible asset. How can courts divide an intangible? Those who are not clear about their fealty to a corporate entity, or about other stability issues, might be advised to choose salary over stock options, or to negotiate to protect their stock options.

The other aspect of the Wendt divorce that bears examination is the unofficial notion that "enough is enough" in dividing marital assets. Since "anybody" ought to be able to maintain herself on $4, $5, or $8 million, courts have been reluctant to award women like Lorna Wendt much more than that. No matter how large the marital estate, some judges have balked at splitting it because "enough is enough." Unfortunately, this is an attitude that trickles down, an attitude that means that not only corporate wives, but also working wives get the short end of the stick when judges view their cases from a patriarchal perch that suggests that marriage is not always a partnership. While many don't care whether Lorna Wendt gets $8 or $17 million, there are social and economic policy implications from other divisions of marital estates. There may be corporate implications as well, which is why the intersection between household and family transcends sociological inquiry to impinge on aspects of corporate finance.

King Features Syndicate, December 5, 1997

SOME WOMEN DON'T HAVE FEMINIST CHOICES
BY JULIANNE MALVEAUX

My seatmate on a recent cross-country flight said she was worried about her 8-year-old son. "He misses me when I travel," she said. "But I travel to make a living." She confided that she might quit her job, but that her husband was worried about his status if his company merged. She mused that her son might have "life-long scars" because of her frequent travel. At some point she picked up the telephone and, at $2.50 a minute, talked to her husband and son and offered them both "wet kisses" over the phone. Then she sighed — "I feel a little better"—and pulled out her laptop, making a set of furious notes. "I'm caught," she said, "between technology and feminism."

I would have forgotten about the woman's pithy remark were it not for the cab driver I got at the airport well after midnight. She was an older white woman who wore her tiredness heavily on her shoulders. "You will probably be my last fare tonight, hon," she said, and pointed her cab downtown. She told me that she drove a cab from about 4 p.m. until midnight, and waited tables at a diner on a noon shift, trying to keep up the payments on her home and to pay overdue medical bills from her husband's uninsured illness. Her time was as tight as that of the executive woman I shared a plane ride with, but technology played no part in her conversation. Neither did feminism. Instead, my 50something cab driver talked about limits, about not having enough time, money, or energy. "I never thought I'd be in this position at this time in my life," she said wearily. "I really never thought I'd be driving a cab at night, waiting tables during the day, and feeling like there are no choices."

Dozens of women policy wonks are talking about the "F" word, feminism, but they are talking more to the woman executive than to the woman cab driver. I've heard women, lately, debating whether or not it is a quality-of-life decision to stay home and raise children as opposed to working. Some of these women look at their six-figure-earning sisters and suggest that those who juggle children, jobs, and cross-country travel need to find simpler lives and just cut back. I wonder if their lens is broad enough to include the cab driver who holds two jobs to make ends meet.

The fact is that too many women don't have lots of choices. Too many still work in low-end, poorly paid jobs. To be sure, more and more women are finishing college, and more and more are choosing graduate education. They can, like my airplane seatmate, look forward to exciting lives and careers and to the luxury of choice. Those who do not finish college, who do not concentrate in science, management, or computer fields, can find their choices extremely limited. They might look forward to low-wage work or unemployment with a safety net now shredded by welfare reform.

The gulf between the women who talk about what women should do and the women who do what women must is often a wide one. The policy analysts, pundits, and talking heads who talk about the role of women do so from a relatively privileged position. From time to time they need to walk in the shoes of the cab driver, the waitress, the clerical worker, the hotel-cleaning service worker. Then they might be more careful about suggesting that people should stay home to take care of their children. Then they might well ponder the question "If women stay home, what will their children eat?" And then, perhaps, they will understand why issues like access to education and public assistance are among the most important feminist issues.

King Features Syndicate, February 27, 1997

FLIPPING THE SCRIPT: WHOSE OBSESSION WITH DIANA
BY JULIANNE MALVEAUX

How could I not care that a 36-year-old woman left two children to mourn her death? I cried my eyes into red rims when I realized that one of my sorority sisters, a woman who was just 40, succumbed to breast cancer and left a husband and two tragically lonely boys, aged 8 and 5. My soror's driveway won't be covered with flowers, nor will those who knew her be interviewed by curious media. Yet her death is as tragic as Princess Diana's. Since tragedy knows no race, no status, how could I not care about what has now been described as an international tragedy?

Still, let's flip the script. As much compassion as I feel for Diana's sons and for her friends, I have antipathy for the way the world has been obsessed with this woman. Indeed, the world's obsession with her says much about the lens through which we view ourselves. Millions tuned in to the television coverage of her 1981 wedding, too many women watching because they, too, wanted a prince. They said it with subtlety and they said it bluntly. They said they wanted to be swept away. Millions of women said it again when they thronged to see the movie *Pretty Woman*. It was about nothing more than their desire to buy into a fantasy of a rich and powerful man who would take care of them. Their wishes flew in the face of feminism, but they also flew in the face of reality.

I am an African American woman. Powerful. Fearless. Impervious to pain. Despite the new line that we black women need to explore our humanity, I am clear about what I can expect from the world. And I am clear that it isn't a prince. The "swept away" vision of a fantasy reality never appealed to me, perhaps because I was born with my feet firmly planted on the ground. The Diana Fantasy always irritated me because it appealed to a woman who was doing too much leaning, a woman who wanted to be taken care of.

The Diana Fantasy was at its peak in 1981 when the Fairy Tale got flesh and Diana married Charles. Whoever believed in fairy tales got their tail smacked around when Charles and Diana waged a media war that pitted one hapless lover against the other, the Rottweiler versus Squiggy or was it Squidgy. Nobody won. Diana took her fantasy back when she left Charles, the toad prince, after much negotiation. She might have lived happily ever after except for a drunk, the paparazzi, and a tunnel. In the parlance of the hood, "the party's over, say goodbye."

But I am compelled to write about Diana less because of her fantasy than because of our nation's collective obsession, and because of what this obsession says about the ways we hang together or stand apart. I remember the first time a friend and I differed about Diana. She said she would stay up all night to watch the fairytale wedding, and I said I'd rather drink muddy water than lose sleep over Di. My friend was sweet and plaintive when she asked "why," and I was mean when I responded. I asked if her life was so empty that she needed to watch someone else get what she thought she wanted, and she cursed me and hung up the phone. We didn't talk for days, or was it years? She was so busy chasing her prince that I hardly noticed when she found, then lost him and drifted back into my life. There were no magazine covers, no trumpets and paparazzi to note her transitions, nor should there have been. She lived enough of her life through Di that she was caressed by the Princess' trumpets and bolstered by her victories.

Our collective obsession about Diana lifts up one kind of woman and, by extension, ignores another. We celebrate the women who are butterflies, who emerge, and ignore those who come strong to the table. We celebrate those who develop a personality in public, as opposed to those whose development is less invisible than their contribution. Through her innate compassion, and bless her for that, Diana figured out that she needed to use her celebrity to help AIDS patients, land mine victims, and others; she is due all praise. So are those who didn't need to figure it out, whose giving has been as much a part of living as it is of breathing.

We must have compassion for Diana, Princess of Wales, without being obsessed by her. We must be clear that any young woman who dies leaves an unfinished legacy in her children. At the same time we must be clear that there is a flip side to this script. There are millions who are not obsessed by Diana, who are mournful, but not consumed, by this tragedy. There is a gap—no, a gulf— between those who are moved and those who are not.

San Francisco Sun Reporter, September 9, 1997

DOES IT REALLY TAKE A VILLAGE: MOTHER'S DAY REFLECTIONS
BY JULIANNE MALVEAUX

"Do you have any kids?" a colleague asks me as she slides into the seat opposite mine nearly half an hour later than we planned to meet. She is harried, rushed, and hoping for understanding. She thinks that I'll understand why she is late, out of breath, and slightly unfocused only if I share the motherhood experience with her. The truth is that I don't have to be a mom to understand the balls she has to juggle. The other truth is that I'm tired of being asked to define myself by my motherhood, or lack thereof, to be asked for understanding on the basis of whether I've given birth.

On Mother's Day I am always happy to offer kudos to those many mothers who bring their children's worlds to life. In 1995, 10 million of them were single mothers. I'm a product of one of those mothers, a woman who shepherded her five kids to museums, zoos, parks and every place else because she wanted to give us "exposure." A divorced woman, she did it alone most of the time, alone, without complaint, and with an eye on the future. My sister, a single mom, has taken our mother's playback and adopted it as a mantra. If there is a camp, a class, an opportunity that her children might be interested in, they'll have it, no matter what it takes.

I appreciate dedicated mothers. But I don't appreciate the notion that those 29 percent of women who are childless are somehow less than women for our status. Our childbearing sisters often look askance at us, implying that we haven't had "real life experience" until we've birthed a child. They use their children like pawns, sometimes, pieces on a status chessboard that often puts us one down. To be sure, most women will experience motherhood at some point in their lives. But some of us are childless by choice, or childless because of circumstance and time. We shouldn't have to take second status because our lives are different than those of other women.

Indeed, we childless women are often part of the village it takes to raise a child. We are sitters and supporters, surrogate aunts and cheerleaders. Yes, we avoided the birthing pains, but we experience the same pain and pangs of disappointment when one of our "special" charges missteps. And we enjoy the same giddy pleasure when our specials have milestones like graduations, promotions, and weddings.

Often we create bridges between parents and children, interpreters who offer neutral ears, fresh eyes, and different perspectives on some issues. We're not about medals, kudos, or acknowledgment. We are available to young people because we understand the human connection, the concept of community. But we are often cut out of community when understanding, or lack thereof, is implied with that simple question, "Do you have children?"

I'd prefer to be defined by answering a different question—"Do you have compassion?" Do you understand, as we all must, that children are our nation's future? Are you willing to reach out to a child, a young person, who is not your own? Is there something you can do to have an impact on their lives?

There are 30 million women over age 15 who are not mothers; some will have children one day, but others never will. While we appreciate our nation's mothers on this Mother's Day, we are mindful that we are also part of the nurturing village that transforms a person from child to adult. This Mother's Day, I celebrate my mom, but also a coterie of women who laid nurturing hands on me, women whose caring is not defined by whether they have given birth. Our concept of community must stretch to include every member of the village, not just birth mothers.

King Features Syndicate, May 8, 1997

BLACK, FEMINIST, OUTSPOKEN, UNINTIMIDATED
BY JULIANNE MALVEAUX

Beverly Guy-Sheftal's masterful anthology of African-American feminist thought, *Words of Fire* (New Press, 1995) is a reminder that African-American women sometimes publicly expressed feminist thought before white women did. Sheftal describes a small group of free black "feminist abolitionists" who surfaced in the early nineteenth century, including Maria Stewart, Sojourner Truth, and Frances E.W. Harper. Anna Julia Cooper said that African American women confront both a "woman question and a race problem," and Sheftal describes this question as the essence of black feminist thought in the nineteenth century. In the late twentieth century, though, black women are often told that we have to choose between race and gender.

Johnetta Cole has the answer to that. In her epilogue essay in Sheftal's book, she likens the choice between race and gender to a swimmer with both arms tied behind her back. Which would you have released? Cole asks. Would you fight racism or sexism when the battle against these twin evils is essential to your survival? Because of the history of racism in the women's movement, many black women find it hard to be "down" with white women, especially when their stories of male oppression don't jibe with what we know and see. But many black women, myself included, refuse to cede "feminism," and the issues feminism addresses, to white women. In the name of women like Maria Stewart and Ida B. Wells, we are obligated to struggle for women's rights, even as we struggle for the rights of African Americans.

There were substantive reasons for some African American feminists, myself included, to oppose the October 1995 Million Man March. If it were merely billed as a black male "love-in," I would have had fewer objections. If black women had not so explicitly been told (not asked) to stay home and "pray and teach" while the men "marched and led," the march would not have had the taint of traditional gender roles. If it had not been cast in the shadow of the 1963 March on Washington, a march that did not exclude women's participation, it might not have been as objectionable. And if it did not take on the conservative tinge of "atonement" and "taking responsibility" in a policy arena when these are exactly the things policymakers are asking of African American people, it would not have been as much a problem for me.

Let me be clear. Despite my objections to the Million Man March, I was intrigued by its spirit. The morning of the march, I was moved by the men who thronged to the Capitol, the sea of black men who moved as if choreographed, courteous, strong, focused. After the march, I also agreed with the significance of an event that could bring more than a million black men to one place. But noting that, I still feel the march was fundamentally flawed, and I still take issue with it.

Many who supported the march decided to make it a litmus test on blackness. If you didn't support the march you couldn't "really" be black. Or you couldn't have the interests of African American people at heart. Many of us who visibly opposed the march were the targets of ugly hazing and harassment, moves that seemed designed to muzzle dissent, to evoke fear. Perhaps this is why so many women only gingerly voice feminist concerns. Consider Pearl Cleage, writing about O.J. Simpson and female self-defense in *Words of Fire*: "I am afraid as I write those words. Afraid that my brothers will read it and be angry with me. Afraid that I will be accused of male bashing, of judging O.J. before he's even had a trial. Of being a part of bringing down another good brother. Even worse, I can hear the howls of outrage that I could even think of advocating that black women arm themselves when our community is already an armed camp."

Cleage drew courage from Ida B. Wells, who wrote about black self-defense. She drew parallels between her argument and Wells' and affirmed her obligation to write about the status of women. She acknowledged that she'd rather write about "love and healing and nationalism and wholeness," but wondered what she would write if her daughter had been battered.

Like Cleage, I'd rather be writing about the economic liberation of African American people than about anything else. And that's usually what I write about, talk about, take positions on. But even as I write about economic justice, the data make it clear that African American women shoulder more than our share of the economic injustice in our community. More than black men? That's not the comparison I choose to make. African American men and women have both been affected by a capitalist patriarchy that devalues our culture, our work, our communities. Our pain has been a collective pain, and we have sometimes inflicted pain on each other. In writing about economic liberation, I would be less than honest if I didn't tackle issues about the status of African American women and the way institutions in the African American community are sometimes instruments of oppression.

I could swallow my objections in the name of black unity, or suppress them to sidestep the angry attacks that so often come when a black woman speaks out. Instead, I choose to voice my objections. In the name of love for black men and women. In the name of truth. And in the name, and the footsteps, of Ida B. Wells, of Maria Stewart, of Anna Julia Cooper, I stand concerned about race and gender. I am black, feminist, outspoken, unintimidated, and claiming Women's History Month as a time for African American women to deal with these feminist issues.

King Features Syndicate, February 21, 1996

SISTERHOOD, NOT CENSORSHIP: REFLECTIONS ON THE MILLION WOMAN MARCH
BY JULIANNE MALVEAUX

I had mixed feelings about the Million Woman March. Anytime African American women get together, there's something good going on. But when they get together on shaky ground—with an ill-defined platform and scant information, it makes sense to raise questions. I raised questions, and shared my skeptism and estimated that "no more than 100,000" women would come to Philadelphia for the march. Not only was I wrong, but if some of the counts are to be believed I was fifteen times wrong! Numerically the Million Woman March was a rousing success, and naysayers like me stand corrected by the actions of the 1.5 million women who braved rain and cold to come to Philadelphia.

How could I have called it so wrong? Part of my call was frustration with the poor organization and dearth of information available to interested parties. Part of it, though, was the fact that I simply underestimated the outrage and pain that so many African American women feel about our circumstances. I underestimated the fact that when 60 percent of African American women working full time earn less than $25,000 (compared to about half of white women and a third of all men), these women have reason to gather. When of the 3.5 million workers with six-figure earnings, only 29,000 are African American women, we have reason to gather. When incarceration rates for African American women have quadrupled in a decade, we have reason to gather. When few black women have been unscathed by the crack cocaine epidemic, by rising rates of breast cancer, we have reason to gather. Knowing African American women as I do, I know that we have reason to gather, but I did not know that we would gather for the rather vague platform that the Philadelphia organizers disseminated.

Perhaps I let my biases get in my way. When the Million Woman March was described as "inspired by the spirit of the Million Man March" I cringed because I didn't happen to think that the Nation of Islam-called Million Man March was, in the vernacular, "all that." I also don't think that women's efforts ought to be so imitative of those of men. The Million Man March was a gathering, and black male voter participation rose after that march, but what other outcomes have there been? There is so much more that organized women can do than walk lock step behind, and in imitation of, men.

I was also confused by a march that, on one hand, called for unity among black women but, on the other hand, rather openly bashed "professional," "middle-class," and "civil rights establishment" African American women. Aren't professional women sisters, too? And are there really enough of us to bash? The distinction between grass-roots women and other black women seemed artificial and divisive, but it seemed a key aspect of march organizing.

Further, I was extremely concerned about the influence that the Nation of Islam had on the Million Woman March. My concerns were justified by the rather toxic remarks from an obscure and delusional Nation of Islam representative who chose, in the spirit of unity and sisterhood, to excoriate just one African American woman—me, for my rather tepid stance on the march. This is typical of the Nation of Islam. If you don't toe their As-Salaam-Alaikem party line, you aren't "black enough" for them. Their attack both confirms my antipathy for the Nation of Islam, and my contention that their influence on discourse in the African American community is, at best, harmful. Their propensity to read African Americans "out of the race" for even mild disagreement with them is so disturbing that it outweighs any positive impact they may have once had because of their economic development work.

My concerns aside, this is one time I am glad to have been wrong. I'm glad the Million Woman March was a success, and that so many African American women felt inspired and empowered by their coming together in Philadelphia. I'd have preferred to see a practical outcome of the march, such as the pledge to boycott just one corporation that discriminates, or the contribution of just one dollar per sister to an education fund, development fund, or other institution-building fund in the African American community. But the women who called the march had a plan, and perhaps an agenda, that precluded practical outcomes.

While my estimate of Million Woman March attendance was absolutely wrong, I was absolutely right (and have the absolute right) to raise questions about the march, its organizers, its platform, its outcome, and the Nation of Islam influence on the event. If I had to do it again, I'd wish the Philadelphia sisters the best and then ask the very same questions. To be silent would be to accept the very limiting notion that sisterhood is censorship.

King Features Syndicate, October 31, 1997

SCHOLARSHIP, SISTERHOOD, SERVICE
BY JULIANNE MALVEAUX

When twenty-two young black women came together at Howard University to form Delta Sigma Theta sorority, their goal was to focus on scholarship, sisterhood, and service to the African American community. A review of the sorority's early history indicates that these young women, and the ones who followed them, did exactly that. Members of Alpha Chapter of Delta Sigma Theta sorority marched down Pennsylvania Avenue in support of women's suffrage in 1917, even though our white sisters hardly welcomed us with open arms. We were (and remain) advocates, activists, and excellent scholars. Our first national President, Dr. Sadie Tanner Moselle Alexander, was also the first African American woman to earn the Ph.D. in economics, and was the first woman to enter the Pennsylvania Bar.

The roster of stellar Delta women is long and distinguished, and the roster of Delta's accomplishments is outstanding. Under the leadership of Lillian Pierce Benbow, the Arts and Letters Commission actually produced a film, *Countdown at Kusini*, because we felt that we should control some of the means of cultural production, and the images of African American women. Our outstanding work complements that done by the other African American women's sororities, and relations between the organizations might be described as "sisterly competition." We all want to be the best, to bring the most to our communities. To the extent that we don't trip over ourselves trying to do the very same thing, and to the extent that we understand that competition notwithstanding, we are all African American women in the struggle, we are an enrichment to our community.

As rich as our legacy is, though, there are issues of membership intake that all of the African American Greek letter organizations must deal with. These issues often tarnish our stellar record of scholarship, service, and sisterhood. While no undergraduate chapters of the sororities have incidents as outrageous as those that the fraternities have, chapters have been suspended because of hazing incidents that violate the boundaries of dignity and sisterhood. Some of the hazing begs the question of African American women's self-esteem. Why should someone be degraded in order to be my sister? It might be "fun" to dress up in silly costumes, but fun can turn ugly when there is no compassion involved in the pledging process. Delta Sigma Theta Sorority has attempted to address some of these issues by changing the membership intake process, but too many young people circumvent revisions with "underground pledging." This unsanctioned activity often includes abuse and physical violence. It is unnecessary, and unworthy of organizations whose purpose is to serve the African American community.

In the spirit of sisterhood, though, it makes sense to review more than illegal activities. We might also review the spirit of what happens as part of the membership intake process. I know too many people whose undergraduate pledging experience was so unpleasant that they have an only peripheral relationship with their sorority now. I know others who are active, but who carry decades-old grudges over something that happened during the pledge process. If sororities say they are a sisterhood, then what are sisters doing to each other to cause all this negative baggage? And what are we going to do about it? (And I don't want to hear that white women have negative baggage, too, because in this context I am not even thinking about white women.)

A recently released study indicated that African American women are at the bottom of the happiness hierarchy in this country, unhappier than whites, as well as African American men. Why? Part of it must have to do with the way black women are unaffirmed in our society. But part of it may have to do with the way that we, black women, treat each other. If we can't model positive relationships in our sororities, where we are supposed to be "the best and the brightest," then what does that say about our experiences outside sororities? If young women can't feel affirmed in a membership intake process designed by black women and for black women, then should we expect to feel affirmed in a larger society that is hostile to us?

To be sure, this can be explained psychologically and sociologically. We can talk about women and competition, about the extra burdens that women often take on when we juggle multiple roles. We can talk about the status of the African American man and the burden attacks on the black man place on the black woman. We can talk about the way black women play status games around issues like skin color, class, employment and even marital status. An infinity of explanations, though, detract from the focus on sisterhood, scholarship, and service, and the bottom line. We can do mo' better.

In her book *Sister Outsider*, Audre Lorde talks about the ways that the rage one black woman directs toward another often has a special, ugly component. The fact that black women experience rage is not surprising. The fact that we unleash it on each other is unsurprising, as well. What is disgraceful, however, is the extent to which we unleash this rage while hiding behind a banner of sisterhood. Our legacy doesn't deserve to be tarnished by this distortion of our purpose and history.

Black Issues in Higher Education, May 29, 1997

CHAPTER 10

VIRTUE, VALUE AND VISION IN A FRACTURED ECONOMY

Sometimes I have to remind myself that life isn't just about politics and policy. It's also about that small, sweet stuff that poet Langston Hughes described as the "sweet flypaper of life." That's the everyday stuff that molds us and shapes us, the peculiar stuff we notice as we meander through our worlds. It's the catching of breath, the meeting of eyes, the sweet dimple of a baby's smile, the swoosh of a basketball dropping through a hoop. It is also the ugly underbelly of the reality of homelessness, the galling nature of inequality, the fatality of futurism.

If the real deal is economic, how does the economy affect our values, the ways that we see each other and live with each other? Or do we get past the economy at some point to simply deal with values and that which is good in our lives? The columns in this last chapter attempt to explore issues of virtue, value and vision, to catch the fly on the wall with Hughes' sweet flypaper.

RACE, RULES, RIGHT AND WRONG
BY JULIANNE MALVEAUX

If Delmar Simpson were my brother, I'd take him in a small room and just go upside his head. Matching my 5'6" frame to his 6'4" one might be something of a challenge, but if I had to stand on a stool, I'd smack that bald head of his and rain my anger down on him.

The conversation would go something like this:

What would make you, whap, think that you could, whup whap, have sex with all those white women, whip whup whap, and suffer no consequences?

Have you ever heard, smack, whap, about the Scottsboro Boys and how they were jailed for reckless eyeballing, smack, whap. Don't you know that your behavior played into every stereotype that white folks have of black men, whup whup whap. Have you lost your whole bald-headed mind?

I don't know how long it would take to make this point to Delmar Simpson as well as to the other men who have pled guilty to charges that range from consensual sex to indecent assault. It is the most important point that needs to be made about the sexual misconduct at Aberdeen.

There is no excuse for Sergeant Simpson's behavior. He was wrong to abuse his position by having sex, consensual or otherwise, with his subordinates. Having said that, I still think race is a factor in the way that Simpson and 11 other drill sergeants have been prosecuted. Race may also play a role in the accusations against the Army's top enlisted man, Sergeant Major Gene McKinney, an African American who is accused of adultery and obstructing justice.

To date, African American men are the only ones charged in these cases of sexual misconduct. At Aberdeen, there are 46 drill sergeants, 63 percent of whom are African American. Is it reasonable to think that African Americans are the only ones who violated the Army's rules about sexual behavior? Have the non-black drill sergeants been investigated as closely as Delmar Simpson was? Have their accusers been as coerced? With the thin line between consensual sex and intimidation, have investigators as vigorously urged those with a gripe against white drill sergeants to make official accusations?

In a race-neutral world, some of the questions I have raised wouldn't matter. Wrong is wrong. But our country's history of unevenly enforced rules has engendered an antipathy for "law and order" on the part of some African Americans. If the rules aren't fair, they are "white man's rules" to be manipulated at will. Understanding this, the NAACP exhibits a profound patriotism in asking for an outside investigation of the judicial process at Aberdeen. They are not for leniency for Delmar Simpson, they are asking for confirmation that the rules are fair.

If the "race card" has been played in Aberdeen, it is only because the rules card has been so compromised. As much as I'd like to smack Delmar Simpson upside his head, I would also like to know that he has been treated fairly in this peculiar investigation that has revealed sexual misconduct only among black men who are drill sergeants.

USA Today, May 8, 1997

WHAT "EVERYBODY," ANYWAY?
BY JULIANNE MALVEAUX

I was standing on the corner a few months back waiting for a limousine. Now, I could have had the limo meet me at the office I was visiting, but you know how, sometimes, you don't want some folks in your business? So I told the folks who were sending the limo just to send it to the corner of 33rd and M Streets, figuring that I'd cool my heels for a few minutes then relax in air-conditioned comfort. No such luck. Instead, I spent half an hour checking my watch, and eventually I made my way to a pay phone and irately called the folks I was waiting for. "But Miss Malveaux," the receptionist said, "you should have used your cell phone." "I don't have a cell phone," I told her. "Everybody has a cell phone," she rather smugly replied. "Even my brother has a cell phone and he doesn't have a job."

Aha, I thought. Everybody has a cell phone. I guess that makes me this side of nobody because at the time, I didn't have one. (I must say that the incident prompted me to purchase one a few weeks later.) Everybody has a cell phone. So if you don't have one you are, I guess, nobody.

A week or so after the cell phone incident, I sat on a panel next to a man who told me that "everybody" would bank by computer by the year 2000. He made the point smugly, pointing out that there was really nothing wrong with the banks that are closing branches in inner-city communities because soon enough "everybody" would be banking by computer. Yeah, right. People who don't make enough money to merit a branch bank clearly don't make enough to buy computers. Indeed, and in fact, fewer than 12 percent of African American households (and fewer than 40 percent of white households) have computers in them. Even if we assume that the purchase of computers will double or triple in three years, highly unlikely, that tripling would still leave the majority of African American households out in the cold. But everybody will be banking by computer. Everybody, that is, that the banks want to do business with.

The two incidents taught me quite a bit about that word: "everybody." The all-inclusive word is too often used in exclusive ways. Pick up the style section of the paper, for example, and note how they write that "everybody" owns a classic little black dress. What everybody? Some people haven't had new clothes in years; does this make them black dress-less nobodies?

Without using the exclusive words, the President and his competitor have a way of implicitly talking about "everybody" and then leaving some people out as they make public policy. When President Clinton runs his game down, a game primarily designed to help middle-income families, he is implicitly saying that other families don't matter. When he offers a $1500 tuition tax credit, he is assuming that "everybody" can front such a sum and then use the tax credit to get it back. But some students at community colleges and other places don't have the $1500 worth of front money. So everybody won't get a crack at that tax break.

I realize that the use of "everybody" is a verbal tic that many of us have been using for years. But I'm not sure we think about the exclusion implicit in the term, and about the ways we gloss over the diverse experiences of others when we say that "everybody" has it, does it, knows it.

And when public policy is delivered from the workplace, we are assuming that "everybody" has a conventional job. Everybody does not. Increasing numbers of people work temporary or part-time jobs, or as "consultants," which is often a kind way of saying that one is between jobs. But health insurance is often delivered through the workplace. So is the family policy that allows workers 12 weeks of unpaid leave for family purposes. Firms, then, bear the burden of paying, implicitly or explicitly, for social policy. And those who don't have conventional jobs get to watch politicians pat themselves on the back for offering something to "everybody."

People will always use the word "everybody" and attempt to use shorthand to suggest that we are all in the same boat, everybody with cell phones, computer banking, tax credits, and conventional jobs. Doesn't anybody get it? There are "somebodies" who don't have access to all those goodies, and they matter just as much as those amorphous everybodies, if not more.

San Francisco Sun Reporter, September 10, 1996

WHO WILL TAKE RESPONSIBILITY FOR THE MCCAUGHEY CHILDREN?

BY JULIANNE MALVEAUX

The birth of every child is a miracle, a blessing. Yet you'd hardly know that to hear policy wonk types talk about the children that are born to unwed mothers. Too often, the blessing of birth is overshadowed by our need to judge the economic and demographic circumstances of parents. Could they afford it? Who will pay for it? Were the parents "taking responsibility"?

To be sure, the circumstances of some births make me want to holler. Why must a 14-year-old deliberately conceive? Why must a woman with no husband and no job prospects have a child? Why must a young, working-class couple who already have a child have seven more? And who will take care of their children?

I am writing, of course, of the McCaughey septuplets, Kenny Jr., Alexis, Natalie, Kelsey, Nathan, Brandon, and Joel. Their parents, Kenny and Bobbi of Carlisle, Iowa, live in a two-bedroom, ranch-style house with their older sister, Mikayla. Their income seems too modest to cover a reported half-million dollar hospital bill, even with the help of their church. The bills for diapers, food, and medicine so dwarf the family's income that one has to wonder what they were thinking when they decided to add to their family with the help of fertility drugs. When I heard about the birth of seven children to one family, I asked the same kind of questions that I hear conservatives asking about women who give birth knowing they will receive public assistance. While it is politically correct to ask these questions of poor women, though, it is perhaps both incorrect and insensitive to ask these questions of a married woman who seemed extremely eager to have a brother or sister for her only child.

The McCaughey children are the only known septuplets in the world, a built-in marketing opportunity for anyone who wants to provide formula, disposable diapers, or other services for them. But where will they live, and how, and what kind of support will be available for their parents? Already the governor of the state of Iowa, a state that is enthusiastically kicking people off public assistance, has pledged to build new housing for them. At whose expense? With state funds? For what reason and to what end? If the state of Iowa can recognize the miracle of septuplet birth and the sanctity of the lives of the McCaughey children, surely it can recognize a miracle in the lives of thousands of others who will not be beneficiary to their largess. Perhaps the same compassion that has moved Governor Terry Branstad to build a new home for the McCaugheys will also move him to keep homeless shelters open for thousands of other families. To be sure the McCaugheys look like a poster family, a family hardly likely to need social services. They are well-scrubbed, white, and likable-looking, her demure smile, and his broader one radiating contentment. They don't look troubled, pathological-like or candidates for the public dole, but if their own scant resources don't cover the cost for raising eight children, the public will help them in one way or another. There's no shame in that. We live in a society with a safety net so that people who need help can get it. I bristle, though, at the notion that the same people who would relieve the McCaughey children as a miracle heap scorn on the children of mothers who have a less "acceptable" look than Bobbi McCaughey. If society can rally around this family in the name of family values, why can't it rally around every other family in need?

I mean no disrespect to the McCaugheys. From everything I've read about them, they believe the message of the African proverb, "It takes a village to raise a child." They will need a village to take seven tiny premature babies and nurture them into adulthood. But every set of parents needs that kind of help, and every child needs the loving nurturing of the village that is our society. Why is the village so eager to embrace some of its children and so reluctant to provide a safety net for others? When people lecture that parents ought to "take responsibility" for their actions and decisions, why am I so sure that they don't have the McCaugheys in mind?

Every child is a miracle and a blessing, and every birth deserves to be celebrated, applauded, supported. Can we learn from the McCaughey miracle that it is important for us to take responsibility for each other? Or is the public outpouring of support for the McCaugheys an indicator of our nation's double standards and hypocrisy?

King Features Syndicate, May 29, 1997

HAVE WE FORGOTTEN THE HOMELESS?
BY JULIANNE MALVEAUX

As I am writing this column, I am anticipating President Clinton's words on affirmative action. He will speak tomorrow, Wednesday, and has asked black leaders from around the country to join him as he talks. I don't know what to expect—more vacillating, perhaps. I do know that while affirmative action focuses on those black folks and women who are working, public policy has ignored the folks who are out of the labor market.

There are a lot of words we don't hear these days. "Homeless" is one of them. But one morning in Washington, D.C., I counted nearly 100 homeless men, all of them African American, in a 20-square-block walk I took before daybreak. How do I know they were homeless? Why else would they sleep on the street? And why is our nation so indifferent to their plight? Here are some of my early-morning observations:

There's a 24-hour gas station across the street from my house, a well-lit space that does brisk daytime business. Late at night the cars slow to a trickle, but the homeless flock to the light and the tiny kiosk where someone sits making change and selling cigarettes. Those homeless have become such an accustomed sight that they have almost blended into the scenery. Except for this night when a woman who has wrapped herself in a vivid blanket seems to moan every minute or so. It isn't a howl or scream—I couldn't hear it inside. But outside there is something about her low moan that put a hook in my heart big as a harpoon and made me want to cross the street and say something, offer something.

I didn't. Nine months on my street have taught me to treat homeless folk with a healthy respect. Speak when spoken to. Don't offer if they don't ask. Set limits with charity. Listen to a moan. No, that wasn't one of the rules, but what if sisterfriend said she wanted shelter. Could I offer it, provide it? Did I know where to take her? I could probably offer coffee or a meal, but even that modest offer would take me off track, and I really wanted to walk. What about money? I'd stuffed some ones and an emergency twenty into my shoe. But what would a buck or two or twenty do to stop the moan? I thought I was walking while I was thinking, but I realized I was staring in the night at the woman with the moan. And so I moved one foot in front of the other, sort of propelling myself forward. In its first few minutes, there was nothing about this walk to put me in the racewalking hall of fame.

Indeed, my feet seemed to be glued to the sidewalk. Then I tripped over a can or something and the eerie silence on the block made the sound of aluminum on concrete echo into the street. The three men sleeping on the church stoop across from the gas station sort of shuffled in their sleep, distinctly enough for me to hear them move. They had covered themselves with dirty blankets and pieces of cardboard and their limbs just sort of moved, like youngsters resisting the intrusion of an alarm clock. The slightest one slept at the edge of the last step that led to the church vestibule, perched so precariously that he looked like he might fall if he shifted too abruptly. But his movement was slight, more a shrug than a stretch, until he opened his eyes and muttered something, maybe one of those sleep sounds that we all mumble in that limbo between full and semi-consciousness. Did he say "good morning"? For a minute, it seemed that he did. For a minute I imagined that his eyes had long lashes, that his limbs had been showered before he went to bed, that his skin was smooth, not mottled, that his hair had been recently combed. Seeing him that way, in a house, not on a stoop, I saw the man he might have been, the young man who was somebody's brother or son. I recognized the man as one of the corner hoods who would boldly block your path down the street at mid-day, cadging coins, talking stuff, demanding a nod or a smile. There is something more vulnerable in his half-sleep glance, something more gentle than the false bravado of a hungry man. There were echoes of a student in those eyes, something about that haunting look that reminded me of someone whose head is slumped over a stack of books in the middle of a study session. There was kinship with my nephew in those eyes, a bond between this stoop-sleeping man and a drowsy boy who has to be jolted from sleep, who moans, mumbles and talks in tongues when it is time to get up. What did the man on the church stoop say? Did he say "good morning"?

What do we say to, for, and about our nation's homeless? Too many of them are people of color, too many of them have skills and productive potential. How many of them are our kin, and what can we do about it?

King Features Syndicate, July 19, 1995

HOLDING HANDS AND HOLDING ON TO COMMUNITY
BY JULIANNE MALVEAUX

Spring and summer are tourist season in Washington. Groups of youngsters storm off buses as if they have been imprisoned on them for months. They storm fast-food outlets as if they have been starved on their journey to the nation's capital. You can't help but empathize when their chaperones and leaders try to huddle them together to cross a light, get into a building, get out of the rain.

The smallest children are often told to hold hands so that they can stay together. Linked chains of children swirl around, stumbling when the leader insists on too swift a pace, and slackening with rolled, bored eyes when the leader slows down. The determination with which the youngsters hold on, once directed, can be impressive. I've rarely seen adults stick together with the same tenacity as children. Grown people seem to know that our sense of direction isn't as fragile, that our existence isn't as vulnerable, that it isn't as necessary for us to hold on. We can make it if we don't. Thus the number of grownups, hefty men and self-sufficient women, who held hands and snaked through the thick crowds at last week's Stand for Children was striking.

"Don't want to lose my family," smiled the young man who was part of a 12-person chain of relatives. "I wouldn't know where to look for them," shrugged the woman who was part of a half dozen coworkers. Like the kids, they held hands and tried to make their way through the crowd, smiling and nodding as they moved through, making eye contact and bumping shoulders with swift acknowledgment. Like the kids, they kicked up dust when their leaders stalled to chat. But like the kids, they didn't let go.

The event was called a Stand for Children, but in many ways it was a Stand for America. Forget the politics and the debate about personal responsibility and social programs. Remember the values debate and the ways that politicians talk about these values. While values aren't reflected in the acrimonious debate that takes place on Capitol Hill, values were reflected by the grown people, weaving through crowds, holding hands, holding on, recognizing the value of community, not only for their children, but also for themselves.

Watching the touching, among children and adults, made me wonder how often strangers actually touch in the context of community. How often do we bump shoulders, hold hands, negotiate space and place? The physical jostling at the Stand for Children might, in many ways, have been a metaphor for the fiscal jostling that takes place on the Hill, when people try to decide which programs have priorities and how conflicting priorities should be juggled. But unlike the Congressional jostling, the jostling at the Stand for Children was peaceful, powerful, spurred by the notion of our collective common purpose.

At the Stand for Children, the people holding hands, the communities of people, asserted that one of our nation's priorities ought to be keeping them together. Through public policy we can support families, or we can cast them adrift, we can hold on or we can let go. Laws that say men must leave families to receive public assistance, for example, often cause a traumatic severing of important family ties. Similarly, laws that provide a tax deduction for child care as long as it is not provided by a family member send a signal about the value that we place on family ties.

More than three thousand organizations supported the Stand for Children. In the days before the event, conservative organizations began to bash it, describing it as a defender of big government. But among the crowds, among the people holding hands, there was no support for bureaucracy, for big government, for programs. There was support for building community, and deciding national priorities. And this support was often communicated by the simple act of holding hands.

King Features Syndicate, June 6, 1996

A STATISTICAL NO-BRAINER
BY JULIANNE MALVEAUX

My accountant looked at my tax situation and gave me three options: have a child, marry someone with no income, or buy a house. That was a no-brainer! It was time, I decided, to buy me a house. Yes, I'm speaking in Ebonics. I know better, but if I'm speaking in six-figure language, I figure I can split as many verbs as I want.

I can split my verbs, but I can't pay late. Never, ever, ever. Buying a house is metaphorically worse than checking into a hospital for invasive surgery. Lenders not only want to know about your spending habits, they also want to know why, a decade ago, you failed to pay for magazines you never received. There are no two sides to the stories that show up on your credit report.

Why did I charge a few thousand dollars at a department store in 1993? I paid it back, I replied. The man asked if I'd consider myself extravagant. Maybe I was depressed, I ventured. Wrong answer. Do not pass "go," do not collect a home loan. I was tempted to refer this banker to my herbalist, therapist, and astrologer, to share my expired Prozac prescription with him. Instead I caustically asked if he'd ever done side work as a proctologist. Point, Malveaux; set, mortgage company.

Another day, another lender. Every issue I've studied hit me upside my head. Redlining. Mortgage discrimination. Bait and switch. There was a silver lining in almost every cloud, though. There was a lender who went out on a limb; a realtor who vowed to make a deal happen; a stranger who shared pages of files and contacts. As an economist, I've looked at fluctuations in home purchases as an indicator of economic strength for years. As a purchaser, I wonder whether my three months of water torture says anything about the strength of the economy. What if

I'd taken another facet of my accountant's advice and brought children into the world or attempted nuptial bliss?

I love the fact I bought this house! I can paint my walls red and stain my floors mahogany, build shelves under stairs and plan for roof decks. This house is mine, mine, mine, mine, mine. It is almost shameful to be so gleeful about owning a piece of the rock.

More than glee, though, is the quiet understanding that statistics are shorthand for the things that poet Langston Hughes described as the sweet flypaper of life, the small special stuff that makes a life worth living. Thanks to banker goodwill, the help of some friends, and my own taut tenacity, I caught a corner of my dream, not as an economic expansion statistic, but as a woman negotiating place and space in her world. Taking that step was a real no-brainer.

USA Today, January 14, 1997

DO SPECTATORS HAVE A COMMON LANGUAGE?
BY JULIANNE MALVEAUX

The extent to which we hang our life on television fantasy is revealed in a recent Wall Street Journal/NBC poll on health care. The poll asked Americans who they'd prefer as doctors, the staff from *ER*, Marcus Welby, M.D., Hawkeye Pierce from *MASH*, *Dr. Quinn, Medicine Woman*, or the doctors from *Chicago Hope*. The *ER* doctors were the clear winner, with 25 percent of those polled preferring them, while only 6 percent preferred the *Chicago Hope* doctors. In between, 21 percent would choose Marcus Welby, 15 percent Hawkeye Pierce, and 11 percent Dr. Quinn.

My first thought about this question on an otherwise comprehensive poll was that it was an indirect way to measure television ratings and that there must be some correlation between NBC's participation in the poll and the fact that *ER* is one of its flagship shows. My second thought was that I needed to do some calling to figure out who Marcus Welby was. Then, I realized that there was just one woman doctor (and an early-20th-century wilderness doctor at that) in the sample, and that there wasn't a single doctor of color, except as part of the *ER* ensemble. Which of the shows' doctors would I choose as my doctor? Try none of the above!

A day before this poll was released the National Commission on Civic Renewal, a bipartisan group that spent 1 1/2 years tracking trends in political participation, trust, family integrity and other aspects of American life, released its report, "A Nation of Spectators," which suggests that we are all too disengaged for our own good. "Never have we had so many opportunities for participation, yet rarely have we felt so powerless," the report said. "In a time that cries out for civic action, we are in danger of becoming a nation of spectators." We are such spectators, it seems, that our pollsters attempt to gauge our medical preferences by using fictional television doctors, such spectators that we know these television doctors because we spend an average of 28 hours a week watching television. Our common language has become the tube. Why not try reality?

Choosing Marcus Welby over Hawkeye Pierce may mean choosing dignity in a physician over irreverent humor. But what does choosing the ensemble of *ER* doctors mean? A choice of chaos instead of serenity? Demographic identification? To be fair, the question was one of several asked, with many of the other questions having far more substance. One of the more notable findings of the health survey was the fact 67 percent of all adults (and more women, African Americans, young people, and Democrats) thought employers should be required to offer health insurance to their workers. Now that's real, not television fantasy. But the fact is that spectator Americans may have to get off of their couches and into advocacy mode to get the reforms in health care that we want.

Is the notion that Americans should get off of our couches and onto the streets too much '60s retro hoopla? I don't think so. There are dozens of reasons why Americans might try activism. Our economy is expanding yet millions still subsist in poverty, earning the minimum wage or a few pennies more. Our nation's corporations are merging at an unprecedented pace, yet consumers aren't getting breaks from these mergers. While many of our cities are experiencing a revitalization, there is a bifurcation in the quality of city life. While some city dwellers are "living large" in high-rise apartments downtown, others cannot get to work because buses don't run their way. Too many politicians are smug, since they don't have to respond to that half of the citizenry who grouse but don't bother to vote. Some don't think they have to respond to voters, either, unless they are significant financial donors.

Everyone doesn't agree with the report, which is just a little suspect because of the participation of former Education Secretary William Bennett, a scolding Republican pundit who has presumed to lecture the American people on their values. The Newton, Massachusetts-based Institute for Civil Society says that Americans aren't simply spectators and observers, but participate differently than they have in the past. I'd like to think the Institute for Civil Society is right, but my experience says there is more apathy than activism out there. And while I'm not about to go as far as Bill Bennett does in suggesting that the entertainment industry should be held "as accountable for civic harm" as the tobacco industry is for physical harm, I am chilled by the way we now use television as a way of communicating with each other.

Why not try language? Why not try reality? Why not find the adjectives to describe the medical care we want than say we'd rather visit Dr. Marcus Welby than Dr. Jane Quinn?

King Features Syndicate, June 26, 1998

OKLAHOMA CITY LESSON: TAKE OFF THE BLINDERS
BY JULIANNE MALVEAUX

If ten black men said that they were stockpiling weapons and designing paramilitary exercises in order to defend themselves against government, the FBI would have infiltrated them quicker than they could say Black Panther Party. Instead of featured spots on our nation's most popular talk shows, the black men with weapons would probably have been featured on our nation's post office walls! The Michigan militias have been treated as a law-abiding, non-alarming curiosity until their links, however weak, to the abominable bombing of the Murrah Building in Oklahoma City were revealed. Now, there are discussions about the need for FBI and CIA surveillance of domestic terrorist groups, or those with terrorist potential. One wonders what kind of racial myopia kept those who catalog terrorist groups from finding white supremacist militia dangerous until now.

Part of the answer is that the spoken targets of these groups are people that our nation has not generally valued. They have talked about doing things like paying people who stop others in the commission of a felony and by implication the felons are black. They have talked about "eliminating" people (but they never use the word "people") from the planet and again, those people are usually black. We have passed laws against bias crime, but seem indifferent to enforcing them. Indeed, government and the media have been more intent in using bias to place blame in situations like the Oklahoma City bombing. For the first 24 hours, the cry was that the perpetrators were from the Middle East, and Arab Americans shuddered because the finger was being pointed at them, yet again.

There are those who will wonder why, in the face of the horrible tragedy of Oklahoma City, matters of race should even enter the discussion. But the speed with which we made the Middle Eastern connection, combined with our sluggish recognition that white supremacists played a role in the Oklahoma bombing, suggests that some of our biases have much to do with the way we see events in this country. We don't want to believe that the "angry white men" we keep talking about are so angry that they will kill. Yet the way we discuss these men stokes their anger, authenticates it, in many ways.

Why isn't anyone saying that white men are angry for the same reasons all Americans are angry? There aren't enough jobs to go around. There is too much economic uncertainty. They are frightened for their futures and the futures of their children, but white male arrogance has no language of fear. Fear turns to rage turns to anger which is legitimized by headlines. Which is acted out in many ways, including the formation of militia.

Why do we know so little about these militia? The media have failed to cover this story in the kind of detail that they might have if, say, a dozen or so black men had retreated to the woods with guns. That would have been dangerous, but too many have treated this militia movement as if these folks are the descendants of male movement icon Iron John. Just strumming some drums, howling and playing with a few guns.

Hindsight is, of course, always perfect. No analysis can bring back the people who were massacred in Oklahoma City, no finger-pointing can restore the children to their families or assuage the grief of those who lost spouses, friends, and relatives. Still, while our nation is stunned into grieving silence over Oklahoma, it makes sense to look at the debacle for lessons. And among the many lessons that we take from this is the lesson that stereotypic is myopia. After Oklahoma, will people conclude that white men are more likely to be terrorists than others? Will newscasters speculate aloud about the next bomb reminding them of "white male" (and not Middle Eastern) terrorism? This Oklahoma City bomb ought to blast away the white male presumption of innocence and remind us, in the most malevolent way, that we are all in this together.

King Features Syndicate, April 28, 1995

BEYOND BITTERNESS
BY JULIANNE MALVEAUX

African American poet Langston Hughes wrote about the "sweet flypaper of life," the little stuff, the wonderful stuff, that often makes life worth living. A pleasant lunch with a friend; the shy smile of a child; the rush that comes with a job well done; the compliment unexpectedly offered; the majesty of sunrise and a new day; all these things remind us of life's richness, a richness that transcends the ugliness of the Contract on America, the racism of police officers like Mark Fuhrman, the poverty that strangles nearly a quarter of our nation's children.

I thought about the sweet flypaper this week when I learned about the death of Dr. Elizabeth Delany, one of the two sisters who were catapulted into national fame with a book, *Having Our Say*, that described their 100 years of life and was turned into a Broadway play. The book is a gentle but poignant reminiscence of how the 10 Delany children grew up in Raleigh, North Carolina, and how Sarah and Elizabeth attended New York's Columbia University before enjoying careers as a teacher and dentist, respectively. The two women lived their entire lives together, sweet Sadie and the more acerbic Bess.

Many wondered at the popularity of *Having Our Say*. When the book sold over 900,000 copies and went on to Broadway, many marveled that the homespun wisdom of the centenarian sisters had reached so many people. Despite their pointed comments about race, the Delany sisters shared a rich appreciation of the sweet flypaper of life, and I think that's what their audiences responded to. Here were two black women who had seen Jim Crow and segregation, who had seen the signs that said "white" or "colored," and had managed, somehow, not to rage. Elizabeth Delany was almost lynched when she talked back to a white man in a train station in the early twentieth century. But she maintained a perspective on bitterness. "It's understandable that colored folks are bitter," she wrote. "The only problem is, their bitterness won't change a thing. It will ruin their lives . . . sometimes we get mad, but there's a big difference between anger and bitterness."

Bitterness eats you up. Anger motivates movement. Bitterness consumes you. Anger energizes. There's a thin line between anger and bitterness, a line made thinner by those who make social policy in a way that is entirely contemptuous of individuals. I've gotten to the point where I can't read a newspaper without raging, where daily life provides too many anecdotes about the absolute craziness of our times. Race-baiting and woman-hating are almost everyday occurrences, and some of life's ironies make me want to emigrate to outer space.

For example, a Towson, Maryland lawyer is defending a white police officer who is charged with shouting racial epithets while beating a drug suspect. Henry Belsky said that Officer William Goodman wouldn't even be charged if the Mark Fuhrman tapes had not come to light. Lots of people are saying Fuhrman's tapes illuminate police racism. This is the first time I've heard it used as a defense. Makes you want to throw your hands up and search for sanity. Makes you seek refuge in the sweet flypaper of life.

On the occasion of Dr. Elizabeth Delany's death, I flipped through the pages of *Having Our Say* once again, humming my agreement, basking in the richness of their wisdom and their words, laughing at their cocky certainty that they had the answer to everything. In rage-filled times the gracious Delany sisters quietly remind us of the personal richness that we can discover in politically imperfect times.

King Features Syndicate, September 27, 1995

LOVING LIFE—THE LEGACY OF BETTY SHABAZZ
BY JULIANNE MALVEAUX

The first time I met Betty Shabazz I was, frankly, in open-mouthed awe of her. I sort of buzzed around her, hovered in her orbit, but didn't say a word. She had been married to Malcolm X, I told myself. And she raised six daughters by herself, after his assassination. She earned a Ph.D. as an adult, and was running a major department at Medgar Evers College. The woman must be awesome, I told myself. So I watched and I wondered when and how I could approach her and share my admiration.

As things happen, she and I ended up at the same side of the pool, our lounge chairs separated by one of those rickety tables that try to support an umbrella. I introduce myself and awkwardly gushed out my admiration for her, so brimming over with hyperbole that I realized I was being foolish. Still, I continued on for several minutes, until a deep chuckle emerged from someplace near her gut. "Child," she told me with a husky laugh, "you had better get over all that."

That's the thing about Betty Shabazz that the obituaries missed, that humor, that approachability, that self-imposed notion that she was not larger than life, but simply life itself. Since June 1, when the news that she was badly burned hit the media, I've thought much about Dr. Shabazz and her approachability, about the way she was able to put everyone at ease, all the while carrying the Malcolm X torch, all the while protecting his legacy.

Betty loved life, which is perhaps why she clung so tenaciously to it, living for three weeks after doctors said she would not make it because of the severity of her burns. Her love for life was reflected in her determination to live it well and wisely, and to communicate that desire to others. As counselor and dean "Dr. Betty" at Medgar Evers College, her love for life equipped her to teach and talk about overcoming adversity. After all, who can say they "can't" overcome when they are speaking to an icon of a woman who has cleared every hurdle that adversity placed in her way.

Betty Shabazz didn't want to be a role model, but she could not help but be. Her life is an example of triumph over tragedy, an affirmation of the way that African American women have "a habit of survival," of "making a way out of no way." As the widow of Malcolm X, Betty Shabazz had to rebuild her life, and redefine herself as a single mother. She triumphed in the process of her redefinition. As professor, educational administrator, talk show host, and leader, she became a role model for every woman who has had to reinvent her life in the face of misfortune.

With her death comes a set of lessons, as well. Her New York City memorial service at Riverside Church brimmed over with mourners, some well known, and some not. Though he has not been a friend to African American people, New York Mayor Rudolph Giuliani brought heartfelt condolences. Because he has not been a friend to African American people, Giuliani was booed. Atallah Shabazz shrugged off her grief for a moment and fiercely admonished the crowd to give respect to someone who came to pay respect to her mother. I could hear both Betty Shabazz and Malcolm X in her dignified fierceness, and was reminded, again, that there is a time and place for everything.

The most powerful lessons came from those who chose to address the delicate subject of the future of Malcolm Shabazz, Betty's young grandson who stands accused of setting the fire that caused her death. Haki Madhibuti and Maya Angelou did not shy away from the subject but implored the crowd to treat this young black man as every young brother, to surround him with the same love that we seemed to surround Betty Shabazz's memory with. "God created him, but we made him," Maya Angelou said poignantly, tearfully. Weeks, months after Dr. Shabazz's transition, we can pay tribute to her by doing the work she did so well, counseling, educating, and guiding our youth.

A few days after Betty Shabazz died, the Supreme Court ruled that people do not have the right to assisted suicide. While I have always supported people's right to choose death over life, Betty's death reminded me of the value of life. The way she lived and the way she died reminded me of something that black scholar W.E.B. DuBois wrote in the twilight of his days, when he looked back over nearly 100 full years of challenge and controversy. From Ghana, where he died, DuBois exhorted, "One thing alone I charge you. As you live, believe in life. Always human beings will live and progress to greater, broader, and fuller life. The only possible death is to lose belief in this truth, simply because the great end comes slowly and because time is long."

Dr. Betty Shabazz may well have written such words. She lived by those powerful life-affirming principles. Those who knew her and admired her have many ways of remembering her. I choose to remember her as life-loving, approachable, Malcolm's widow, but so much more than that, as mother, teacher, sister, leader. Betty Shabazz was a sister who loved life so much that she clung to it, even in the midst of tragedy.

Black Issues in Higher Education, July 8, 1997

THE JOY OF PIDDLIN'
BY JULIANNE MALVEAUX

A few days ago, I had the delight to give a speech at the Chautauqua Institution, a gated community in the southwest corner of New York state that has a nine-week educational summer program. Each week has a theme, and the theme for my week was the economy, so I delivered an hour-long lecture and answered half an hour's worth of questions. Other than that, I sat on the porch and simply enjoyed the clear weather and nature. At some point, I ate lunch, and at another point I took a walk. And then, because no grass grows under my feet, I was back in D.C. managing my crazy life.

I could not help but notice, though, the idyllic nature of Chautauqua, and the quiet serenity that so many of the people there exuded. Why not? The hardest decision they had to make was whether to have seafood Newburg or blackened catfish for lunch, whether to play volleyball or sun themselves in the afternoon. There was supervised care for children of all ages, private piers with small and medium-sized boats, manicured lawns and sprawling Victorian mansions. In many ways, this is the life.

I talked to a man who comes to Chautauqua every year for simple "renewal," bringing his family of three children to enjoy the amenities. Another extended family, a dozen or so of them, come for several weeks each year and spend their time "getting to know each other again." There appeared to be little stress, little anger, little hostility from anyone on the premises. Indeed, even the most critical of questions for my lecture were couched in gentle terms.

Did I mention that I didn't notice many people of color at this idyllic place? There was an older sister, who told me that her daughter, about my age, would be coming up in a few days and was sorry to miss me. But there were at least a thousand people in attendance at my lecture, and I didn't see many of "us" at all. Not that it matters. This is just an observation. But it struck me that these are environments that would be idyllic for everyone (or anyone). And, more than that, it struck me that exposure to some of this kind of serenity might reduce some of the harsh hostility that erupts into violence so often in our communities.

I know young African Americans who have never had the luxury of simply piddlin'. They are on survival alert almost all of the time. They are often worried about their parents, worried about their environments, worried about getting shot, worried about their lives. A very special young brother I know, at 18, does not know whether he will live to be 25. He has already been shot once because he was in the "wrong place, wrong time," standing on a corner near a store shot up by drug dealers. His neighborhood is a pastiche of danger zones, places he dare not go or cannot go, houses away from things he calls "safe places." Just a week ago, on the Baltimore pier, the young brother spoke to a woman he found attractive and exchanged telephone numbers with her. Moments later, he was confronted by her angry boyfriend and his posse, two of whom were carrying guns.

For some reason my young friend sprung to my mind as I watched an elderly woman ponder the luncheon choices at Chautauqua. I don't know if he has ever leisurely looked at a buffet and taken five minutes to figure out what he wanted. I do know that he has only rarely left his Baltimore home, and that he has no feeling of the limitless nature of options and life. For the first time in a long time, I was reminded why so many cities have funds that send children to camp, getting them outside their environment, out of their boxes, into nature and into the range of things that life has to offer.

My morning on the porch, riffling through my notes, enjoying nature, and listening to birds sing, was both a blessing and a lesson for me, too. My quiet time reminded me that life does not always have to be a hurry hustle-bustle crazy rush to the next appointment, last-minute attempt to squeeze in one more thing to do. It reminded me that life is good when there is a balance that may include periods of frenetic activity, but also periods of simple, sumptuous rest and piddlin'.

I don't know that I can take my young Baltimore friend to Chautauqua. I do know that when we talk about what black people need we often speak of jobs and economic development. We also need to think and speak about the quality of leisure time, about our environment, about the need to recharge our batteries, to rest ourselves, to piddle.

San Francisco Sun Reporter, July 30, 1998

IS FUTURISM FATAL?
BY JULIANNE MALVEAUX

What will the year 2000 look like? I don't know how many conversations I've had with people who are trying to project what we will be doing just a few months from now. No, the year 2000 is not some faraway date that will happen sometime in the distant future. It will happen in about fourteen months, give or take a few days. So why all the mystery?

So many of us are dependent on computers that we've been caught up in the Y2K quagmire. Will our computers turn to dust, or turn us back a century on January 1, 2000? I know folks who are planning to leave the country with their cash in their suitcases to escape what they consider the inevitable glitches that will come when we move from the 20th century to the 21st. Unless I get a better offer, I plan to spend January 1, 2000 with a nice glass of Dom Perignon, at my computer, doing my favorite thing, writing.

What will the year 2000 look like? It will look just like 1998 unless we do something about it. Futurists use past trends to make their predictions and projections months and years out. If the number of women incarcerated stands at 100,000 and the increase in incarceration has been 10 percent a year, we can reasonably say that in five years, there will be more than 160,000 women incarcerated. Then we can do one of two things. We can decide to build more prisons to accommodate the extra 60,000 women, or we can decide to reduce incarceration rates by revamping the criminal code so it is more effective, and by doing other things (like providing drug treatment) to come up with alternatives to criminal activity.

What we tend to do is behave as if predictions are written in stone and concrete. We behave as if the way life has been is also the way it has to be. For black people, this is the equivalent of having had some 1855 fool say that there would be so many million slaves in 1875, not taking things like the Civil War and emancipation into account. For some, the point is obvious. Others, though, spout off about the future as if no one has any control over the way the future will turn out, as if no collective action can redirect the "inevitability" of the future.

To be sure, we know that some things will happen as certainly as the sun rises and sets. Population will fluctuate as people are born and as they die. Immigration also has an impact on domestic population, but immigration is also influenced by world conditions and by the legal climate. How easy it is to move from the "natural" to those natural things, like population, that can be influenced by the structural and legal. If it is that easy to make the shift with issues like population, what about other issues, like race relations?

According to demographers, by the year 2010, there will be more Latinos than African Americans in the population. Some suggest this means that African American political influence will wane as we become the nation's second-largest minority. Certainly, shifting demographics suggest that all peoples of color might work more closely together in coalition when our interests intersect. Reality bites, though, and we know that our interests don't always intersect. Does this mean African American influence will necessarily wane? Has African American influence reached its maximum level yet? Are the maximum number of African American people voting and participating in politics and civic affairs? It seem fatalist that we should simply assume that a demographic shift will strip us of power we have yet to maximize!

Had anyone predicted that the Congressional Black Caucus would balloon in size from just over 20 to 38 by 1996? The CBC size is a direct result of the way district lines were drawn in several states. Indeed, some have been so incensed at the growth in the size of the CBC that they've attempted to turn the clock back to draw district lines more to their liking. In one district a white man had the nerve to sue, alleging that his civil rights were violated because he had an African American Congressional representative. Imagine what would happen if every African American with Caucasian representation sued! More importantly, understand the impact that discrete action has on future outcomes.

What will the year 2000 look like? Just like 1998 if we don't do anything about it. We can easily predict that by 2000, 40 percent of all black children will live in poverty, black unemployment rates will be double white rates, cities will face more economic challenges, and the public education system will be weakened by vouchers, charter schools, and other alternative plans. Based on the growth of computer use among African Americans and among whites, it is easy to predict that the technology gap will grow. If these predictions are unacceptable, then we need to do something to change them. There's activism, legislation, litigation, and interventionist tools not yet imagined. But unless we conceive an alternative to challenging forecasts, we simply surrender ourselves to a fatal future of dire predictions.

San Francisco Sun Reporter, October 22, 1998

Acknowledgements

It has been a fascinating and frustrating exercise to compile this collection of columns. Reading through them reminds me of the issues that have concerned me over the four years this collection represents, 1994-1998. This time has also been a personally challenging time, as I moved from one coast to another, made a series of employment-related transitions, and learned to make change something to embrace, not avoid. In the middle of change, one thing stays the same for me, I write.

Though I am not aided and abetted, I am surrounded and supported by a loving immediate and extended family. My mother, Proteone Marie Malveaux, is an "uppity woman" and a constant source of inspiration. My siblings, Marianne, Mariette, James and Antoinette, are sounding boards and loving friends. The little ones in my family, Anyi, Armand and Kuwan, provide hope and joy. Extended family members Lulann McGriff (1943-1998), Barbara Vance, Barbara Skinner, Cora Masters Barry, Ramona Edelin, Barbara Reynolds, Kojo Nnamdi, Mark, Cheryl and Matthew Brown, Sade Turnipseed, and others who will forgive me for not acknowledging them by name provide tone and texture in my life. My extended family also includes the sisters of the National Association of Negro Business and Professional Women's Clubs, Inc., who provide me the challenge of leadership and who are often, as I travel the country, "the wind beneath my wings." During the Spring semester of 1998, I held the Sister Catharine Julie Cunningham Chair at the College of Notre Dame in San Mateo, California. My students and teaching partner, Dyanne Ledine, brought richness to my work.

I offer special thanks and gratitude to Karen Beasley Young, an extremely supportive, wonderfully giving sisterfriend. She prodded me into productivity when I was overwhelmed, flew across the country twice to help me put this manuscript together, and has been an extremely positive influence in my life. I am blessed to know her.

My personal assistant, Lorna Foote, has also been a tremendous help in the completion of this project. Lorna is a master magician who answers the phones, works the computers, manages the schedule, and still finds the grace and patience to deal with an often-harried employer. Thank you, Lorna.

I am also appreciative to the people who have edited, published and supported my work, especially Paul Hendricks at King Features Syndicate, Amelia Ward at the *San Francisco Sun Report*, my many supportive colleagues at the *San Francisco Examiner*, Frank Matthews and Cheryl Fields at *Black Issues in Higher Education*, Cynthia Smith, formerly of WLIB radio, and Rochelle Lefkowitz of ProMedia.

Denise Pines is the best publisher a writer could ever ask for. She is patient, kind, firm and fun. I am grateful for her friendship and professional support.

I am also grateful to the people who read my work and who share their feedback with me. Left-of-liberal African American women writers like me sometimes feel that we work in a vacuum. I enjoy those who watch, read, listen and share the fact that I gave voice to their thoughts.

Finally, and most importantly, I must gleefully and gratefully acknowledge the power of Almighty God, from whom all blessings flow, and give thanks for the prayers of my Metropolitan Baptist Church family in Washington, D.C.

About the Author

DR. JULIANNE MALVEAUX is an economist, writer, and syndicated columnist whose twice-weekly column appears nationally through the King Features Syndicate. She writes weekly for the *San Francisco Sun Reporter*, and monthly for *USA Today* and *Black Issues in Higher Education*. Her work has also appeared in *Ms.*, *Essence*, *Emerge* and other national magazines. Malveaux is a frequent national affairs commentator for television and radio, appearing as an analyst on *MSNBC*, *CNBC*, *Fox News Network* and *CNN*. She is a regular panelist on the PBS program *To the Contrary*, and the WHUT program *Evening Exchange*. She has also been a radio talk-show host at WLIB in New York, and on Pacifica radio.

A former college professor, Malveaux was coeditor of the book *Slipping Through the Cracks: The Status of Black Women* (Transaction Publications, 1986), and is the author of a collection of columns, *Sex, Lies and Stereotypes: Perspectives of a Mad Economist* (Pines One Publishing, 1994). Popular on the lecture circuit, Julianne Malveaux speaks to civic, academic, business, and professional groups each year. Active in civic affairs, she was listed by *Ebony* magazine as one of the nation's 100 most influential African American organization heads. She is president of the National Association of Negro Business and Professional Women's Clubs, Inc.

Julianne Malveaux is a native San Franciscan who lives in Washington, D.C.